What Others Are Saying...

"This book goes directly to the heart of why enterprise architects often fail to make the progress they want. The author provides deep insight into the challenges we face, and propose practical yet innovative architecture and career solutions for aspiring as well as experienced enterprise architects."
—Dr John Gøtze, Co-founder, International Enterprise Architecture Institute & Lecturer, IT University of Copenhagen

"A must read for anyone new to the architecture field or who wants to grow their career. Sharon's book is a helpful and easy-to-read resource that you can start to use and profit from immediately."
—Scott Bockheim, Manager of Commercial Architecture, MillerCoors

"It's often said that enterprise architecture is a journey, not a destination. In fact, enterprise architecture is multiple journeys – a journey as an evolving discipline, a journey as an emerging profession, a journey for an organization as its enterprise architecture matures, and finally the journey of an individual practitioner's career and professional development. It's this personal journey that gets the least attention and is thus the least well understood. At last, we have a resource that not only maps out this journey for you, but gives you advice as to how to travel it in style. As such, Ms. Evans' book is a welcome and major contribution to the state of the art."
—Leonard Fehskens, V.P., Skills and Capabilities, The Open Group

"Finally! A book for career architects with insightful no-nonsense advice that goes beyond the typical frameworks and models discussion to get to the core of what it means to be a successful enterprise architect. New and seasoned architects alike will want to read this book."
—Jeff Scott, Forrester Research

"This book leaves the realm of models and frameworks to educate the reader on what it takes personally and professionally to succeed in the world of architecture. It allows the reader to candidly assess their readiness and suitability to this role that balances technical mastery with business acumen. You won't find this critical information anywhere else."
—Stephen Farr, Chief Architect, National Life Group

If you aspire to be an Enterprise Architect, Zoom Factor explains enterprise architecture and lays out a roadmap for achieving your career goal in a common sense, easy to understand format. Zoom in with this book before somebody zooms you out.

—Stuart Charles, CIO, Workers Compensation Board of Manitoba

At a time when doubt grips the world economy and companies face increased competition Sharon Evans' book provides a definitive path for IT Strategy. This book is an essential toolkit for any IT Architect looking to ensure the long-term viability of their company and their own career.

—Michael J. Daniel, CTO /
Senior Vice President of Engineering, AR Publishing

I have no interest in enterprise architecture as a career, but I think that this is a great book. To me, it's a book about striving for excellence and achieving success in any endeavor – business or personal. It just so happens to be applied to the EA world. Using her extensive technical experiences, her business acumen, and her keen awareness of human behavior, Sharon plots a clear path to success. She continually points out in her book that if you start to do anything, you should strive for excellence in that endeavor.

If you want to be an EA, then be an excellent EA. But, the book's message is universally applicable. If you want to be a teacher, then be an excellent one. If you want to be a friend, an author, a husband, a gardener – then be an excellent one. Start by aiming high (excellence), develop a plan, monitor and measure your progress, continue to grow personally and professionally, and give to others (mentor or coach – they are two way avenues to growth) – that's the path to success in any field.

This is not a technology book. It's a personal, business, career mapping and improvement book focused on a technology related activity. It's lucid and crisp with a simple message – achieving success does not have to be complicated. But it does involve commitment, hard work, and a flexible plan. Anyone who wants to be successful can learn something from Sharon's narrative.

—James M. Livelsberger, Program Manager, EMBARQ

Zoom Factor

FOR THE ENTERPRISE ARCHITECT

How to Focus and Accelerate Your Career

Sharon C. Evans

Acknowledgments

I would like to extend my appreciation to the architects with whom I have worked over the years, many of whom contributed by reviewing these materials or by participating in countless discussions we shared. Several of those conversations became articles or presentations and then formed the basis for the framework upon which this book is based.

Thanks to all of my reviewers who graciously read chapters and shared feedback that helped me to make this book better. Thank you to John Zachman, Jeff Scott, Jeanne Ross, James Livelsberger, Allan McLeod, Stuart Charles, Dr John Gøtze, Scott Bockheim, Cam Loepke, Randy Wood, Nick Curry, Michael Daniel, Leonard Fehskens, Stephen Farr, Cindy Genyk, Michele Taylor, Jean Bernard Trouve, Sylvain Trempe, Robert Gauthier, Pat Smith, Glen Douglas, George Paras, and Larry DeBoever. You have all provided insight and leadership that resulted in these pages.

A heartfelt thank you to my parents Bill and Marian Evans and to my family for believing in me, supporting my education, encouraging me, and forgiving my absence while I brought my perspective to print. To my husband Ron, who continually spurred me on to finish this work and guided our son while I just took ten more minutes to tweak it. To Harvey and Shirley, who were always available to pick up our son so that I could squeeze a couple more hours out of my day. Most of all, thanks to all of those countless IT professionals and architects who kindly gave me their time for more than twenty years, especially those whose insights and experiences were a factor in bringing this book to fruition. Finally, thanks to the Canadian Information Processing Society of Manitoba for giving me my first opportunity to speak on the topic of enterprise architecture so many years ago.

Warning – Disclaimer

This book is designed to provide information on enterprise architecture, the process and the career of the enterprise architect. It is sold with the understanding that the publisher and author are not engaged in rendering legal, accounting or other professional services. If legal or other expert assistance is required, the services of a competent professional should be sought.

It is not the purpose of this manual to reprint all the information that is otherwise available to existing and potential enterprise architects, but instead to complement, amplify and supplement other texts. You are urged to read all the available material, learn as much as possible about enterprise architecture and your career, and tailor the information to your individual needs. For more information, see the many resources referred to in this book.

Every effort has been made to make this manual as complete and accurate as possible. However, there may be mistakes, both typographical and in content. Therefore, this text should be used only as a general guide and not as the ultimate source of enterprise architecture and the career. Furthermore, this manual contains information on enterprise architecture and the career that is current only up to the printing date.

The purpose of this manual is to educate and to inform. The author and Firefli Media shall have neither liability nor responsibility to any person or entity with respect to any loss or damage caused, or alleged to have been caused, directly or indirectly, by the information contained in this book.

If you do not wish to be bound by the above, you may return this book to the publisher for a full refund.

Preface—Note to the Reader

Many information technology architects will experience feelings of loneliness, fear, and isolation when they first take on the role of the enterprise architect (EA). They are not sure what the role entails or even how to do the work. They are concerned whether they can even do the job. They worry they don't know any of the terminology, methodologies, or anything else about the models their clients will want them to create.

Even though most architects will feel they have been doing architecture, most will second-guess their ability to do the job. Who pauses to ask how they might do a job well before they accept the job? This book is designed to fill that hole: here is your personal invitation to dive right in and get the information you need. You'll find most of the information you need to assess your career prospects as an EA within the confines of these covers. Occasionally, we'll jump off through a link to the book resource site that will give you the information you need or to do some work to design a career you'll love.

The secret of joy in work is contained in one word—excellence.
To know how to do something well is to enjoy it.
—Pearl Buck (1892–1973), The Joy of Children, 1964

What does this all mean to you? By reading the contents of this book, you'll take comfort in what you already do know and learn how to apply your knowledge to your work at hand. You'll receive a road map through the steps you need to become great and reduce the pain and frustration you might feel from being overwhelmed by all that might seem important when you first become an EA. Within each chapter, you'll find guides and checklists for what you will need to do, which will help you save time and money.

Each chapter is designed to be an easy read and is divided into digestible chunks. It is laid out in an order that should minimize your challenges along your career path, but you can also easily skip to a step you might immediately benefit from.

Contents

List of Figures

INTRODUCTION

The Book's Intended Audience

For New or Aspiring IT Architects and Enterprise Architects

This book will help you understand what is in store for you if you are a new or an aspiring EA. Step One will help you assess whether you are qualified to do the job. Steps Two and Three will help you learn the skills and abilities you need to excel in the role as well as help you define your future in the role. In these steps, you will read and learn information about deciding to pursue a career in enterprise architecture. Steps Four and Five will allow you to visualize and think like a master architect. They will provide a step-by-step approach to gaining the hard and soft skills you need to be in the top 10 percent of all enterprise and IT architects.

For IT Architecture Managers and Chief Architects

If you are a leader, manager, or director responsible for direction and career development of an architecture team, you may use Steps One and Two to identify potential architects and hone development plans for your teams. You'll be very interested in Step Three, where you'll learn about team design as well as how to plan for soft-skill development. In Steps Four and Five, you will learn how to eliminate barriers to advancement, how to assist others in career mapping, and how to drive your careers, departments, and organizations.

For Chief Information Officers

Step Five of the book will likely hold the most interest for you. Skimming through the entire book and reviewing each chapter's Zoom In and Zoom Out sections will provide you with a chapter summary. More importantly, reviewing these sections will give you great insight into methods your teams can use to gain efficiencies.

The strategies presented will allow your teams to plan and implement architecture strategies that provide stakeholders more value by saving time and money. In addition, you might be very interested in reading the chapter on architecture teams as well as the step on soft skills for EAs.

The Book's Approach

The premise of this book is simple: there are five steps to building excellence as an EA. The goal of this book is to help you focus on those steps and build the first skills you need to accelerate your career in the most efficient way possible. Following a very precise order, the book presents a variety of distinct knowledge areas common to architects who possess traits of excellence. The architect who is centered in his or her learning endeavors may leap ahead of colleagues by learning only the most important information in a focused manner. You will find opportunities for decision points where you can decide whether a career as an architect is right for you along the way.

What you'll find here is a system for training the best EAs. It is not based on any curriculum you'll find at any university. This system was born out of personal observations and experience in working with well over four hundred architects over a career span of nearly twenty-five years. I travelled many paths in information technology to gain this insight, and along the way, I had experiences with some of the most intriguing projects and people. From what I've observed, it seems that the architects who are able to get the attention of the business and provide the most value are those who seem to possess these similar characteristics and traits.

This book is a culmination of the mentoring, coaching, training, and consulting work I have done as an EA. Over the various projects I have had the joy of working on, people have raised many questions regarding the roles, teams, skills, and paths they should take to become an EA. Through training classes, assessment programs, as well as many articles and blog posts aimed to arm the architect with knowledge and effective decision-making tools, I decided I could sum this up into a career path and a description of the most common skills and abilities you need to possess to become a great EA.

After observing these traits in the best architects I had the opportunity to know and work with, I reflected upon these traits and merged them into what I call the Matrix of Excellence. As the list grew, I wondered whether the common thread among those first-class architects was a particular industry vertical or even a technology background or discipline, but that wasn't the case. My curiosity then morphed into an intense study.

I went on to list every company I had worked with, whether as an employee, consultant, or mentor. That number grew to more than one hundred companies. I was shocked but not surprised, as I've spent many months travelling to work as a consultant. My work as a road warrior allowed me the privilege of working with many great teams over my nearly twenty-five years of experience in information technology. As I remembered my experiences, I realized the key characteristics of these great architects were indeed similar.

This similarity couldn't be mere coincidence, I decided. To tip the scales and decide whether I was onto something, I grouped them and then categorized their skills and traits. What else would an EA do? The results were a matrix that resembled a framework in appearance, much like the Zachman framework. Born of coincidence? I think not. Once an experienced architect, the mind tends to work in this way: slicing and dicing, ordering, categorizing, and separating.

Structural Overview

It is my goal, intention, and dream that you will get as many benefits from this book as quickly as possible. Because this work is a daunting endeavor, I have chunked it into smaller parts so it doesn't seem quite so overwhelming. Thus, I decided to separate the knowledge and skills an architect needs to take to become excellent into categories or steps and make some sense of it. What does that look like?

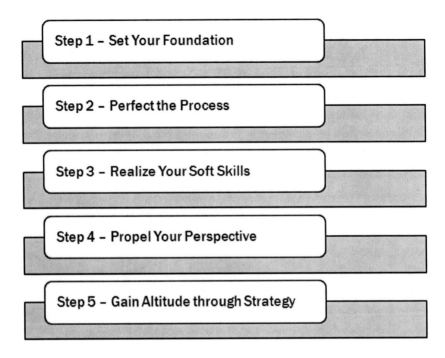

Figure 1. Five Steps to Enterprise Architecture Excellence

These steps are aligned with the parts of this book. Each part contains multiple chapters, and in each chapter, the focal point is either a knowledge area or a characteristic an architect must possess to become excellent. Keep in mind that you do not need to possess each characteristic to be excellent. However, the more of these traits and knowledge areas you possess, the higher the position you're likely to attain in your career as an EA. This position may be the level on which you contribute or operate, and it may include levels all the way up to executive positions.

The first step is establishing a solid technical foundation. You must have a solid base on which to become a practitioner. Thus, Part I of this book describes the basic information and proficiencies you need to excel as an IT practitioner. These are the prerequisites you must possess, combined with experience and a journey through a company's IT department or the business, to become an EA. This part includes the topics of research, analysis, and others from an architecture perspective.

The second step is developing a solid grasp of the use of the architectural process in the most efficient manner appropriate to the context of the problem and business strategy. You will most likely appreciate and use the architecture methods and process intuitively as you move through your work and the projects in which you participate. An abridged guide of information you need about the architecture process is covered in Part II. It covers the critical information you need to apply to sort through the various and confusing architecture methodologies prevalent today. This part includes the topics of modeling and engineering from an architecture perspective. It includes abstract and pattern thinking, and we will discuss in depth the mapping and blueprinting activities great architects use in their everyday work. A review of the skills you need to compartmentalize and organize chunks of information and requirements into systems and solutions in the context of frameworks rounds out this part.

The third step is mastering the use of critical soft skills. We reach a major crossroads here—one in which you, the architect, may decide to further your career as a lead project architect or choose to follow a path in enterprise architecture. Soft skills such as leadership, politics, consulting, and specific communication methods are key components that will lead to success in the EA role. Part III shares a description of the critical knowledge areas as well as the ways in which you may gain experience in these areas from various project assignments. This part will review some of the most prevalent soft-skill areas you must master to negotiate the curves and turns of the EA career.

The fourth step to architecture excellence is cultivating the ability to maintain various perspectives of a situation from the correct angles that will allow you to see the best path to an optimal solution. You will have the ability and the knowledge to take steps backward and forward to view the situation from multiple perspectives. Part IV introduces architecture perspectives such as vision and big-picture thinking. It also addresses the concept of using road maps to broach the subject of moving from current to future state from both project architecture and enterprise viewpoints. This part also includes a way of using realist filters to test recommended solutions, and it provides a checklist method that will help budding architects ensure solution integrity, demonstrate their skills, and gain credibility as an expert. It concludes with team design, construction, and leadership, as they are typically the key areas for enterprise architecture coaching.

The fifth step is taking it to the top. Part V includes critical knowledge areas you must master to attain full excellence and recognition as a chief architect or chief technology officer. This part includes topics and specific activities, such as strategic planning and fostering alignment between business and IT, and it discusses the various components in the alignment process. Part V also shares techniques that will help you prove quality in the architecture through metrics and portfolio planning. It also focuses on the key business knowledge areas you must strive to learn to gain the respect of and to work alongside business experts. The topics of the EA as a master of change and the next steps an architect may take to gain even more expertise close out the book.

Successful EAs make excellence and quality their goals and part of their overall shared vision. First-class practitioners have incredible insight in strategic planning and the use of strategic measures. To succeed and play the role of a management consultant, you must be viewed as a key business strategist. You must master many facets of business and strategy and possess entrepreneurial skills. You must know how and when to apply specific methods in the pursuit of the design, development, and realization of the road map to the future for your enterprise. This book covers all of these elements and more.

As you read, you'll notice two features worth highlighting within each chapter summary. The first is the **Zoom In** section. This component will outline some tools and tips that will help you become more efficient. It will allow you to think and perform some architecture activities more quickly, thus providing more value for your client or company. Following each Zoom In section, you'll find a **Zoom Out** component. The focus of this feature is the big-picture perspective you need to keep the most prevalent points of the chapter in mind. You can use it as a refresher when you return to the book for reference in the future.

Zooming In

My goal was to recognize the traits an architect exemplifies that signal greatness and pass this information on to you. With this information, you may also be able to distinguish behavior patterns that inhibit excellence in the EA and gain awareness so you can avoid them. You should also be able to glean knowledge about how you can design the organization and enterprise architecture team to provide the right atmosphere to promote creative and visionary performance. You'll soon realize what activities and traits you may exploit within the team context to become a great architect. You'll discover how the EA can exhibit value and lead to excellence both as an individual team member and in the enterprise architecture program.

Throughout the book, various checklists and diagrams will assist you operate in the most efficient way possible. Various suggestions and tips are available to help you plan your career so you can make the right moves to achieve the most satisfaction and growth within your vocation. Flip through the book from start to finish and explore the checklists. See which are relevant to you now, take them, and adapt them to your specific work or task at hand. Again, the goal of this book is to help you to become more productive immediately and learn the most efficient way to bring value to your company.

After you have skimmed, read the book in its entirety. Skim steps you feel you already have mastered, or read them anyway to see whether there are any additional tips or suggestions that you might pick up. When you are done, you might want to check out the book's website or the links scattered through this book; you can get even more leverage by taking advantage of the online tools and downloads available with this book. You'll need to log in to obtain access to these tools, as they are just for those who buy this book. I regularly use these tools and tips with my coaching clients, and you'll be privy to some great information that otherwise would not be available to you.

Zooming Out

The topics and ideas presented within this book have been laid out in a specific order. It might have been just as easy to plainly state that there are just five steps to becoming an excellent architect. The reality is, you should focus on several concept areas, and there is only some semblance of order in which an architect may master these skills. While acquiring all of these skills will ensure that you become an excellent architect, this book's intention was to share and illustrate these keys for another reason: my utmost goal is to share the straightest line possible to that pinnacle in your career.

At first, an aspiring architect must face the question of how he or she should do this. How do you become an architect? What does an architect do? How do you do it? You may or may not have gone through this process in your career already. If not, within the first few chapters of this book, you will find help to answer those questions. If you are like many EAs who are reading this book, you are more than likely asking the question how do I do this well? This book aims to provide you a pathway to achieve excellence.

We are reaching a point in the business cycle where quality will again become the focus. We've recently seen iterations of "do it fast," and we've also gone through waves of "do it cheap." This is likely what we are experiencing now in combination with "do it carefully." At some point not too far in the future, it will cycle back to "do it well and with high quality." If you are concerned about your employment status, quality should be foremost in your mind.

Another consideration of your career will have you facing a question of your personal value. Today, many of us are thinking about what really matters and rethinking our values. If you are going to look inward to find ways to do things at the utmost levels of quality, now is the time. This book provides one such perspective.

Website

www.zoomfactorbook.com

Visit the site to get instructions for accessing the book's bonus information and updates online.

Career Road Maps

At various points within this book, you will be directed to access additional information online or to refer to diagrams and information to map your career.

PART I:
SET YOUR FOUNDATION

In this part

- Chapter 1: Architect Your Career
- Chapter 2: Exploit Your Expertise
- Chapter 3: Scope the Problem
- Chapter 4: Analyze as an Architect

Part I of this book describes the basic information and proficiencies you need to excel as an IT practitioner. These are the prerequisites you must possess, combined with experience and a journey through a company's IT department or the business, to become an EA. This part includes the topics of research, analysis, and others from an architecture perspective.

CHAPTER 1:
ARCHITECT YOUR CAREER

Every day I remind myself that my inner and outer life are based on the labors of other men, living and dead, and that I must exert myself in order to give in the same measure as I have received and am still receiving.
—Aristotle

Designing a career for yourself should include mastering the most basic skills an EA has in his or her tool kit. Your company made you an architect—now what do you do? You are most likely to going to dive in and take whatever assignments are sent your way. In no time flat, you will have missed the opportunity to make this a great career by design. Time will fly by; projects and initiatives will come and go.

Other than your new job description and a list of generic education requirements, no clear qualifications for the IT architect exist. Some certification programs are improving their lists of skills and activities the architect will possess upon completion, but most programs are technology-, methodology-, or framework-specific and cannot be applied universally as a standard.

Also, we as an industry inconsistently define the role. Career paths and road maps are seemingly nonexistent. Persons with a great wealth of experience in business and IT can alike land in this job. Why not ensure that you are qualified for the journey? Take the road to architecture excellence.

Let's face it—past technology practices of gaining new skills and approaches in information technology have been backward. You study a new technology and attempt to find out all you can within it to become an expert. You research and compare all the frameworks and approaches available, and then spend a lot of valuable time trying to figure out which one would best match your organization, style, and budget. After you are done, you attempt to get funding for programs and then spend more time defining roles, responsibilities, and programs and seeking support and funding.

What's wrong with this picture? It seems like reinventing the wheel yet again. What if you were to learn the foundations of your work so that you could put them into action now? What if you knew which skills and knowledge you personally needed to achieve more success and help your company achieve its strategic goals at the same time? What if you had a laser-focused list of the twenty most important skills you'd need to put architecture into action as quickly as your company is dying to realize?

People who create their own success ensure they know what they need to do to succeed. What if you knew now which skills and knowledge you should focus on so as not to waste your time? What if you had the foresight to plan not only how you would gain this knowledge, but also to plot a journey in excellence for yourself and your career? In the first step of the journey to excellence as an EA, there is a long list of skills and experience you will need to set as the foundation for your work, knowledge, and career. As you review them, if they are missing from your personal inventory, you must figure out how to gain them. Save some time: try some of the suggested resources included in this book and make your life a little easier. Make your ground floor rock solid and enjoy the ride!

Why must a great EA have a solid foundation in information technology?

> ➤ Possessing firsthand project experience in the trenches is key to understanding how all of the pieces fit together and the art of the possible.
> ➤ Proven, deep skills in one of the core domain architecture areas—business, data, solutions, and technology—are almost a prerequisite for excellence in enterprise architecture.
> ➤ Respect from your peers for your judgment, abilities, contributions, and teamwork goes a long way toward the leadership you will need to exhibit.

> ➤ Track record in superior quality solution creation, project development, and management gives you the depth and understanding you'll need to create viable architectures.
> ➤ Practical understanding of many facets of your industry and the methodologies and processes used in the various technology and business domains allows you to be empathetic to the requirements and needs of all who will contribute and use the architecture.

Your Capacity for Excellence

You can achieve excellence by understanding the differences between good architecture and great architecture. An organization needs to create the right landscape to give an architect the room to enable and make actionable what will become the perfect blend of change, technology decisions, and competitive distinction. As you go through this book, you will find you have the capacity to achieve the traits and skills presented. You'll recognize how to apply the skills you already possess and gain confidence in your existing abilities. Many new architects lack this confidence.

Acknowledge your existing talent as your journey in the role of EA begins. Use each step to identify your personal strengths—know yourself and assess your skills honestly. Identify your weaknesses in the same manner. Accept where you need additional knowledge and reflect how an EA would apply the skills you may possess from an IT-architecture perspective. A great example is in the area of analysis. Systems analysis and architecture analysis are different. Know the difference and plot your growth path.

Deep technical skills are not as important for the EA as soft skills. Human factors have become increasingly important today, especially in the area of business strategy. Emotional intelligence or neural linguistics has become a popular topic evident in many areas of business.

In addition, it is more important that EAs possess a wide range of technical knowledge than specific expertise. It is crucial that they at least possess general technical knowledge on most subjects, as they are going to work toward putting together large solutions. They need to appreciate the moving parts to understand the risk and the need for deeper technical viewpoints from other experts.

Great EAs will typically be great leaders, communicators, and politicians. They grow past the need to solve intense technical problems and are more interested in bigger-picture business challenges. When EAs select their favorite technologies out of habit or technical religious preferences, it actually hampers their efforts. The technology-neutral EA who selects the right technology or solution for both the context and requirements of the business problem becomes a much more valuable asset.

Overall, EAs should be visionary and passionate about the reasons enterprise architecture is critical to the business. They realize why we shouldn't argue the benefits and the value of architecture. After truly understanding the benefits, it is difficult for them to operate in any other way. They are capable of looking past their personal preferences and just want what's best for the business—plain and simple.

The Reason Your Company Needs Architects

There are many theoretical, scientific, and business reasons your organization needs architects as IT professionals.

➢ Architects are trained to collect the type of requirements that analysts don't collect, to see the big picture, and to conceptualize.

➢ Architects look beyond immediate requirements to design flexible solutions that will adapt to changing business needs.

➢ Architects can solve problems creatively from various viewpoints.

➢ Architects gain more opportunities to understand the business when they are involved at the earliest planning and strategy stages, allowing them to develop creative solutions that realize time and cost reductions.

> ➤ Architects gain efficiencies and save costs for their companies by maximizing investments made in technology.
> ➤ A well-designed architecture solution can reduce investment costs now and increase long-term value in the business.

As you start your career in information technology architecture, you need core technical foundations and qualifications as a baseline. Though the backgrounds of all great architects vary greatly, if you dig deep enough into their starting points, you'll find at least one commonality: almost all of them can list at least three great initiatives they have worked on in the past.

Your Claim to Fame

In most great architects, some common key skills and expertise are present. Expertise comes through application and practical experience. Your skills and experience, in addition to passion for your role and your company's advancement, will define your future. The most common theme in great EAs is point of origin. The candidate EA is most typically an expert in one of the various domain architectures, such as data architecture, system or solution architecture, or perhaps technical architecture. Consider where you have spent your time and what types of things your past holds for you now that are leading you to this point in your career.

Your experiences might have been born through key involvement in a large enterprise solution, such as enterprise resource planning software or a portal solution. As illustrations, my personal examples include a portal selection project and e-Business design for a large financial company. These are just personal examples at the roots of my career that allowed me the incredible opportunity for intriguing work with respect to data governance, metadata, and standardization. Both led me on a global cleansing adventure that allowed me to interact with organizations as massive as the UN and see the world and company from an enterprise view. The work included the global leader in grain marketing as well as in a technology area with a huge database and infrastructure initiatives. As for you, perhaps you completed a business or data intelligence initiative, enterprise data modeling, data warehousing, or a massive data integration initiative.

My personal history includes a multiyear project as a consulting domain architect lead with an amazingly gifted team. Our project was the design of a model remote operations center, its infrastructure, technology, and processes. Perhaps you might even include your own business process renewal project where your strength lies in the business architecture role or that of a business strategist. Many architects have acted in roles without the garden-variety architecture titles. For a diverse list of architecture roles and titles, check out the information at www.zoomfactorbook.com/book-resources. Individuals typically start their careers working as analysts both in systems and in business or in programmer developer design roles.

Your Three Defining Moments

Architects typically come with a breadth of expertise and experience. Something in common is usually a strong track record, including at least three great undertakings. Many potential architects will have more, but this is a common denominator. Most can recall at least three turning points in their careers that have allowed them to become great.

In addition to these great projects, you may have experience on a problem response team, tiger team, or "SWAT" team. Typically, companies form these teams as an emergency response to a large problem that has many technical specialists scratching their heads. These problems are typically multidimensional and are too challenging for many to solve without the brainstorming schemes of many people and a cohesive strategy. Recall some period in your life when you were asked to solve a very large problem. This was likely one of these turning points in your career—a beacon for destined greatness. What are the things that really stand out in your memory— the things you are very proud of?

Innovating Your Way into the Spotlight

Perhaps you are a real innovator and you have created something different or great. Maybe you came up with a new way to test or prototype an idea and saved time and money in the process. These types of experiences typify the great architect. It could have been the planning or transition of new technology. Do you recall a time when you were co-located with other systems engineers, a great team of developers, or perhaps even a cross-functional team? You had a massive problem to solve or a big project with many technological unknowns. You were thrown together to feed off each other's energy and ideas. There is nothing quite like it when you reflect back to that point in your life and your career. Do you recall how you felt when others believed you were capable of being innovative and creative? Your organization trusted you to come up with solutions.

It is the highest level of respect to allow the architect the space to innovate. Depending on the type of industry in which you work, you may get more opportunity than others. Of all of the IT roles possible, the architect is typically given most credit for providing this type of effort. Your management team has put you in the position to put together a solution to a large problem. As you move toward the role of the EA, this becomes an even bigger responsibility. Pretend for a moment that management sent you to work at the puzzle factory— not just to pick out the pieces, but also to decide what shapes, colors, dimensions, and quantities you need. Your track record has earned you this latitude.

Your Boardroom Impressions

Have you ever made a big impression with a company and caused heads to turn or made positive moves that resulted in somebody requesting that you be accelerated in your position? You might have forgotten, but if you go back through each step in your career, you may recall some point where you were asked a very critical question. Influential individuals were listening, and perhaps your response caused eyes to widen or your superiors to sit up and take notice. Your method of describing an idea, solution, or problem was defined and succinct, and people noted your contribution.

As a technical specialist with strong core technical expertise, you may have contributed to big wins at your organization. These might have been a large cost savings, heroic budget cutting, or focused pioneering of a process or method that resulted in positive results for your organization or clients. Your curious nature might have prompted you to prototype or test such a new theory or method and learn all you could about it.

You may have been positioned as a groundbreaker or great leader in the area of processes and methods at your company. Someone may have also asked you to present the work you did to others. Your behavior caused a shift in the thinking of the individuals around you at your organization. These are signs that an architect possesses the keys necessary to become excellent. You were in the right place at the right time, and you conquered.

Your Strong Analytical Mind

Your potential greatness as a leader in enterprise architecture lies in your strong analytical mind. This natural ability is near the top of the list for those with the potential for greatness. It is a skill you can learn, and an individual who does not possess this great skill naturally must be open and willing to learn and desire to become expert in it. The individual must have great strength in problem definition and methods and have an uncanny ability to very accurately set the scope in context.

If you are an individual destined to become an excellent EA, you will always keep your eye on containing problems so they do not grow in complexity or number. Predictably, you are the one in the meeting ensuring and reminding those who are all trying to get a problem solved that you must stay focused to put context and structure around the problem.

Your Vast Experience

The EA comes from great experience, practices, and a wide array of background roles in both business and in information technology. Your career might have originated as a member of the ranks of mid-management or as a project manager or lead. The positions and roles are not as important as the experiences and initiatives. So many potential career paths lead to IT architecture; the links at www.zoomfactorbook.com/book-resources include the most up-to-date information on potential architecture career paths. Typically, a role based in technical knowledge is the person selected as an architect. This individual is usually the one who becomes an architect without evolving through the business area. A recent exception is the small number of EAs who start from the strategic-planning department, born from business areas.

You are characteristically strong and have deep knowledge in one of the domain areas—business, applications and solutions, information, or technology. Most likely, what differentiates you from other technologists is that you also have a wide variety of general technical knowledge in most of the other areas or domains. If you were to become a very strong solution architect, you are typically very skilled either in the technical side or on the data side. If you are very skilled in the data area, you may have decent skill in the business area as well.

Typically, you have sharp business and application insight with a perceptive eye for process. In the end, as you will see on your journey throughout this book toward excellence, the architect possesses or builds very strong psychosocial skills.

The Roles That You'll Play

The Role of an IT Architect

A search for a consistent description of the role of an architect might leave you frustrated and perhaps even confused. Descriptions you might find state skills and traits the architect must possess, as well as some of the behaviors they must emulate. But here's the most important part—the role may differ slightly in each organization. The IT industry seems to have made a business out of redefining and recycling terminology. Rather than focus on this obscure nomenclature, it is simpler to evaluate the variety of the talents, behaviors, skills, and traits of an architect who will fit into any organization and match many job descriptions. Take what you see here as a high-level, generic version.

Problems are less well defined for architects, and they must spend time to ensure that a problem's context, scope, and boundaries have been defined before they assess it. The architect's primary activity is to focus on the implications of technical choices for the organization. The architect must understand all of the overarching dynamics and impacts in making such choices and lead a team of developers, integrators, and implementers along the prescribed path.

Architects must sustain an overall system view at all times while designing a solution. Architects build models of the problem and the solution space and apply their analytical and conceptual minds to visualize how the pieces may fit together. They recognize patterns and apply experiences and concepts they know from their past when they approach new solutions.

Architects explore alternative approaches to almost every solution presented to them. They must view and take into account all of the different aspects within the organization, such as people, process, technology, data, and applications when determining which approach they will take. Architects spend a great deal of their time preparing documents, positions, presentations, and diagrams, and they must be very strong in communication, diagramming, and documentation skills.

They must be very good modelers and be able to adapt to varying levels of tools available for the prescribed deliverable. Architects must have a strong business sense and the ability to scale down or tailor explanations of architecture for sponsors and stakeholders as well as technical staff. Their skills range from providing technical detailed descriptions for technology staff and implementers to higher granular levels for the business stakeholders to demonstrate that they understand the business problem.

Success for an architect depends on skills and characteristics not typically emphasized in university curricula or on-the-job training. Architects gain experience during their years of experience within information technology. They merge experience they may have gained from various careers and depend on their experience and their keen business sense to propose solutions. They diagram and document their solutions and solve the largest and most complex technology problems for the organization. For more details on the roles in IT architecture, visit www.zoomfactorbook.com/book-resources.

The Role of the EA

It is difficult to come to a consensus on a formulated role. Most organizations realize now that they need such a role or team, but there are many differences as to whether this person is rooted in information technology, a strategic-planning department, or the project or program management office. With the adoption of privacy acts and regulatory changes in the economic environment, companies are making the case for better definition of such a role.

At any rate, EAs are leaders and must be good communicators and listeners. They are visionaries and agents prepared to promote and deliver change to their organization to make their companies more efficient and effective. EAs believe in change because they have an enterprise view.

EAs work in an aligned manner with leaders, business resources, and technologists to build an enterprise view of the organization's strategy, business requirements, processes, information, and infrastructure assets. EAs analyze the links between the business drivers of an organization to the information technology domains using models or views from both a current and future state perspective. The objectives for EAs are to achieve efficiency, flexibility, and agility. They play a central role and typically manage the creation of many solution blueprints for the components they oversee. The EA's role is further characterized by analyzing some of the parameters in which the EA works. Minor differences appear based on the department in which EAs work, their reporting relationships, and the motivation for creation of the architecture. Chapter 10 includes more descriptions of the various types of EAs and their roles.

The Career You'll Design

IT architects know the value of laying a good foundation. As with any career, it is important to know the qualifications for the job and the various paths you might take to achieve your goals. Your career can take various paths depending on your desires and abilities. Your career road map is yours to create, and the conclusion of each step of this book is a logical point at which to reevaluate your skill levels and desired direction. Your primary focus in this step will be laying a foundation to ensure you have the basic skills and qualifications you need as an IT architect. As you progress through this book, you will focus on the enterprise and what you need to succeed there. It is important to honestly assess your abilities and your motivation underlying your career goals. These goals might include recognition, growth, advancement, and financial security, just to name a few.

Charting Your Career Road Map

In Chapter 17 on teams, you'll learn how to recognize architecture skills in potential candidates and how to excavate to find EAs within your organization. You'll want to pay special attention to the ways in which you can pick up assignments to help grow traits and skills in the areas you need for this role. Your leaders, managers, and mentors can give you tools to foster your growth into an excellent architect. You'll have to decide for yourself which path you want to explore and honestly assess your skills, strengths, and weaknesses.

If you want to grow toward an EA role in its full capacity, you'll need the entire slate of soft skills covered in Section Three of this book. For now, let's make sure you have the solid knowledgebase you need to exist and mature as an IT architect.

Zoom In—Action Steps You Need to Succeed

Here is a questionnaire to help you determine whether you are ready to be an architect:

- ☐ I am skilled at designing solutions.
- ☐ I am interested in the business at my company and have a decent understanding of their goals.
- ☐ I am intrigued by business in general and have good business application and solution insights.
- ☐ I have worked on at least three large or significant projects in the past.
- ☐ I am able to communicate well both with more technical people and less technical people than myself.
- ☐ I enjoy showing someone what my design or vision is with a solution either by drawing a diagram, model, map, or picture using a whiteboard and computer tools.
- ☐ I have deep knowledge and am an expert in one of the four key domains: applications, systems and solutions, data and databases, or technology and infrastructure. If I am not an expert in any of these domains, I have been a leader on the business side and am expert in business process and process design.
- ☐ I am process oriented and believe in following a proven method.
- ☐ I have acted either in an official architecture role or in a senior leadership role in solution, system design, or project management.
- ☐ I have a strong analytical background.
- ☐ I excel in solving problems with creative solutions.
- ☐ I am good at setting boundaries around a problem and knowing where to set limits for the solution.
- ☐ I am able to get focused, refocus, and stay focused.
- ☐ I am known in my company as an action taker, contributor, driver, or a star. I get things done.
- ☐ I have strong social and personal skills.
- ☐ I have good variety in my educational background and am committed to continued learning.

☐ I use a wide variety of career experience and practices to help guide and steer processes, standards, and principles needed for an architecture program.

☐ I have good general knowledge in the technical areas in which I do not have deep levels of experience.

☐ I have taken on a variety of roles from doer, team member, planner, leader, and troubleshooter.

Zoom Out—Big-Picture Concepts

Wouldn't it help if you knew what you did best every day? In formulating many of the plans for your career, it helps if you know your strengths and how you can exploit them. Leveraging your strengths has become a common theme in business today. Use your instinct-based actions to determine what you do best every day.

By leveraging your personal, instinctive strengths, you can isolate how you can tap into them to provide your customers greater value. By staffing around areas where you are not as strong, you can put together the best team.

Ten Reasons You Need to Know Your Instinctive Profile

1. It tells you who you really are.
2. It helps you make career decisions.
3. It hones your competitive edge.
4. It lets you tap into your mental energy.
5. It spotlights your natural advantages.
6. It helps prevent conflict.
7. It reduces stress on the job.
8. It maximizes your productivity.
9. It helps you be a star.
10. It makes work fun.

Visit the link at www.zoomfactorbook.com/selfassessment for a true analysis of yourself, which will guide you toward what you are best suited to do.

CHAPTER 2:
EXPLOIT YOUR EXPERTISE

Experience is one thing you can't get for nothing.
—Oscar Wilde

As you start your journey into IT architecture, don't lose how you became qualified. It might already be obvious to you how you will use your current expertise to create deliverables and artifacts shaped and aligned differently than pure technical specifications. You might feel overwhelmed that you have been named as an IT architect or even shocked that someone has asked you to take on the EA role. If you are like most people, you aren't sure what you're supposed to do next and how you should engage.

You might even be feeling a sense of panic. Are you unsure because you don't know what the process is? Are many terms a little fuzzy? Are those artifacts you've been told you'll have to create a very daunting proposition? Are you worried about how your colleagues will treat you? Rest assured. Use your expertise, experience, and obvious star talent to boost your confidence. Take a moment to make a plan to take advantage of your experience. What has changed? It will take some introspective thinking. EAs are selected, delegated, and nominated for a variety of reasons. One thing is for sure: your experience and expertise won't go to waste.

The important matter is that, by relying on your experience and knowledge, you will be confident to focus on getting the job done. Take your core technical stardom and build on it; if you have more than one developed knowledge area, great. As Marcus Buckingham said in his book *Go Put Your Strengths to Work*, "Either resign yourself to a life in which your strengths are largely irrelevant; or, instead, learn how to make them relevant. Learn how to put them to work. It is your choice." You'll soon see how the skills that made you great as a technologist will become largely irrelevant as you pass into the world of architecture. Even so, those skills still have great value, so you should learn how to use them to your advantage.

No one talks about where architects come from and how they use their expertise. There used to be a premium on your technical skills. It is what made you the great resource that you are. Now is time to consider the skills you'll need to round out these skills. This isn't a debate about reducing focus on your weaker areas. You might be driven to know to learn more about other technical areas in the IT domain. If you were a stellar data architect, don't try to be an expert now in networks or hardware. Panic often sets in for new architects because they feel everyone is going to expect them to know more about everything.

You'll need high-level, broad knowledge in each of your non-strength domains, but only enough to understand how all the pieces work together. Build on the solid technical baseline first. You are establishing the context for your career, studying the parameters, and setting the perimeter. Focus on what you should spend your time learning and developing. Your goal should not be to learn all about the other areas of technology. Your job is to look outward and upward. Think about architecture from a broader perspective rather than from a narrow, technical view.

Throughout the course of this book, you'll find specific lists of the knowledge you'll need to gain and the skills and processes you need to learn. Many topics have intentionally been omitted. You'll learn a lot about technologies not on your forte list without having to go into a full study. You'll gain perspective through projects, research, and initiatives, and you already possess the talents you need to learn what you'll need as supplements to your knowledge.

Until this point in your career, you have tried your best to hone and maintain your technical expertise. You've attended seminars, read periodicals, and attempted to get the best assignments at work. You will have gained and earned the status of a technical expert in the career you deserve. You either are a natural talent or have worked hard, but that's the way your career has naturally evolved up until this point. You have some deep knowledge in an area of business or technology and are a domain expert through the expertise you have gained.

Now, you also have some broad knowledge in other areas of business. Perhaps this is a vertical subject matter of expertise within your organization, such as finance, accounting, marketing, sales, or another core area of your business. Perhaps this is manufacturing or technology itself. You may have some broad knowledge in another areas, perhaps from your post-secondary studies or from a personal interest, and again, this is going to become very important later on in this book.

At some point, you've also become great at other business skills you have sampled. You have some core skills closer to the soft side that will make you a better all-around employee. Perhaps your skills may include something like communication, either written or verbal, or even leadership. You may possess some kind of political skills enabling you to work collaboratively with other people or to notice some of the trends and behaviors around you and your organization's culture.

Whatever your other talents are, you have them. Know that. You may just not acknowledge or recognize them, but you are most likely very strong in one or most of these other areas. Let's leave that for a moment, but let it percolate in your mind.

Use Technical Experience as a Foundation

Use your technical expertise as a launch pad and build a platform from which you will propel into architecture. All of your problem-solving skills and technical knowledge, combined with your experience, will culminate in work you'll soon know to be architecture.

Your experience in a specific domain will help guide and steer the process, standards, and principles you need for an architectural program. You may not recognize some of what you have learned and used so far, but it is indeed process. You may be well aware of what might be standard in your organization. At this very early time in your architecture career, you typically haven't heard much of the architecture terminology. You will see that you know more than you think once you get exposure to the process in Part Two of this book.

In the meantime, we've got some work to do.

Form Your Frame of Reference

You should be able to see key issues in your dominant technology specialty due to your experiences. This is one frame of reference as you move forward. For example, if you started your career in the area of application development, you will knowingly or unknowingly relate back almost everything you will learn about technology or about data to what you know about applications. It is your main point of reference, and you should feel secure in using that to your advantage.

The same is true if you have a basis in the area of data. You will associate everything you will hear from any others in your organization in terms of data. When somebody explains a problem he or she is having to you, you will wonder: So where is the data? How did you get the data? How did you save the data? How was it designed? Take these as very simple examples with respect to setting your frame of reference. Use this as your comfort zone.

The Roles You Played

Another common phenomenon occurs for all technologists during the earlier part of their careers. It will have occurred over the period when you have gained your vast experience as an expert. You've taken on various roles in your organization. You most likely started as a student learner or as an apprentice at your organization. From there, you moved toward being a doer, team member, or planner, and sometimes even a team leader in a project setting.

Aside from that, one thing is for sure. As an IT practitioner, you became a troubleshooter. This can also be true if your area of expertise is in the business area. We've all been asked to solve problems, and that's why you are typically doing the job you are doing. Consider the culmination of all of this—some deep knowledge and strength in at least one of the architecture domains as well as some very large project or initiative experience. Combine this with implementing technologies in a variety of conditions, and you will have well learned and put down a very solid foundation in the setting in which you are now working.

Potentially, you've built this up over the first few years of your career within a single industry vertical, and you have strong industry knowledge. Whatever it may be, you have formed the basis for the variety and expanse of experience needed for an EA. Later on, we'll look at the variety of other skills necessary in the EA's role, but at this point, we'll presume you have formed the necessary footing.

Gain Experience Through Career Transition

If you have changed careers over your lifetime, you will have deeper experience with respect to industry verticals and the core areas of business industrial knowledge. The depth will depend on the number and reasons for the changes. Various skills are brought to you through career change—either within the same role but at a different company, or in varying roles within the same company. Today, employers look for this breadth of experience when they review resumes prior to hiring for architecture positions.

Nearly twenty years ago, lack of tenure at one company was viewed in a negative light. Today, companies do not view it this way. For those of you who are still in the same organization where you started your career, congratulations. You are loyal, enjoy stability, or have had a fortunate number of opportunities within your organization. Employers view many pluses in you as well, especially your dedication. Something you will want to highlight is the broad experience you've gained from participating in various projects and acting in various roles within your organization.

In short, there are upsides to being in both positions.

Apply Practical Business Experience

There is no replacement for the lessons learned through the teachings of real business experience. Over your career lifetime, you will have seen many projects planned, started, ended, and cancelled. Your technical expertise may have been born in a variety of methods. If you started off in the area of business or systems analysis, you should have some skills in the area of business process mapping or modeling. You should be able to break down business functions into chunks, and you should be able to group and analyze them individually.

Depending on how close you have been to large projects, you should have been in and around the activity of collecting and identifying both the core components of the system as well as nonfunctional analysis. Your experience should have led you to view all parts as a whole and to understand the need for all such parts. You know the benefits of putting these parts together in the specific manner in which they were assembled.

If you are an individual who has experience or some background in business, you should have also experienced business-requirement engineering or process re-engineering activities. These are core experiences with respect to business analysis as well as the system asset life cycle. If your architecture career originated on the business side, it is likely you were one of the business subject matter experts on a large project or assisted in the area of database development or business intelligence.

Plumbing 101 (Infrastructure Planning)

Another source of your technical expertise may have come from the roots of your technical specialty. You may have been in the role of an infrastructure planner or technical specialist. These gurus are what people first think of when they hear the term architect. This is primarily because of the wiring nature of many of the diagrams they produce. A good example might be a network diagram.

A few years ago, if you asked corporate executives what they thought of when someone said the word "architecture," most would come up with a picture in their mind of some technical spaghetti, which was probably a network or infrastructure diagram. In the years I worked with architects at some of the biggest telecom organizations in North America, I witnessed spaghetti like you've never seen. With the common magnifying glass or the zoom feature on a computer, we determined these folks were a different kind of genius. What looks like a big hairball at 100 percent view often looks like pure brilliance at 300 percent.

Infrastructure specialists have been forced to coordinate with many infrastructure teams and manage plans on a regular basis. Most often, they are trying to replace the carpeting without moving the furniture. Infrastructure projects are among the most difficult to plan in information technology today. If your experience is here and you toiled in large-scale replacements, consider yourself fortunate and well trained. Many IT professionals spend time in the disciplines of infrastructure or technical support services at the very beginning of their careers. Some of today's experts may have started in such basic operational support roles. They could have worked as help desk analysts, answering telephones or doing basic technical support. The career paths introduced in Chapter 1 highlight experience with respect to more advanced positions within architecture.

Education Through Development Platform Transformation

During the time you have worked with information technology thus far, you have cultivated expertise in the areas of various development platforms and frameworks. The more technology cycles you have seen and products you have experience with, the broader your understanding and ability to see the similarities and differences. The more projects and companies on which your experience is based, the greater your experience will be multiplied.

You will have experience in many development and design tools depending on the number of companies you've worked in and the number of platforms and projects you've dealt with. Many times, this depends on the size of the companies in which you have worked. Many organizations do not invest heavily in tools, so if this has been the case for you, you are not alone and likely have experience only in the most common office productivity tools. Development tools will be either purchased or homegrown, possibly built by you and the teams with whom you worked, depending on your background and the type of organization where you work.

An example of this might be in modeling and development tools. In my personal experience with a complex marketing agency that relied on databases, I grew up with some of the largest scale and most sophisticated modeling and development tools. Over time, I worked with smaller and more-budget minded customers, which helped me evolve toward simpler and more widely used tools. The system development environments you may have used or perhaps even participated in constructing at your organization are another massive differentiating factor for many architects. Today, many architects come from Java, Microsoft, or even an open source development shop. In most cases, the software or system architect will construct some sort of a framework so that each individual component or piece of code can build up on something common among all of them to save time. Experience through involvement in such frameworks is invaluable in your career.

Focus on Patterns

Some other experience that is part of a technical expert's core is in the area of software or solution engineering. If this is your background, you'll most likely be an advocate of patterns, whether or not you know it. Patterns are known to be at the center of efficiency in a solution or application architecture. You may have been a user, designer, or contributor of such patterns in your organization.

This means you may have created a piece of code or a solution that will be copied or replicated over time. You may or may not have been skilled in actually being a good pattern provider. In fact, your pattern should be very well documented with the intent to reuse it. If this is the case, your experience level will be higher than that of many architects. You are off to the greatest of starts, and it is likely you already have the Zoom Factor.

Learn Through Leadership

During the time you spent in information systems, you may have become a technical lead on a project or program area. Be it informal or formal experience, you may have acted as a leader of a project and dealt with some of the softer skill areas in the area of IT.

Some of your experience with these skills might include areas such as leadership, basic project management, and people management. These areas are at the root of every project. Architects will have to become skilled at conflict or team management out of necessity as they often try to sell their ideas and promote their designs. You may also be gifted at coordinating and the brainstorming of solutions as well as prioritizing some of the business requirements and requests for the solution.

Zoom In—Action Steps You Need to Succeed

Not everything you have developed as a skill can or should be used at the EA level. Look at this list and consider these areas within your experience as ones you should leverage or reuse in architecture. If it is not on the list, consider leaving those roles to your company's other technical experts. You'll have more conceptual and strategic matters to attend to, so carefully consider what skills you continue to develop.

Pack it up to bring to the role checklist:

- ☐ Knowledge of methodologies
- ☐ Knowledge of nonfunctional requirements
- ☐ Knowledge of development and system environments
- ☐ Modeling, diagramming, and prototyping skills
- ☐ Problem-solving skills
- ☐ Technology skills
- ☐ Patterns
- ☐ Handling abstract concepts
- ☐ Orientation toward solutions, as well as championing and promoting the solution

- ☐ Broad subject area domain knowledge—applications, data, technology, or business
- ☐ Soft skills such as leadership, facilitation, team building, communication, political handling, relationship management

Zoom Out—Big-Picture Concepts

Consider how you would relate your expertise to an architecture team. Consider the possibility that there is one subject matter expert in each of the domains beside you.

- ➢ What things do you do now that you would drop or leave behind for the other experts?
- ➢ How would you do this?
- ➢ What would you need to learn to interact and communicate better with these experts?
- ➢ How could you let this type of work go?

Activities you should plan to let go:

- ☐ Problem solving at the technical level
- ☐ Buddy systems with developers
- ☐ Database analysis
- ☐ Call lists
- ☐ Vendor relationships
- ☐ Configuration of anything
- ☐ Price negotiation with vendors
- ☐ Anything system or configuration management-related (third-level support)
- ☐ Staff management

There are exceptions for almost all of the items on this list. For example, the size of your IT shop might dictate that you are managing staff. Know that it is very difficult for you to make the time you need to do any architecture work when you have several resources dependent on you for allocation of work, performance reporting, and advanced troubleshooting.

CHAPTER 3:
SCOPE THE PROBLEM

If I were given one hour to save the planet, I would spend fifty-nine minutes
defining the problem and one minute resolving it.
—Albert Einstein

What makes architecture analysis different from most IT or business analysis is that you'll need to view problems in a whole new manner. Architecture is a combination of problem solving and decision making. Most often, architects are asked to participate when significant change is required for both business and information systems. Change is typically precipitated by problems, which the architect must distill and simplify, then revisit from a more granular perspective.

To perform effective problem analysis, definition and sizing of the problem are key. It is critical that you set the context before trying to solve the problem. Does the problem affect the corporate strategy? The IT strategy? Will it change the current transition road map? You can use this information to shape the requirement-gathering activity and to research potential components and services that will compose the solution space.

An Architect's Approach to Problem Definition

For EAs, problems become decisions to be made. A good decision will have structure, process, and documentation for the purposes of communication and reuse. As an EA, you will need to be able to adapt to change and stress at times when problems are deemed emergencies, when crises surround you, or when you are exposed to periods of great risk. Initially, your first glance must be broad brush. In other words, you must go with a wide perspective before narrowing down to deep details. Skilled EAs are careful not to eliminate alternatives too quickly. This requires that you hover at twenty thousand feet to survey the situation and consider all factors from a broad, general view. In these situations, time-boxing analysis can help expedite your analysis.

Complex problem solving offers yet another opportunity for you to add your skills and experiences. You must break down the problem into pieces, much like system components. Your method for solving problems should start with context setting and evaluating the circumstances under which your company is experiencing the problem or might encounter it. Following that, you need to align all of the problems that can be similarly grouped to a single or a few business drivers in the strategies you have prioritized at the top of your executive's lists.

Define the Problem

Many of the best EAs will start by defining the problem when they are asked to participate in any activity. Perhaps it is to gauge their time and effort, as well as fit in their schedule, but the most relevant question of all is "What is the definition?" This is typically where people struggle to begin with because they tend to get emotional or overwhelmed at the beginning of each architecture initiative. Many people will react to what they think the problem is. However, a calm, collected, process-oriented method of resolution is the key. You must choose to understand more about the problem.

To start the process, you might look at each domain perspective of a problem and consider what you might do or collect in each. For an example, you might review the main business functionality to result from a solution, the main data entities or stores associated with the functions, the systems available or required to perform the processes, and the technology needed to deliver them. If you use a method such as time boxing and spend a set time, such as one to two hours, to consider each perspective, it will allow you to focus on what is important and get used to moving quickly from one perspective to another in reviewing a problem.

Investigate the Root Cause

Most common problem-solving methods include a round of problem verification before jumping into solution mode. It is usually helpful to consider similar past situations where these types of problems have occurred, as well as to confer with colleagues on technical forums or at other companies with similar infrastructure or environments. Focusing on why this problem is different from those previously encountered typically saves time, money, and effort, providing value more quickly.

First, you should aim to describe the problem and to understand the possible causes as well as the business drivers and context for the specific problems. EAs are skilled in evaluating information by filtering out the background noise, politics, and extraneous information. If you are strong in problem identification, you may see opportunities to create a solution that may solve more than one problem.

Your ability to efficiently and effectively define problems, then organize work efforts to research and analyze the problem space, is critical to your success. As an EA, you must find out what others think is causing the problem and what supporting evidence they have. You should also seek out the circumstances and timing of the problem as well as the method. Ask questions to isolate specific cases of the problem, either by user group or in conjunction with other activities. A critical juncture in the process is drafting a written description of the problem. You should write a synopsis before recommending that any action be taken, let alone an architected solution.

When you solve problems, you must know when to call for help. Typically, EAs will call in an expert, consultant, colleague, or a mentor to discuss potential solutions. You should deal with root causes only and avoid dwelling unnecessarily in the specifics around problems. In short, you should take a pragmatic approach and filter out the extraneous information, such as history about why the problem happened or the politics around who caused it.

Determine the Solution Requirements

You should be skilled in using elicitation techniques when gathering solution requirements from business subject matter experts. Their accumulated experience allows them to better conceptualize various scenarios and solutions. EAs are characteristically good negotiators; in this role, it will be important for you to weigh the opinions, resources, and analysis of various parties.

As an EA, you will also be required to move from being a technical problem solver to becoming a big thinker. You will not be able to completely walk away from this role, but it will change your perspective on problem solving. You will need to approach the earlier stages of problem solving from a different vantage point—one of expecting problems or of preventing them by designing robust solutions.

Guide the Nonfunctional Requirement Process

Typically, you will be more involved in nonfunctional requirements than in functional requirements. As an architect, you may know these as quality attributes. You will need to get the basic understanding of the core functionality of the possible solution and an even deeper understanding of the business drivers behind it. This will put you in an even better position to gather those quality attributes. Because you will glean information from both technical teams as well as business teams, your skills will evolve. Before you analyze situations, it will become more critical that you do some advance planning, organization, and research.

Creating scenarios with respect to quality attributes to offer the technical and business resources will lead to success. Phrasing questions in terms of known trade-offs is another technique you can use to frame the expectations of users who may have difficulty defining the specific nature of the solutions they require. For example, if you ask a user, "What type of response time are you expecting?" the user will almost always respond with "fast." However, if you ask whether a two-second screen refresh time is acceptable, that question puts the element in a framework the user might better understand and also places context around the potential solutions.

Another perfect example is one in the area of availability. Asking the business for the number of seconds, minutes, or hours of acceptable downtime per month, accompanied by a dollar value for the loss, is much better than using a popular catchphrase like five nines or 99.999 percent uptime. Everyone wants it, but only a few understand the implications or costs of promising such resilience.

Prioritize the Problem

You may determine that there are several problems to review. If you determine they are related, you must prioritize the ones to tackle first. You also need to differentiate between important and urgent problems. It is easy to consider a problem urgent because of the noise it is getting, the number of people asking for help to solve it, or the risk of publicity or executive attention. To prevent distraction, avoid being involved in such problems unless officially requested.

Determine the Architect's Role in the Problem

Is this problem one that deserves architecture attention? Typically, emergencies are flagged as areas that should be avoided in the future. These types of problems should all make it onto your radar, but you won't be able to solve most problems in an emergency. "There are no emergency architectures" is a favorite saying of mine. Except in rare circumstances, I don't believe architects have a place on the call list. Typically, your involvement should be reserved for disasters. Disasters are typically caused by unforeseen circumstances, and you will need to play a role in recovery or resumption planning. The only architecture that you can really apply on short notice is tactical.

Set Context, Scope, and Boundaries

You should set the problem's context, parameters, and scope to constrain the solution space. Disciplined architects keep this rule in the forefront of their minds for the entire time they are performing architectural analysis. They filter and apply the problem to the business context and determine what would be best for the organization's future. Thus, you should understand there may be both tactical and strategic solutions and know you must weigh the longevity of the solution. The element of time is the prime criterion in solution selection.

Whether you use brainstorming techniques, lateral thinking, or a more formalized named method, such as Kepner-Tregoe or perhaps Edward de Bono's Purpose/Input/Solutions/Choice/Opinion (PISCO), you'll need some structured skills for your problem-solving activities. As you go through the architectural process, you will discover more information that will influence your perception of the problem. Use your experience to help set context. What is reasonable within your defined context?

As you examine potential alternatives and narrow the details of your preferred solution, you may have to revisit various aspects of the current situation where there are requirements to confirm your approach. These practices will show that your first review of the current state or situation should be time bound and not be time consuming. Time boxing is a method of doing problem analysis, decision making, and various other activities. It is meant to constrain the solution visualization process to a small amount of time you have available. Analysis and a plan for your decision making as well as your problem solving must fit within your allotted time. Often you can gain amazing foresight when a deadline drives you: then, only the necessary tasks survive.

After time passes, a great deal of research around your problem space may contribute very little value; this is one of the biggest traps in analysis. The seasoned architect will spot an obvious trap that you might otherwise waste time investigating and limit the investigation time and research. To avoid this trap, you need to organize research and interview processes differently than if you had a blank slate. For example, if you have a standard set of infrastructures at your organization as well as a limited number of solutions potentially able to solve your business problems, you will be able to put some sort of plan of action in place to get the right people to review each of the vantage points and put limits around their work.

To set the right context, it is necessary to think of the solution and its surrounding environment. The fit with this environment largely determines the acceptance and usability of the delivered solution. A common approach to documenting context is using context diagrams and models. Various types exist for IT architecture. Whether they are value network diagrams, big-picture business context diagrams, system context models, or information context diagrams, all are contextual and demonstrate the potential solution space and business drivers. They give the viewer a great visual of the boundaries of the solution to be defined. Often interfaces and both external and internal integration points can be shown to define influences on the solution.

Generate Alternatives and Hypothesize Solutions

It is better to know some of the questions than all of the answers.
—James Thurber

Problem solving generates alternative solutions to a particular problem as a specified set of requirements. Your perspective on the problem will be the focus on the strategy and the risks and impacts of the most convincing solutions. Consider components as assets and attach financial values to both the risks and the possible solutions. Questions such as "what should we do differently this time" or "how should we structure this solution to best support our business" are fundamental to the type of thinking you'll need to do.

Architects are typically able to keep an objective approach and won't eliminate alternatives because they aren't favorites or because technology biases exist. Skilled architects are adept in generating a varied list of alternatives and in narrowing down a short list of alternatives to only those that match compulsory criteria while discarding all others. This is particularly useful when the number of alternatives is quite large.

The more skills and practice you possess, the quicker this process becomes. Your talent lies in accelerating the process by knowing the specifics of what won't work, which allows for clearer decision making. You should have an ability to see patterns in requirements, match them to viable solutions, and fit them into the context. During the architectural process, you will undoubtedly have to make trade-offs as you evaluate various alternatives. No alternative is ever perfect, and you must choose what you are willing to sacrifice to get the greatest potential value from the solution for the business.

Use Criteria and Principles to Narrow the Scope

You will use criteria and principles to narrow the scope. Most often, these will come from your business resource customers—cost, functionality, timeline, and a cast of common nonfunctional requirements such as reliability, availability, and performance. Other considerations include software licensing and operational costs, hardware costs, equipment rental costs, matching standard environments, recovery and integrity levels, and the ability to scale or move to future platforms.

More common today is the ever-growing need to take into account a list of security and legislative concerns. Many solutions have become so proprietary that often some of these matches are difficult, and a large number of trade-offs become inevitable.

Weigh Criteria to Choose Solutions

Selection criteria should be as objective and measurable as possible. A method proven very common and dependable over time is the use of the weighted matrix. If this is a new concept to you, weights are calculated across a number of criteria against a number of ratings.

Difference	Weight	Current Architecture	Alternative #1	Alternative #2	Alternative #3
Desired Feature #1	8	2	3	2	3
Desired Feature #2	6	4	3	2	5
Desired Feature #3	5	0	5	0	2
Mandatory Feature #4	6	3	4	6	5
Mandatory Feature #5	8	5	6	7	2
Total Scores	33	14	21	17	17

Figure 2. Weighted Matrix Template with Sample Data

This method might be too complex for some situations, but you can simplify it to work in most circumstances. You can calculate ratings for each option via consensus within groups, and you can average them to come out with an optimal choice. Typically, you give each criterion some kind of a weight or importance and weigh these against the various available alternatives.

The size of a weighted matrix depends on the number of alternatives and the number of grouping of alternatives. You will keep score and tally a weighted score to compute a final rating for each solution. This can be a time-consuming process, but it is relatively quick compared to some of the other available decision-making methods. Very often, you'll come up with a weight and then the decision will end up coming down to a gut feeling—a feeling about things such as the vendor, trust, or fit with the environment, and, all too often, about the politics in or around the decision or the solution.

Do a Sanity Check

Solving problems requires you to remember and review many different facets of analysis. You can refer to the Zoom In and Out sections at the end of this chapter to save some time with these quick reference lists. If you refer to your lists consistently, you become more efficient. If you don't have a defined process in advance, the selection and validation stage can become very unyielding, time consuming, and even overwhelming.

Troubleshoot or paper test your architecture as one means to validate your solution. Requirements don't lie, so testing each one against the chosen solution will be valuable substantiation that you've made the right choice. You will be confident you've made the right decisions and have matched the business needs to the best of your abilities. Consider all of the possible failure points to take the negative perspective on your selection. Since you will have the widest view on all of the dimensions and components, your biggest responsibility as an architect is to make sure the entire solution hangs together with few known deficiencies.

Using a checklist will help you consider the dimensions you must review and will help you think about such things as project types, risk levels, politics, timing, budget, and resources for your solution. Weigh the various approaches you might take to complete your analysis and match them with the solution's cost, complexity, and risk. The underlying key in problem solving is to adequately understand and research the problem, make accurate assumptions, and then form conclusions that are sound and acceptable to the stakeholders and sponsors as well as the team.

Zoom In—Action Steps You Need to Succeed

Use this quick checklist to analyze problems and move toward solutions:

- ☐ Define the problem.
- ☐ Determine the root cause of the problem by asking many questions without attributing blame.

☐ Verify your understanding of the problem(s).

☐ Prioritize the problem(s) and potential solution(s) while matching them with the business goals and perceived value by the business partners.

☐ Determine the architect's role in the problem and the solution.

☐ Set the context, scope, and boundaries for the solution.

☐ Identify the approach and options for solving the problem and generating options.

☐ Extract solution requirements.

☐ Analyze nonfunctional requirements.

☐ Identify alternatives for the candidate solution set.

☐ Use requirement criteria to narrow the scope.

☐ Identify trade-offs that need to be made for each valid solution.

☐ Weigh the solution set using a weighted matrix approach to choose the optimum solution.

☐ Validate your selection/decision and do a sanity check with stakeholders, requirements, colleagues, industry, and research.

Zoom Out—Big-Picture Concepts

There are many questions you should ask your subject matter experts or research during analysis. Use this question set to short-circuit the context-setting exercise:

☐ What is the implementation cost of the status quo/alternative?

☐ What is the operational cost of the status quo/alternative?

☐ What functionality must be provided to solve the problem?

☐ What performance level must the solution meet?

☐ What is/are the reliability service level(s) expected?

☐ What is/are the availability level(s) required?

☐ Which standards must the solution meet?

☐ Which systems/solutions/components must the alternative be compatible with?

- ☐ What is the portability requirement among your environments, platforms, and geographic locations?
- ☐ What is the recovery cost and time required?
- ☐ Which integrity levels must be met?
- ☐ What scalability requirements must be met?
- ☐ What is the maintenance cost of the solution at the data, application, and technology levels?
- ☐ What security levels are required from the solution?

These are just a sampling of the non-functional criteria that should set context for the available solutions to solve your problem and guide your decision-making exercise.

CHAPTER 4:
ANALYZE AS AN ARCHITECT

If the facts don't fit the theory, change the facts.
–Albert Einstein

EAs provide architectural-style analysis to ensure that business drivers and objectives exist in the functional requirements. You also ensure that system criteria meet nonfunctional criteria while being packaged as a flexible and viable solution. You will also need to know what the company needs through strategic work and use process to confirm or investigate and get the research details from the business resources.

As an EA, you must be a good decision maker who knows how to generate options and also how to do just the right amount of data gathering, research, and analysis. You will need to understand how to perform analysis to help the business transform strategies into capabilities. You will work at levels appropriate to generate alternatives and potential architectures.

Here are the basic analysis steps you will be required to perform as an EA.

The Basic Architectural Analysis Process

Step 1: Identify the values at stake in the organization and set goals to achieve them. You can achieve these values through either the enterprise architecture strategy document or understanding overarching values of the highest level of the enterprise. This activity should be performed at a level appropriate for the architecture initiative.

Step 2: Gather information to understand the context and circumstances in which the goals are to be achieved. Setting context is another way to set scope around the problem at hand. In doing this, you create boundaries so that you may gauge the quantity of research required and know when to stop gathering information and when to start analyzing the data to create information and generate alternatives.

By gathering information, you must be careful not to filter out extra information along the way. You will apply appropriate judgment as to the level of detail and use instinct to discard data or information that is extraneous or that leads to an unworkable solution.

Step 3: Create alternative ways to achieve the goals and create practical solutions. The analyst will review and analyze the data and gathered requirements and generate a list of potential solutions. As you start to move into step four, you will sort and move the information around using a categorized method—one that will match the approach you are taking in this particular analysis project.

There are many ways to work through and rank the alternatives; weighted matrix, heat maps, models supported by detailed documents or presentation notes. In any case, fact-based analysis is what is important.

Step 4: You will analyze the alternatives, decide which one best meets the goals, and discard those you deem impractical, unsuitable, or out of scope. This is where your strength lies. You will be very quick in understanding which alternatives will meet the architecture, the infrastructure, and the style. You will also determine which method of solution is best suited technology-wise. Finally, you will bridge the analysis into the business. You will understand both functional requirements and quality attributes.

Step 5: This step is critical. Here, you will document the process across all decision points. This way, you'll avoid wasting time in the future while rehashing the thinking process you used to derive this analysis. Good architects will learn through process that decision documents are critical to their work and to the process itself. You should house these specific documents in a repository for the architecture and always list the solutions or alternatives you discarded before short-listing. As well, you should prepare a detailed account of the vendors you reviewed and the type of thinking you used to arrive at the decision.

Keep a list of all of those involved in the analysis in various stages. Later on, if the solution does not work out, you need to protect yourself from undue finger pointing. At some point, you will probably pick up pieces of projects that were abandoned or those that have gone wrong. You will want to rework and use the most valuable or workable parts of those projects in the future. The converse is also true—by documenting the people who supported the decision, it allows decision makers to see those in favor of the solution selected. It rallies support behind the recommended solution and eliminates the possibility that individuals will flip-flop with their support.

The method for gathering the information is typically an interview process with business users by systems analysts. Often you will interview information technology users as well as business stakeholders or observe the regular systems analyst interview process. One tactic you should apply is breadth versus depth, so skim, highlight, and read information instead of actually going very deep and getting into a whole lot of details.

Over time, the amount of information you collect and review will increase the amount of confidence in the amount of data. Your accuracy will start to dwindle at some point when performance starts to lag because of an excessive amount of information or data overload. To improve data gathering, include some kind of confidence level in the estimates to be made and in the amount of data collected. The remainder of this chapter includes some tips and techniques you may use while working through the basic process.

Gap Analysis

Gap analysis is one of the most common differentiators in the analysis process between traditional systems analysts and architects. You will review the current and target state architectures and do a detailed comparison to scope the various solutions required to make the transition.

Here is a list of steps you may take in performing a gap analysis of the architecture:

1. Analyze current and target architectures
2. Identify gaps
3. Assess severity and context of the gaps
4. Assign priority to the gaps to close
5. Assign tasks and areas of improvement for the completion of the architecture
6. Target resources for solutions (both monetary and human)
7. Create estimates (often the project's responsibilities)
8. Plan gap closure projects/transition

Gain Value Through Feedback Loops

You will also need to provide feedback to people for them to gauge the type and volume of information you reviewed. A very typical example in the area of architecture analysis is to list the number of possible solutions you reviewed, possible patterns, and potentially the number of vendors. List the ones you discard right away and the reason you discarded them, explaining why you left the remaining ones on the short list.

A rationale around the short-list creation is also valuable; an example might be to follow one of the highly regarded quadrant solutions or matrices for the top vendors or products as per industry analysis. You must make sure you have documented your findings to get the most reuse out of the information.

Time Boxing Is the Secret

When we met with the client, we set a limit on the time we spent speaking with the executives. You'll find that you can obtain all of the critical information you need from very high-level executives in a two-hour time frame if you are able to get them to speak frankly and precisely. To do so, you should give them some kind of a boundary as far as how many options you want to generate and ask them important questions, such as what kind of reports or information they rely on most. We requested the types of numbers and metrics that were critical to them, as well as what kind of measurements they relied on daily, weekly, monthly, and annually. We also asked them what pie in the sky would look like and what they would say was the first capability they needed tomorrow. We wanted to know their ultimate goals as well as their biggest pains.

The succeeding part that you need to include is the one listing options. State the alternative strategies and list the advantages and disadvantages of each. You should streamline this list to only strategies that are reasonable, likely, and relevant. A laundry list of anything imaginable is good only when that list is specifically requested. As well, state each option's estimated cost and assign each a very high-level style ranking, such as small, medium, and large cost. If you have any additional information to include, such as specific dollar amounts or estimates, provide that too.

Following this, list what remaining analysis must be done. So, for example, include "for alternative #1, further research in area X is required to proceed." Alternatively, you might list what needs be prototyped or the proof of concepts that must be run for you to have a level of certainty that is required.

Perform Analysis at Internet Speed

Some time ago, I worked on a couple of projects that required me to do analysis at a very rapid speed. This was in the late 1990s, and at this point, the Internet boom was just ramping up. I started to refer to analyzing at Internet speed as situations when the business or project demanded a very quick, rash amount of analysis and research.

When your analysis is required at hyperspeed, you should optimize your approach by shortening some steps while adhering to the process for the critical items based on your vision. The first tasks are to create some kind of vision statement, to determine the type of deliverable(s) needed, and to develop a set of templates or a framework for your analysis. A template page would represent each function or focus area that you wish to analyze and match a person or group with a limited time for the data gathering and analysis.

You need to be clear on the goal of the analysis: write it down and share it at the beginning of the cycle so you and your team keep it in mind throughout the process. The goal should be your ultimate desired result. To do analysis at Internet or warp speed, set a time limit. You might refer to this as time boxing your analysis. Start with a short, rigid time frame and see what you can get done. To quote Steven Covey, "Begin with the end in mind."

The most vivid example I can recall is when I was sent to do some analysis several thousand miles away at a remote client's office. I had only three days to interview every VP in each department within the company. Our goal was to design the back-office sales tracking and resource calendaring systems for this entire organization. We gave specific instructions for each of the VPs with respect to the questions we'd be asking and the materials to bring to the meetings. In four days, we had enough to build a vision of the entire system and more than enough to get the first three iterations designed.

Label Thy Solution

Something else that is helpful is labeling each potential solution. In a recent situation, I used tactical, strategic, short-term, and long-term labels on a solution that would also help the decision makers determine what type of analysis and recommendations were made. Caveats as to the extent of the analysis in any written documentation provided to decision makers will help set context too.

Two important pages in the analysis document might surprise you. The first is a title page that includes the details of who was interviewed and very detailed information about the type of process used to describe the context of the work done. Your final page should be a recommendation, listing assumptions, stating the situation, and evaluating which solution or multiple solutions are feasible.

If you recommend one or more of the strategies, include a summary of the results if things go as proposed. Add a "what to do next" or "next action" items list as part of the synopsis. The final component of analysis is actually the refined research notes. Each analysis project will include research, some of which will be collecting information from internal users, including business subject matter experts or other users, while some should be from external influences, such as market surveys, vendor representatives, and various other sources. Several pages of appendices at the back of a document provide great supporting material.

Qualify Your Research Efforts

The first stop in the area of research in architecture analysis should be pattern selection. Review the solution patterns already implemented in your company. What is being used now that works? What has been done before that is similar? What might you be able to find externally or through partners or industries similar to yours?

Do you know anyone who has done similar work? Explore and determine the right sources for that information. Will you get the information from a vendor for a product, from a technology area, or from some specific expert? Decide in advance what the approximate amount of research will be. It will be best if you set some strict boundaries for your research team. As well, post a definite and strict time when your team should complete the research.

Maintain Focus Through Questions

It is beneficial to know what the objectives are for use of the information before you set out to do the research. You'll gain benefits from deciding what kind of format you will use as your collection vehicle for the information. Do you already know what you are looking for? Are you researching or generating alternatives? There is a big difference in just surfing the net, hoping an idea will pop into your head based on a few keywords, and targeting a type of solution. What will be the presentation style to share the findings of the analysis? Is there any way to collect information in a format close to what is needed for use in the next steps?

Who are the stakeholders? Who are the people who will review the information? Do you have to summarize everything that you find? Who is going to participate in the research project? Do you need various viewpoints? Is it critical to get the credibility you need, or do you need it because of sheer volume or time frame? Set up some sort of templates or receptacles for collecting and consider how you will limit the research and analysis completed. In other words, how will you know when you are done?

An example might be a daily reminder or a daily scrum with the research team considering where you are currently and where you will go today. Questions to ask might include the following: What do I know today that I didn't know yesterday? How many alternatives do I have so far? What am I going to gain today by doing this research? These are just examples of information you might collect and methods you might use to do research during the architect analysis phase.

Over your career, you will have many opportunities to explore a variety of solutions and technologies. Keep in mind that this can become unwieldy unless your process is formulated and repeatable. Tracking and framing the analysis form the basis for decision points, and it saves rework later if you deliberately plan for and construct a framework to collect it.

Zoom In—Action Steps You Need to Succeed

This chapter closed with a focus on questions. Here is a question checklist that will allow you to ensure you ask the questions required by an architect in the analysis of just about any solution:

Quality

- ☐ How will we back up the application code and data for the solution?
- ☐ How will recover from the solution? What is our fallback plan? How will we test through all of the system interfaces?
- ☐ How long will we keep data, and what are our archiving requirements?
- ☐ What environments are required to move the solution from development through to production, and how will we manage the moves and the versions of the sources?
- ☐ How are we ensuring data integrity within the solution?
- ☐ What are our availability requirements? Have these been addressed through the technical infrastructure with a view to the budget required to support them? What are the required support hours and acceptable maintenance windows?
- ☐ How will we confirm the reliability of the behavior of the system functions? What are the audit and logging requirements from the quality and legislative perspectives?
- ☐ What risks are there to this solution? Are they documented? Have we prototyped the risky components? Are the risks acceptable?
- ☐ How manageable is the solution? How will we ensure the continued quality of the data, components, and infrastructure?
- ☐ How maintainable is the solution? How will we identify and monitor flaws, how long will they take to fix, what records do we have to keep, and what are the life cycle costs of doing all of these things?

49

☐ How will we manage change in the application, components, and infrastructure? Have we added these considerations to our organization's system management practices?

☐ How easy is the solution to use for operations, technology, development, business, and customer users?

☐ How will we document the system for its design, development, transition, and maintenance?

☐ How does the solution meet usability and appearance requirements—language, sight impairment, screen flow, color, layout, etc.? Are errors and exceptions handled gracefully with a standard method or solution?

Performance

☐ What performance levels are required? What volumes and capacity are needed? Can the solution meet our peak business times? Infrastructure times?

☐ How accessible are the components? What time frames are required to obtain replacements?

☐ Does the solution meet all operational constraints? Can the solution be operated in the environments required by the specified users?

☐ What response times are required? How will we determine, test, and monitor the solution? How will we fine-tune the solution if these are unacceptable? What fixes are available as the solution grows and evolves?

☐ What are our security requirements for the data and solution use? Do we need to buy additional components to ensure these levels? Do we have any known security exposures with this solution?

☐ What is our agility factor? How easy are data changes? Application changes? Business rule changes?

☐ How portable is the solution? How will we move to a new infrastructure if required? How will we handle technology upgrades? What is proprietary or inflexible that we know about now?

☐ How can we use the existing infrastructure, tools, and methods for this solution? What must be changed?

☐ What is our vendor strategy regarding availability, replacement, support, etc.?

Cost and Value

☐ Does this solution fit all of the user's functional requirements? Which are not met? What is the priority of those that were met and that were not?

☐ What is the cost of procurement of all of the components? Where does this solution fall in the price range of all solutions?

☐ What is the relative cost of maintenance of this solution? Consider human resources, operations, development, infrastructure, and user support.

☐ What are the life-cycle maintenance costs?

☐ What other projects must be completed to implement this solution?

☐ Where does this solution fit in the investment portfolio of IT assets?

This list is by no means exhaustive. Your architecture design should respond to all of these required behaviors; if not, you should make known and document compromises and risks when they are deemed cost prohibitive, when they require too much time, or when they exhaust too many resources.

Zoom Out—Big-Picture Concepts

Here are a few big-picture questions you can ask yourself about the potential solution:

☐ How will this add value to the business?

☐ Can I say this is a robust solution?

☐ Do I know of any faults in this solution? Have I made the best trade-offs in selecting this option?

- ☐ Where does this solution fit in our business resumption or disaster recovery plan?
- ☐ Does this solution comply with our current standards?
- ☐ How does this solution match the key business strategies my company is trying to implement?
- ☐ Is this solution bleeding edge or mainstream?
- ☐ Are any of my colleagues using this solution?
- ☐ Does my gut say this is the right thing to do for the company or that this would be pretty cool to try?
- ☐ If I were retiring in three months, would other architects think this was a good choice?
- ☐ Does this solution fill an existing gap or create a new one?
- ☐ Does this solution make the best choices for reuse of known, reliability patterns, and components?
- ☐ How comfortable or nervous would I be to present this solution to a team of developers? To be available during development? To present this solution before a peer group of architects?
- ☐ How risky is this solution to myself, my architecture team, the development team, the project schedule, the implementation team, the operations team, and the business?
- ☐ How much vendor risk is involved in this solution? Are they going to be around for a while? What is their reputation both in delivering the goods and in supporting the customer later? Are there any legal considerations I need to bring forward when proposing this solution?
- ☐ Will service-level agreements with third parties be required?

PART II:
THE PROCESS-DRIVEN ARCHITECT

In this part

Part II covers the critical information you need to apply to sort through the various and confusing architecture methodologies prevalent today. It includes abstract and pattern thinking, and we will discuss in depth the mapping and blueprinting activities great architects use in their everyday work.

This part includes the topics of modeling, engineering, and others from an architecture perspective. A review of the skills you need to compartmentalize and organize chunks of information and requirements into systems and solutions in the context of frameworks rounds out this step.

CHAPTER 5:
DRIVE SUCCESS THROUGH PROCESS

If you can't describe what you are doing
as a process, you don't know what you're doing.
—W. Edward Deming

Everyone who has been asked to perform as an architect thinks he or she has likely done some architecture before. But when it comes time to officially start, it is easy to draw a blank and be unsure of which step to take next. Basic skills and abilities in the architecture process are those typically learned and nurtured through both education and experience. These basic techniques, processes, approaches, and methodology root themselves in best practices. Depending on the type of architecture work you are doing, you will need to take one of various approaches, which are outlined below. First, you'll find generalities of architecture in systems and architecture and then a move toward the specifics of enterprise architecture.

When companies initiate the architecture process, they create a vision for a specific outcome. Business drivers and context shape all architecture initiatives. Once you have defined the problem space and stakeholders are committed, you will begin the requirement-gathering process. In this process, you will make decisions and create specifications to document the journey and details of the architecture's development. You will take various perspectives from the conceptual through to the logical and physical, so that all who contribute have the details they need. You will select and validate the architecture solution, and then the iteration cycle begins. As the process continues, you will refine the architecture until you deem it fit for transition to reality.

From a general perspective, various organizational features exist in architecture. These include initiation and commitment activities as well as development activities, such as leadership and teaming. Architects scale and tailor the process to fit the project or initiative at hand. For general architecture, you frequently will take a project approach. Examples are Agile architecture, model-driven architecture, and process-driven architecture. You will emphasize artifacts, frameworks, design, processes, standards, and development.

If you move to the enterprise architecture perspective, you will use a slightly different process. Now you will emphasize planning and developing the architecture, and you will consider strategy and business drivers as well as capabilities and context. You will take a principle-driven approach, and often will take an Enterprise Portfolio Management (EPfM) approach, rather than one of project management. Value for stakeholders is a key consideration, and organizational features such as governance and business alignment come into play.

Frameworks and transition road maps are additional elements that are slightly different. This is not to say you don't use frameworks in the general case with applications, solutions, and infrastructure, but they are more common from the enterprise architecture perspective. Focusing on driving out the future state is paramount, and hot topics include when, how much, and what to include in the current state models. A transformation road map is often the penultimate step in the process, followed by the implementation and management of the enterprise architecture.

Can you see the differences between these two approaches? In the enterprise architecture process, you look at the scale and perspective from a higher-level viewpoint and less from the project position. Since planning is a critical differentiator between the two processes, documentation sets are present but quite distinct for both.

Master the Architecture Process

This is your first major stop on the journey as an architect. Getting this right is critical. Many of you flipped to this step right after purchasing this book to see whether the answers to your questions about the architecture process are in here. When you get started, you absolutely need to know a few basic things about all architecture processes, and you may adjust them depending on your differentiators and situations. Right now, you don't need to decide now whether enterprise architecture is for you. Get the basics down, and the door will be open for you in the future.

When it comes to an architect's skills and abilities in the area of process, some behavior patterns exhibit greatness. Excellent architects require a base knowledge of the process, the willingness to apply the appropriate amount of process to their work, and the ability to figure out what is appropriate. EAs will easily apply process in a consistent and repeatable manner. As a new approach surfaces, they are able to apply the basics and assess whether anything new will improve their methods. They recognize what is similar from one trend to the next.

Now, your next question may be whether you should be process-oriented or goal-oriented. One is not necessarily better than the other, but you should consider the goals of architecture. Goal-oriented people strive, fight for, and move for the sake of attaining a goal. Likewise, process-oriented people process, strive, focus, and move as they look for approval. Both types will likely achieve their goals, but unlike process-oriented people, goal-oriented people often reach their goal and then are happy to rake in the accolades.

In contrast, people who are more interested in growing, creating, and building something that they can point to forever are more suited to architecture as a long-term career. Knowing which type of person you are will help your career immensely.

To determine your type, first ask what your major talent is. What is at your core? Earlier, you learned about Kolbe. When I evaluated myself, my profile told me that my natural talent was defined as a theorist and my cognitive ability or creativity was in originating concepts, innovating systems, and initiating trends. It told me I was a highly productive and creative person and my truth was that I was to be a catalyst, a generalist, an innovator, an entrepreneur, and a promoter or an impressionist. I have always been intensely immersed in process since the beginning of my career, so this is an example of one such link.

Where do your talents lie? Can you apply your analysis to the types of practices you are strong in and enjoy doing? Will it help you determine which type of architect you are and what your approach will likely be? Keep your results in the back of your mind as you explore process through this chapter. It might not make a lot of sense to you right now, but these are the critical things to ponder at this point in your career.

Which Architecture Process?

So what are the architecture processes? For a new architect, the choices may seem cloudy and muddled. Consider the motivation or origin of those who own or have created the process. They will typically come from an industry sector or community or from an association or a company created solely to deliver educational conferences for a fee. There is nothing wrong with this, but you need to know what is motivating these groups and driving their processes. You'll also find that some of these processes have been born out of a need by government and civic organizations. Typically, you will find these processes are quite different from those used by proprietary companies.

You should understand a little about what is available. Later in Chapter 8, you'll find processes intertwined with frameworks, but first a focus on pure approach and process at the model level is necessary. You need to determine which process is important at which time. By focusing on architectural process, you are using a time-proven system or method to approach your problem. W. Edward Deming believed the best means of efficiency is to use a time-proven system. So far, our challenge in architecture is there are many systems or approaches, and many argue which system or approach is time proven.

Of these approaches, here are five of the most common:

1. Project-driven approach,

2. Process-driven approach,
3. Model-driven approach,
4. Framework-driven approach, and
5. Architecture-centered approach

You can also use any combination of these when you construct your architectures, and many organizations will combine them. When would you use them? And why do you need to know about them at this stage of your career? You will advance much faster if you realize these approaches and methods exist. If you are able to apply what's appropriate in a given period and understand your situation at your organization, you'll be better able to readily adapt to what's going on and get your work done appropriately and efficiently.

Project-Driven Approach

To be honest, there is typically little room for architectural processes from a project-driven approach because of the time factor. Great project managers understand that repeatable and proven processes are about the only way to achieve objectives within a tight deadline. A balancing act is required to manage those who are new to the process and are earnest about following it to the letter.

An architect who is new to a given architectural process will take longer to get it done; unless there is a good balance of project team members as far architecture experience is concerned, the time sometimes will outweigh the advantages. Often, this falls beyond the allowance any project manager has at his or her discretion. Review the time and evolution of the project and the hype cycle of the new process with the project manager.

If you plan to use a process new to you, the company, or the team, allow contingencies for the architecture. If you use a tried, proven architecture process, allow more leverage for the time to exercise it. The project manager should budget for architecture time, especially if you can show it was a proven method in a past similar project.

Process-Driven Architecture

A process-driven architecture approach includes processes such as the Rational Unified Process (RUP), Agile Process, model-driven architecture, as well as rapid application development processes. These processes are most often used for software or solution architecture projects rather than enterprise architecture projects.

Process-driven architectures provide a visual representation of the process and process systems within an enterprise. They offer strategists and planners a high-level view of the activities of the enterprise as a whole. The benefits of these should be clear: gaining an overall view of the enterprise makes it possible for planners to identify strengths and weaknesses and allows them to identify areas that need improvement.

Process-driven architecture offers the ability to develop strategy to best exploit the strengths of the enterprise and support the business in the desired strategy. Process architecture serves as a road map by which process planners can devise best practices for high-level and basic processes to ensure all processes align with the overall business strategy. Knowing which process is appropriate at which time is important. For example, The Open Group Architecture framework includes process (TOGAF) and may more often be appropriate for project and solution architecture than it is for enterprise architecture.

Why is being a process-driven architecture advantageous? The focus on processes at the start of architecture is a proven way of representing the business and therefore tying the architecture solution to the business. It allows the business to get what it wants. Businesspeople who get what they want are happy businesspeople.

The Model-Driven Approach

Model-driven architectures are used for systems specifications that begin with the modeling process. The Object Management Group introduced this idea, which is known as model-driven architecture (MDA). RUP is considered a model-driven method, and many of the tool vendors advise this approach. Let's face it: you need models.

You will typically choose these approaches when you take an object-oriented project, but this method been adapted and used in many other situations.

It was a breakthrough in our modern times and architecture and modeling history to see a unified global group select the Unified Modeling Language (UML) as a modeling standard in the late nineties. Consider what the past ten years of architecture would have been like if you were haggling over notation and languages for your models.

Framework-Driven Architecture

Framework-driven architectures are another popular approach in architecture process. Rather than this chapter become a primer on frameworks, it is more useful to list a few better-known approaches using frameworks. A framework is simply a prescribed specification of how to organize and graphically represent different views and perspectives within the architecture. John Zachman created the most popular framework based on his work at IBM in the 1970s. He formally presented his version in the 1980s, initially introducing it with a five Ws approach.

The Zachman framework is an analytical model or classification scheme that organizes the descriptive representation. It does not describe an implementation process and is independent of specific methodologies. Over time, it has become common to use specific UML models to fill each cell in the Zachman framework as a process unto itself. To follow on that, two approaches that combine a framework as well as a prescribed method to complete it are TOGAF and the MDA.

Another approach is a variation of a framework called a reference model. A reference model is an abstract approach, clarifying things such as entities and relationships within an environment. This approach is especially good when the focus is on standards. It works best for industry verticals and government. The most well known is the Federal Enterprise Architecture Framework (FEAF). It consists of various reference models such as the Performance Reference

Model (PRM), Business Reference Model (BRM), Service Component Reference Model (SRM), Data Reference Model (DRM), and Technical Reference Model (TRM).

Frameworks are covered in more detail in Chapter 8. At this point, it is necessary that you know at a minimum the basic premises behind the Zachman and TOGAF process and frameworks, or FEAF if you work for the US government. The other methods and approaches will combine the use of frameworks with a road map to help you do your work.

Architecture Approach or Architecture-Centered Approach

This approach is the belief that the architecture should be the center of all development and all things IT. There is a time and place for everything, and you should select the appropriate approach depending on the specific situation. Architectural deliverables and artifacts are the main output and derived value from the architect. You will select processes and approaches to complete artifacts, documentation sets, and deliverables.

A Basic Fundamental Architecture Process

Let's face it: this is confusing stuff, and it can be overwhelming. It is more important that you understand the core elements of the two major frameworks, Zachman and TOGAF, and know there's no need for you to understand everything and the history of all frameworks before you make your choice. Worry about the rest at some point later in your career unless you are now in a situation where another approach or framework has been prescribed.

Each organization will use a mixture of approaches and adapt them for its specific use. It is a common misconception to believe that by understanding everything about all of the architecture frameworks, you will be able to open up your decision and make the best choice when choosing a framework.

A very basic simplified architectural process will enable you to adapt it to any of the other methods, approaches, and frameworks you will come across in various projects or organizations in your career. It is both simple and a basic architecture design process, based on best practices in their most organic state. It is where I start with those who are new to architecture, as it is the easiest for them to grasp.

You may apply this process to either enterprise architecture or system architecture. If you want to apply this to an application, data, or technology architecture, you may need to abbreviate some pieces. In general circumstances, this is how you may proceed:

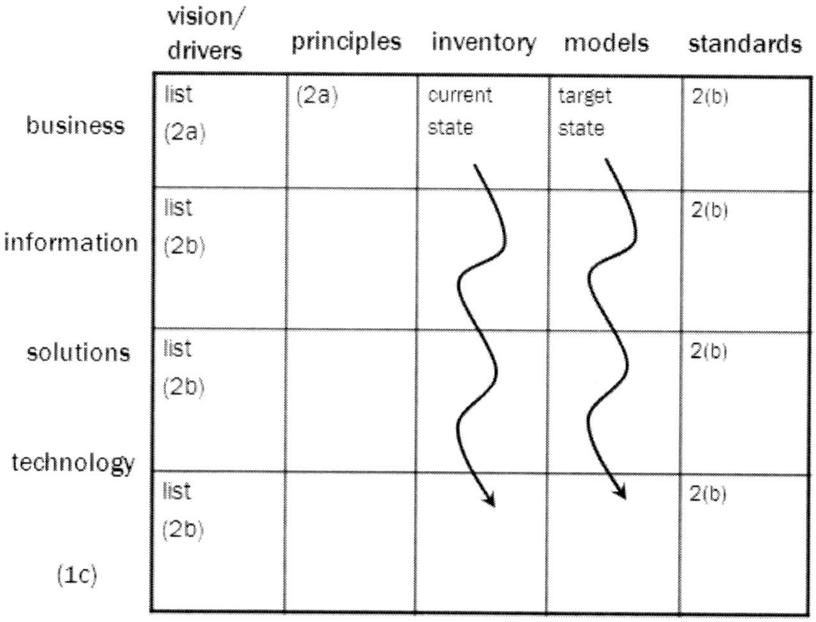

	vision/ drivers	principles	inventory	models	standards
business	list (2a)	(2a)	current state	target state	2(b)
information	list (2b)				2(b)
solutions	list (2b)				2(b)
technology	list (2b)				2(b)
(1c)					

Figure 3. Simplified Architecture Process

Basic Architecture Process

1. Create or choose the framework. If you are developing a system architecture document as an artifact, you may choose to create a template based on an existing framework. See www.zoomfactorbook.com/book-resources for an example for starting your framework based document set deliverable. You must complete some of the steps below:

a. Define the intended use of the architecture. Include things such as vision, purpose, objectives, and probable methods for completing the architecture.

b. Determine the scope of the architecture. Include items such as considerations for technical boundaries, resource constraints, and time frames within which you will complete the architecture.

c. Complete and select the system dimensions or views with the system model.

> If you are using a very simplistic model, you may just be able to select the business, information, technology, and solutions.

d. Consider the extra views or domains that might be likely or prevalent in your organization, geographic region, or project. These things might be security architecture or an organizational or operational architecture included with these other frameworks, and you may want to have this as a means of dividing the information and work you have to do.

e. Establish executive or stakeholder buy-in for using the architecture design process. Some of this will require extra funding or the project manager's buy-in.

2. Develop your strategy to dictate your starting point for the architecture. Here, you'll need high-level details and a baseline or current state architecture, including at the very minimum the business architecture and a simple inventory for the other domains.

a. Add the business and the design drivers for the architecture.

b. Determine things like the data required to support the architecture development, as well as principles, entities, criteria, linkages, and standards required for you to complete the architecture.

    c. Current state models and artifacts should be created for those areas affected most by the business strategy and require knowledge of what is to determine what should be.

3. Expand design components by starting to work on your target architecture. You may have created more than just business in the area of the current state for the previous step. You may have a requirement in the area of the technology architecture to outline what you already have in a current state. Complete what you are focused on changing.

    a. In this third step, you want to create a vision document. .

    b. Use design models to gather requirements for new solutions. Use cases for functional and nonfunctional requirements and other models such as activity and sequence diagrams to populate the architecture where appropriate. You will need to focus on the data, application, solutions, and technology, and at the next step add standards components or processes or some artifacts you've previously delivered.

4. Validate the target architecture. Do this by prototyping and evaluating linkages between domains. Test by using either paper prototypes or actually physically testing some of the pieces that are technology risky or new. To evaluate linkages, traverse the architecture domains and compare them against the other vertical domains to see where the relationships and linkages lie.

To compare data versus business, ensure there are sufficient models or information to convey what you want to do in the future state as well as the minimum you need from the current state. The same is true in the area of the application or solution. Compare this against the data and against the business to make sure you have sufficient information to proceed. Continue by comparing technology against data, applications, solutions, and the business. Add any standard components that you know.

5. Create your transition plan. How will you get there? Perform a gap analysis to create a sequence plan for the deployment of the architecture.

Perform a gap analysis. Do this by reviewing your strategic business drivers, capability requirements, and IT initiatives that have been mapped to the categorized and prioritized business desired functionality. If you have an IT strategic plan available, use it here. If you do not, this activity may create the basis for it.

a. Use your keen eye to determine which large solutions and technology components would best fill the holes. One method might be to group business strategies and then apply them against existing departments or functions at your company. Look at which functions are affected most by the new strategies and those that would be affected.

b. A grouping and prioritizing exercise will follow to help you lay down your target. Consider all of the enterprise-level components that would be required to support your business strategy and the planned solutions. Use trade-off analysis alongside your vision and budgets.

Put some order to some of the steps for the items you want to create. Typically, you should group some of the future state items into categories, such as projects and groupings, and time them to match your program portfolios as well as your IT budget.

In sum, there are just five steps for laying down your architecture. Choose a framework or layout for your documentation, create a baseline for your current state, and complete it with current business information. Expand it by adding a target state architecture including a vision, standards, and principles. Validate the architecture by comparing and examining links between each of the domains. Prototype some of the components depending on the focus for architecture creation, and subsequently create a transition plan. Choose an approach such as an architecture-centered process, and examine and inventory each domain architecture to fill in the details.

The Role of Architecture Principles

Architecture principles are a basic set of rules and behaviors an organization uses as a guide to decision making. Principles govern the architecture process and implementation of the architecture. During the architecture process, it is a best practice to first establish a set of principles to use as decision-making guidance for designing and developing information systems. They affect development, maintenance, and use of the architecture.

Architecture principles are the cornerstone of our enterprise architecture and the enterprise in which you work. One of the drivers toward determining the principles you require is the business needs. A common principle is "buy versus build" or "capture data nearest the source." These are overarching statements included as part of the enterprise architecture and perhaps in system solution architectures.

Principles come in varying levels of statements, in that there are those that apply at the enterprise level and then finer-grained principles that apply to each domain perspective. Architect teams should know the implications and use them to drive toward document standards and guidelines. The principles also drive the actions you will take. You need to provide IT resources with information on how they may achieve these principles, especially when they are vague. A common way to present such principles is with an implications specification or one that details the recommended steps to achieve the principle.

Principles form the base for our enterprise architecture policies and guidelines. They serve as a road map and as guideposts to develop the enterprise architecture. Always create them first so that you can keep them in mind as requirements for the enterprise and for your construction of the enterprise architecture plan. They will keep you aligned with the drivers of your architecture. Renew and refresh them each year to make sure you keep in alignment with the business drivers you have addressed and exposed through your business strategies.

Principles are common across organizations. During my training sessions, I recommend not trying to reinvent the wheel, but instead browsing a large list of industry standard principles. You will find such a list at www.zoomfactorbook.com/book-resources. These are principles I have either seen in other architecture plans, principles I described in enterprise architecture presentations, writings, and documents, or principles I collected over ten years of consulting engagements. I typically use these as my starting point. Choose a subset of the enterprise-level principles. Ultimately, principles will emerge from business strategy discussions with executives at your enterprise, from IT strategic-planning sessions, or from the architecture plan.

When reviewing this list at a first glance, you may want to include all of them as they are generally good ideas. Try to find the ones that best match the organization's objectives. Try to see whether you can limit your list to ten. I attempt on the very first cut of an architecture draft to narrow down to five, but typically, I don't get any fewer than seven. Ensure this list aligns with the types of business drivers you see emerging from your organization.

Zoom In—Action Steps You Need to Succeed

This chapter contained a basic process that covers and overlaps a variety of industry standard approaches. Here is a checklist I use to get any architecture plan started quickly, whether it is as small as a solution architecture or as big as an enterprise architecture plan:

Basic "Zoom" Checklist for Fast Results:

1. Create a placeholder document based on your framework for your architecture plan. This will hold your decisions, models, and documents and may become your road map, and you may use it to guide the process.
2. Define the purpose or use for this architecture project.
3. Define the scope and constraints for this architecture project.
4. Identify the core architecture views you wish to include in this architecture project to prioritize and evaluate the work required—business, information and data, applications and solutions, and technology and infrastructure.

5. Establish and identify your stakeholders and get buy-in for the project.

6. Determine the strategy to be used to complete the architecture deliverables.

   a. Will a complete current state architecture be necessary?

   b. What is the team composition for the development of the work?

   c. Will the work be done as part of other projects or as a stand-alone enterprise architecture project?

7. Determine the target state deliverables and approach.

   a. Which models and deliverables are required, and what is their priority?

8. Gather and complete the models, deliverables, and artifacts.

   b. Validate as you are doing the work. Always ask "what has changed" and "is there still value in this work?"

9. Evaluate the gaps between current and future state.

10. Create your transition plan and your architecture road map.

Zoom Out—Big-Picture Concepts

Why not expand on the above-mentioned work? The chapter outlined a few approaches to develop an architecture. Here are a few big-picture questions you can use to zoom out and determine how you will fill your framework or develop your architecture. Do so by considering your answers to these questions:

1. The framework I will follow is _____ or the framework(s) I will modify are _____. If I do not have a framework, the process I will use to choose the framework is _____ and it will take approximately _____ days to complete this work. The selection shall be completed by _____ (date).

2. Which projects are planned at my company or are in flight that will contribute artifacts to the architecture?

3. What is the process I can use to fill the architecture current state? How much can be mined from our existing inventory? From various IT and business departments? From vendors of solutions we utilize? What can we leverage to complete the future state architecture? How will I conduct the work to create it?

4. Which modeling tools and methods will I use to complete the architecture?

5. Which standards and approaches will I use to complete the architecture?

6. Which repository and tools shall I use to complete the architecture(s)?

7. Where will I store the results of the decisions we arrive at while building the architecture?

CHAPTER 6:
THE MODEL AND ENGINEER

A picture is worth a thousand words.
—Napoleon Bonaparte

Another trait that signals architectural greatness is being a known model genius. People comment about great architects' models. These architects are typically known around the company as the killer slide creator or the master of spaghetti. Strive for the former. Killer slides are often capable of telling an entire story in a two-dimensional picture or page. They are the ones people carry around, refer to, and talk about long after the presentation is over.

Here is a snippet of one of my favorite architecture stories. The CEO of a company attended a presentation in which an architect presented him with an executive-sized slide deck outlining a recommended multimillion-dollar solution. It included the infrastructure, audience, content, solution, and values. Within that deck was a single slide the executive himself could take away, walk around with, point to, and use to communicate to other executives. It is a great sign when the most senior executive can promote a model within a slide deck and then claim he or she owns it.

What would it take to create such a work of art? A great model will:

1. Demonstrate context about the key strategic driver the executive originally sought out.
2. Require little or no explanation due to its simplicity (at least, the second time).
3. Emphasize the main factors on which a decision can be made.
4. Label or call out rather than describe most of the text.
5. Need no glossary or legend.

A single page that includes a model allows us to focus on a message. It's less distracting than a large text document or words on a page. It provides the big picture by delivering a visual image.

The Modeling Effect

This section will not be a comprehensive course on modeling; rather, it will discuss the general topic as a skill for the architect. It is a mandatory skill for you in any business or systems environment. You will find that models are essential, but they normally cannot stand alone. You will embed documentation with model diagrams to show traceability, to illustrate why decisions were made, to demonstrate how the architecture addresses concerns, and to provide critical information.

You need to have solid modeling skills because a great deal of your role includes communication, exploration, and design. A diagram is the fastest way to communicate a solution, and you will draw many over the span of your career. Very often, these activities will be ad hoc, in meetings or discussions, and never hit the digital world. Consider them a communication device critical to your tool kit.

Why Should You Model Software or Solutions?

Models are a powerful way to create visualization and interaction for an architecture solution. In its Architecture Center website, Microsoft states enterprise architecture is a "comprehensive set of cohesive models." Similarly, Rational Software depicts architecture as a set of models from different perspectives. As an architect, you will use models to make complex things simpler and to bring order to the chaos of all you need to consider. Your models should always be value-based, meaning you will derive some benefit by putting your effort into gathering the requirements and drawing the picture. Using models, you will capture context to understand the business drivers, internal and external influences, and risk impacts. Your models should always achieve a goal. Since your goals will evolve, so should your models. Finally, you will communicate with stakeholders and your teams through models.

You can use models to optimize or verify various components of the solution being proposed. Models help to facilitate communication of a high-level design or architecture. Through models, you can show large and complex solutions in a one-dimensional perspective. By using models with reduced detail, you make it easier for an audience to grasp the assignment of significant system responsibilities to high-level structures. Models allow those who will implement the architecture the highest-level understanding necessary to set context, as well as a detailed understanding of the specific, narrowly scoped pieces of the system they will work on. Models increase speed and efficiencies by decreasing the time it takes an organization to understand the intent of the architecture and to agree on the solution.

Architecture models show how you can effectively partition work. At times, you will create them to communicate solution designs before committing additional resources. Sometimes you will use modeling software to enable you to communicate and discuss potential scenarios using a solution or technology. Models enable you to trace design back to the requirements and help ensure you are building the right system. Whenever you see the term "model," analysis is not far behind: these two activities are often paired during architecture activities. As you analyze, you will model your findings, and as you detail your findings, your models will grow.

Models come in many shapes, sizes, and styles, and the method and technique you use to create them will correlate with the purpose for which you create them. You will draw some models to show context of the architecture, highlighting boundaries and interactions between components. You might draw other models to elicit conclusions from the viewer, or you might use models to document findings and capture the results of investigative efforts. Models will allow you to practice interactive development in which models and other higher levels of abstraction facilitate quick and frequent changes. If you model each change as you move forward, you will be able to see the evolution and the possible implications of your decisions.

You might create models when you are unsure of an outcome. If you record what you research, the picture may allow you to draw conclusions that would otherwise not present themselves through words. Models are decision-making tools, in that you may create various viewpoints to see your choices.

In summary, modeling is an incredibly important component of an architect's role in any systems environment. So when should you model software or solutions?

When Do You Model?

It is a miracle that curiosity survives formal education.
—Albert Einstein

You use models to better understand the business situation or problem space. At various points of the program or project life cycle, there will be prescribed times and subjects for which you will need models. The overall goal is to improve the enterprise and the systems you provide it. You will model when you want to build and design a system architecture or solution or if you want to create visualizations of code or other forms of implementation or technology solutions. In other words, modeling is one way to provide better solutions.

You will include models within your design documentation sets to describe a potential solution. Some examples will include:

➢ Data models to illustrate and define the enterprise's data stores and depict their relationship with one another.

➢ Application models to depict applications, their parameters, and their integration that controls the data.

➢ Technology models to define the technology of the infrastructure that lies beneath both the solutions and the data.

Various aspects of the current state as well as the future state for your enterprise architecture programs and portfolios will require models. At times, you may not need to model the current state at all. Consider modeling it only when there is significant value in studying the current picture to more accurately plan for the future. Often, inventory lists and rough diagrams can fill this need.

Models you choose to create should focus on areas of great concern and importance. One of the most crucial decisions you'll make as an architect is whether there will be value in creating the model. Most failed architecture programs come from a misinformed need to model everything and start from the beginning. Questionable efficiencies come from modeling on that which is volatile and changes too often to keep an accurate picture up to date. Model when and only when there is a business need and the known expected value is critical. There is always a prescribed need for models in the enterprise architecture or a solution. For more information, see www.zoomfactorbook.com/book-resources .

What Do You Model?

There is no single prescribed architecture model. An interrelated framework includes such models as the information architecture models that allow the enterprise to create a common and consistent data resource. It includes the business models that show the processes that demonstrate how business is conducted. Solution models show linkages between data and the business and how they are constructed and distributed. Technology architecture models are infrastructure-based and align with each of the solution, business, and data architectures. The framework you select for your enterprise architecture will dictate which models are appropriate in the view or approach you are elaborating. You'll have to consider those that are of the most value and prioritize your efforts.

You can create a current state, or an as-is, model to better understand the business situation and to obtain the understanding needed to craft a better system. This improved system will be your "to-be" model or the future state model. You will model when you want to build and design a system architecture or solution and if you want to create visualizations of code or other technology solutions. Design models are included within your lists of potential solutions and things you may wish to model. You must consider the appropriate level of abstraction based on the amount of detail dictated by the view you take. You will weigh this against the amount of effort you can afford for the exercise.

Models may be divided by those that are conceptual, logical, or physical. Each category will be used for different purposes. You will choose the appropriate model type based on value and purpose. You'll use conceptual models near the beginning of your architecture initiative, and you'll opt for physical models closer to the blueprint or just prior to construction. You may use them for simulations, for visualization, or for deriving formulas within the solution. The level of detail and accuracy you will need in the model purely depends on the intent and future use of the model.

How Much Do You Model?

A word about the extent and volume of current state modeling is appropriate here. Many look at the Zachman framework and wonder whether they need to do it all for the current state and then again for the target state. The answer is an emphatic no—you will need to exercise much judgment here with respect to value of the activity and need. Typically, you will need two copies (current and target) in areas that are complex and necessary to understand today's situation to plan for tomorrow. A lighter version of models is optional for the various cells where there is value to obtaining some current state knowledge. Complete omission of a current state model is an option where it would provide no value.

You might consider the value of a list or drawing versus a model in such situations. If you were to consider the time it would take to create an application model for each model in your current state, you would quickly realize you might never finish, or you would definitely need to revise it before you could complete it. You must carefully and diligently consider which perspective to model and why.

The second step after documenting the current state is to create the target state architecture. You may do this within the chosen methodology of process, which is called the system development life cycle (SDLC). Architecture process work is generally done within portions or artifacts the SDLC requires. The most common modeling approach today uses the UML. Many tools today are based on this standard language.

How Do You Model?

You can learn how to model. As an architect, you will construct models to explain business capabilities and requirements. You have often heard the old adage that pictures are worth a thousand words; models are worth even more. The tools architects use to model range anywhere from paper and pen, to a blackboard, a whiteboard, software tools, and even photographs of whiteboard sketches.

The usage and selection of modeling tools vary from company to company. They range from full-blown enterprise architecture models down to the simplest drawing tools that come with office productivity software. Today's architects often use UML modeling tools or simple office tools known as EVPW (Excel, Visio, PowerPoint, and Word. The Visio tool kit comes with so many standard diagrams and components for infrastructure that it is hard to beat the speed in which you can create a model.

You will create models at both the behavioral and structural levels. Behavioral models will allow viewers to see the various components and interfaces and get a solid understanding of how the architecture works through collaboration and sequence diagrams. Structural views will expose a central perspective, allowing the consumer to see the components and their interrelationships and externally visible properties through an architecture diagram, as well as component and interaction diagrams.

You will create models to depict the different views you need to understand the architecture and to pinpoint specific concerns. Best practices suggest creating models in varying levels, progressing from enterprise-level conceptual views, such as the architecture diagram and context diagrams. The logical architecture follows, where you will add more expanded models and diagrams as you develop the detail and gain precision. At this level, you will move into the blueprint stage with component and collaboration models as well as interface specifications. Finally, you will create physical-level models and diagrams for the purpose of depicting implementation details at the process and deployment levels, such as deployment models and server layout and physical database diagrams, just to name a few.

Your initial step will be deciding on the model's form. Various types of models and diagrams are available. The organization will dictate the model and diagram style unless you are the pioneer in this field. Models are often categorized as UML models and "other." Various standard UML models fit specific needs and are encouraged where applicable as they provide standard notation. In the "other" category, architects use matrices, bubble diagrams, stacked blocks, overlapping spheres, images of various components, and boxes and arrows to graphically depict the intent.

Size, shape, and placement of objects in models and diagrams allow the modeler to imply many messages such as relationships, order, dependency, and importance. For example, you can use matrices to contrast and compare criteria. Three-dimensional models can add a professional appearance to diagrams and imply depth. Show multidimensional and intricate concepts with the appropriate focus in the right places.

Use color to add more dimension to your models. You can highlight comparisons and contrasts simply by adding color to your model. A good example might be what is described as a heat map. Picture an infrastructure model colored with shades of red, yellow, and green. Red might indicate a need for replacement or suggest that attention to urgent issues is required. Green might mean it is an approved standard within the organization; yellow might indicate caution or change to the technology.

Give It That Engineering Style

Great architects add a robust engineering style to their solutions. As an architect, you will find the most difficult part of systems design is knowing how to make trade-offs and balance various components. You need to be concerned about how well things work together. An architecture solution is the logical representation of processes, functions, and information that reflects the business goals and objectives.

The engineering process requires measuring the solution to determine how well it satisfies business objectives and how well it will work. Recall those quality attributes the architect needed to collect during the analysis? You need to understand there will be trade-offs and balances among various components. You will prioritize the requirements you've received for the engineering activities. Using models and prototypes, you will evaluate alternative solutions, put up boundaries, and set scope limitations within the solution. You may test some or all of the quality attributes to determine whether a solution holds water and how satisfied you are with the conceptual and logical architecture. In essence, you are stretching things to see whether they will break.

Your process considerations may include:

➤ Reliability: Why and how often will it fail? When will it fail? Which considerations? How can you measure and track failures?

➤ Availability: How long must the system be up? How can you measure this? What would you have to invest to make it available longer?

➤ Adaptability: Can you adapt the system to different needs? Can you change platforms?

➤ Manageability: How will it be managed operationally? How much will that cost?

➤ Maintainability: How easy will it be to enhance and repair the system?

➤ Performance: How well will it perform? Can you scale it?

➤ Security: Is the system secure? Will it meet all regulations and audits?

The engineering component allows you to draw a line between what will be automated and what should be done manually through human resources. Your engineering experience will allow you to plan for the implementation of the solution in various stages to save time and effort during the actual construction process. You will break down models and diagrams into steps, and you will show layers and working models of pieces for the solution. These are often known as solution blueprints. You will also include the methodical steps used to test and provide proof.

Modeling and engineering skills include prototyping. You may apply various prototypes for the riskier components of solutions. Worthy candidates are those that are complex and are planned using unproven solutions. Suitable contenders will be new technology components and approaches untried in the organization. It is not uncommon for architects to lead a proof-of-concept exercise in which they try pieces of the solution in lab situations at a vendor's facility or bring them in house to try on a company's infrastructure. All are performed with the intention of reducing risk and eliminating the potential for major components to fail during the construction or implementation phases.

Zoom In—Action Steps You Need to Succeed

You must measure and validate the design you are proposing. You can use models to test and confirm the feasibility and the benefits of the initiative for the business. These activities allow you to impart realism and prudence among your activities for your stakeholders. In some cases, models become proof to those who must construct the designs. Impose a time limit for your modeling activities that matches the value you plan to achieve from your activities. Models can always use something more, so keep the value proposition in mind.

Modeling can be a time-consuming exercise, and it is critical that you become more efficient in modeling exercises. To speed up your efforts, maintain and employ a modeling checklist. A modeling checklist includes lists of models and type of models and situations in which you might use a model. You should also note some tricks about your tools and questions to get you going each time you start the activity. Using these techniques to keep the process moving is incredibly helpful.

The EA's must-have (bare minimum) models list:

1. The lists of things important to the business or an activity diagram that shows major business functions or business

processes—both current and future state. Use your required capabilities list to generate your future state context model.

2. The business context model, diagram, or list using a package or class diagram that depicts your current and future states. Again, think capabilities wherever possible.

3. The semantic or conceptual data model—a class diagram or a bubble diagram. Use this to depict your information value chain

4. The business process model—activity, state, or interaction diagram. Gather existing models for current state inventory and create future state versions when required for important business transitions.

5. The business location model (or list). Include the network diagram between locations.

6. Logical data model for any future state transitions only.

7. Integration model for the major systems in your organization.

8. Activity diagrams for major new solutions that are part of the transition.

9. Infrastructure topology diagram (commonly known as a technology stack diagram).

10. Service model diagrams for all services you consume, have in your inventory, or wish to create.

Zoom Out—Big-Picture Concepts

There is great value in creating and maintaining a kit of sample models you use on a regular basis. Dan Roam's great book *The Back of the Napkin* focuses on the subject of problem solving and selling ideas with pictures. Within his work, he built a set of standard diagrams and situations in which to use them. This is a good practice for the architect as well. Each modeling exercise should start with evaluating the purpose of the prospective model. Knowing the expected value well in advance for each model will get you off to a great start. It is not enough just to fill in a cell within a framework. You need to know why to fill it in. Ask yourself, "Which three pieces of key info do I want to convey?"

Limit the content you convey in each model. Remember, it is meant to be a communication vehicle. If you reflect on the work that it takes to create the model and then further to maintain it through future expected changes, you will see what the cost in time and value are. Here is a list of situations that are often too volatile or of too low value to model from an enterprise perspective:

☐ Current state logical data models
☐ Current state application and solution use case, class, sequence, activity, or component diagrams lower than the package level
☐ Hardware diagrams (get them from your supplier)
☐ Low-level network diagrams
☐ GUI/presentation diagrams
☐ Current state deployment diagrams
☐ Current state system or technology design models below the level of context or conceptual
☐ One-time only projects
☐ Data conversion models
☐ Models that do not communicate any value beyond what an inventory list would achieve
☐ Models where relationships between components are not as important as the objects themselves
☐ Models that are invaluable unless they are 95–100 percent accurate
☐ Models where you may not include enough detail to provide value
☐ Models that would not likely be updated after their concept has been communicated
☐ Models that can be drawn once on a whiteboard and a photo image would deliver needed communication

Exceptions exist of course, but you may use this list as a sanity check before taking on the process.

CHAPTER 7:
WHAT'S YOUR ZOOM FACTOR?

Everything should be made as simple as possible, but not one bit simpler.
—Albert Einstein

It's time to explain the original premise of this book. One of the biggest differentiators between most IT resources and architects is the architects' ability to think in an abstract manner. Excellent architects who become EAs also possess what I've named the Zoom Factor. Some never even realize they have this skill, and most will never name it. It is the ability to zoom in and out while you are speaking and listening, and to see the big picture in the back of your mind while you process the finer details at the very same time. The ability to focus is highly regarded in most professions. The ability to focus on two perspectives at the same time is rare.

Where does this fit in the big picture of architecture in your profession? It is crucial to consider many perspectives when you plan and design. Escalating your view to twenty thousand feet is necessary to see all that will affect the enterprise with solutions you are considering. Knowing when to drop down to ten or even one thousand feet is a critical skill you must gain to communicate with others about the architecture, as well as to maintain your vision necessary to create it. Oscillating between levels of granularity in perspective should become an automatic behavior. It enables you to improve your speed and effectiveness in developing artifacts. Using this skill along with the many checklists provided throughout this book, you will formulate an efficiency level that will put you head and shoulders above the rest in your field.

Why Architects Think Differently

Re-factor Problems

Architects are able to spontaneously re-factor problems and subsequently solutions in their mind and on the fly. Re-factoring is defined as a disciplined technique for restructuring an existing solution, altering its internal structure without changing its external behavior. To reuse the term with respect to solutions, it means to make them easier to understand and modify. It is absolutely essential for you to be able to restructure components of architectures and other patterns and solutions in development that have been provided over time. It is the heart of the series of small behavior-preserving transformations.

You will need to be able to see solutions both as a whole and in parts. Your Zoom Factor allows you to see how you can re-factor parts in ways to solve other problems and create other solutions. You need to see ways you can re-factor solutions to improve the solution itself as well as larger solutions of which you are part.

Ability to Focus

You will possess the ability to focus on the challenge at hand while still seeing the future state. You may put a placeholder in your mind for the construction of a road map for the future state architecture. You will need the ability to adjust and refocus as automatically as a camera lens, using an array of auto sensors in your mind to determine the level of focus required. Future images will appear in your mind as solutions and will be present while you are still seeing the details. You will demonstrate the ability to focus on the problem at hand while still seeing the future state.

Another skill to mention in this area is the ability to zone out just to dial in closer. Consider three-dimensional puzzles that appear in color in weekend newspapers. To see a clearer picture in the background, you cause yourself to zone out and blur your vision. This analogy fits this skill perfectly. You'll use this same disassociation skill to improve your visioning performance.

It is all too easy to have a clever solution pop into your head when listening to others describe their own problems. It will take the utmost in discipline for you to reframe your thinking and allow your mind to zoom out to see all of the implications of such a quick fix. You'll need the ability to zoom in for the details and then dial out to see implications. You will use that same skill to know when to articulate details of the big picture and, based on your audience, decide whether additional details are required.

The Pattern Seer

Where are the patterns? And why are they important? Patterns are well-established solutions to architectural problems together with a set of constraints about how they may be used. Experienced architects know reusing a pattern has been a long-standing and proven way to architect a successful solution. You will collect requirements and analyze the set of required characteristics for the solution, and your Zoom Factor will enable you to quickly pare down options within the problem space to create a more narrowly defined set of architecture options.

You will see the pattern forming in your mind as you review what is needed. How does this help you? Specific matching occurs with specific requirements. Discipline in the area of architectural process allows you to avoid grabbing the wrong pattern too quickly. The speed of design and selection with using a known pattern reduces complexity and also fosters a sureness the solution will succeed. Rarely is something 100 percent new. Typically, you will assemble a solution from a variety of patterns and fit it with the new context.

You will need to be careful not to identify verbally what you see too early. This will put you at a disadvantage as a stakeholder, and users may believe that you jumped to conclusions too early or that you have not been listening carefully to all of their requirements.

You will also possess the ability to create a blueprint for a solution through multiple views. You can use this skill to recognize risks or similarities to other patterns that you can apply to this solution.

Architects use business patterns as another method to drive an acceptable option list. The name of the game here is infrastructure reuse. As you narrow down the list of alternatives, you will win with reuse when you choose well-established and tried architectural models. Reuse has been long touted as the primary reason for using the architecture approach. One of the best ways to achieve value and benefits is through recognition of associated risks, costs, skills, time, and nonfunctional requirements.

You should become practiced in seeing patterns in political situations. Your senses should tell you that politics may be at work with the selection of architecture to a solution. You may not be able to see into the future as to all that will happen, but very often you may recognize patterns in others' behavior similar to one of your past experiences. Risk patterns are also common sightings for architects, and you will find them quicker to recall with more experience. When recognizing a pattern, part of your risk identification practice should include identifying and quantifying the risks as soon as possible. Include the size, manner, and likelihood of risks that could materialize and potential actions you would recommend to ensure they don't.

Other patterns that architects recognize are those in the category of IT failures. This list includes projects in development and infrastructure. These are unfortunate but all too frequent. Reviewers responsible for plan approval and budgets see the amount of time planned, and they ensure the dreaded failures of the past are repeated by cutting the time allotted. Deadlines are missed, and IT is assigned yet another failure. All you can do is to demonstrate how patterns and architectural process will help reduce cost and risk. The extent of your control is trying to convince the business and IT managers to take the opportunity to prototype the riskiest parts and reuse what has been already proven.

Abstract and Conceptual Thinking

Reality is merely an illusion, albeit a very persistent one
—Albert Einstein

Organizations that best use architects grant some time for creative thinking. They give architects the tools and space they need for germination of great ideas. If you wish to become excellent, you will need to consider the natural need for thinking time. You may inquire during the interview process as to what an organization does to develop these skills. Space and time to prototype should also be a consideration.

Conceptual modeling time is important and should occur during the inception time of a plan for a business initiative. Conceptual and context diagrams in the enterprise architecture, as well as domain models in the data architecture space, are prime examples. They are critical for visualization of the development of solutions. As an architect, conceptual thinking will be your primary mode of thinking. It is much easier to put the pieces together at a higher level when you think at a conceptual level. Working through options later that don't fit requirements will demand intensive work both in terms of cost and time. You will use your ability to recognize recurring themes within the business strategy. This will help you find common ground between groups when considering viable alternatives.

When you think conceptually, you strive to understand the problem and then see patterns and commonalities forming as you collect the requirements, problems, issues, strategies, and goals. Architects often use conceptualization to frame the project requirements. If you understand a situation by identifying patterns, it is easier to note the key underlying issues and factors. An example here might be considering a rules engine to drive complex applications rather than to plan annual projects to update hard-coded rules within the application. Out-of-the-box thinking leads to innovative solutions, such as matching up ready-made components with pieces of pre-made software applications.

Think with Framework Style

The Zoom Factor is at work when you think within the context of a framework. To "slice and dice" when dividing up a problem and visualizing solutions can assist you clarify your thinking. After being an architect for any period, you will get used to thinking in terms of columns and rows. Very often, an architecture problem has a three-dimensional perspective you must articulate, draw, and model to communicate with those who are to support the solution.

Frameworks are a great way to break down a body of information into smaller parts. You examine it from different viewpoints so it may be better understood. Zachman's framework is based on the premise of the separation of concerns and viewpoints and is still the original method of analyzing enterprise information. Jaap Schekkerman's extended enterprise architecture framework (E2AF) applies yet another variation on Zachman's framework, turning it on its side. The columns take each of the aspect considerations, such as why (contextual), who (environmental), what (conceptual level), how (logical level), with what (physical level), and when (transformational), and allow you to apply these varying perspectives to each of the four major domain views—business, data, application, and technology.

After acting in an architect role for several years and learning about frameworks, it would come as no surprise that you can view many concepts in your life as well as work this way. Many different adaptations of simplified frameworks will come and go, including the 4+1 View (logical, development, process, and physical views.). They are all different ways to organize and divide the work you must do and the information you must collect. They provide a container-style repository for collecting the information and models you'll need to make decisions and plan for the future. For more information on these various frameworks, see the links at www.zoomfactorbook.com/links.

Your Initial Hypothesis

Give me a place to stand and a lever long enough and I will move the world.
—Archimedes, 200 B.C.

Your ability to "helicopter over" the big picture and then hover above the details will allow you to quickly go back and forth to scan for viable options. It is a skill you will find absolutely critical and necessary for your success. A skill in this category is that of an observer. As an architect, you must astutely assess a situation, determine the progress being made, and sense the pieces that are missing to fulfill the future state.

Future images appear in your mind while you are still seeing the details. For example, if you're conversing about problems with a service bus with several designers, you can apply this knowledge in relation to discussions you have recently had with your executives. You may have been involved with an industry organization that tries to list common problems that many are experiencing.

You may know about bigger changes planned and small details that may have been overlooked. Developing the ability to continually oscillate between the big picture and small details is priceless when it comes to the architecture value you will provide your organization. You will have the ability to create an initial hypothesis for many solutions to be created at some later date. Solutions not immediately planned can live in a repository. Your ability to accurately size and scope the situation will become better over time, and your ratio of valid hypotheses will go up.

See the Change Before You Change Your World

Seeing that change is needed is another skill you'll need to acquire in the area of observation skills. This does not mean you should make change for the sake of change or suggest change to business executives and other IT senior level people while speaking with them.

Knowing change is inevitable, you'll design strategies and architectures to facilitate change. It is an iterative process, and the great architect facilitates the design of the architecture to build the solution once and evolve it many times.

You'll need to know when to tuck things away so you can later pull them out and synthesize them when change is required. Often the architect can use these as both proof and research when a change is being considered. If you can safely protect areas for change until a solution is required to realize the change, you'll be better positioned to formulate a great solution that will meet the needs of both current and future users.

Techniques to Strengthen Your Zoom Factor

It is probably a good time to mention the importance and need for you to take regular breaks. It is also probably one of the cruelest realities and probably the most stifling means to architects' creative abilities to seat them in a place that has no window. Visualizing potential scenarios or seeing paths into the future while letting your mind percolate gives you the opportunity to see things more clearly. Architects need to strive to protect ample time for thinking in their schedule—by taking breaks, meditating, and creating great variation in business.

Participation in a variety of groups, including social functions and external activities, gives you different situations and perspectives to apply to current business problems. Your ability to apply various life experiences to the problem at hand is important to becoming an excellent architect. Participating in various activities such as sports and social and charity organizations not only gives you the skills and experiences on your resume that benefit your employer, but it also can give you the chance to fill in the gaps, observe a variety of behaviors, and round out both your experience levels and your ability to do your work.

Strong architects possess wide experience both in business and life. Your wide array of background roles in both industry verticals and within IT prepares you for the work ahead. As you become more senior in your role, your job will become less about what you know and more about your character traits. Finding opportunity to build these traits and apply your Zoom Factor becomes even more important.

Zoom In—Action Steps You Need to Succeed

As has been a recurring theme throughout this book, you can save more time using checklists. Here is a list of some architectural concerns that you should review when considering some of the ways you can architect a solution?

- ☐ If you were to put this solution up for review by peers, how would it rate?
- ☐ What are the most important facts that a developer should know about this architecture solution?
- ☐ Which software patterns does this solution use?
- ☐ Do the patterns match our standard technology infrastructure patterns?
- ☐ Do the software patterns match our standard database infra-structure patterns?
- ☐ What are the components of this system?
- ☐ Are the components easily distinguishable?
- ☐ Have the components been built with an eye for reuse?
- ☐ How does the architecture measure for ease of integration?
- ☐ How will components and services be added at a later date? How will they be decommissioned?
- ☐ Will the components, patterns, and solution selected meet capacity needs? What is the horizon? What is the expected shelf life of this solution?
- ☐ How will the solution be deployed? How will the components be deployed to both human processes and machines?
- ☐ Where are the components being deployed? How will the timing of deployment be handled once the solution is operable?

☐ What aspects/resources of the solution share an environment? Have impacts of change and downtimes been assessed? How are loads shared for this solution?

☐ Have alternative methods of deployment been considered for this solution? How will hardware and platform changes be handled for this solution? How will business and IT processes be handled with this solution?

☐ How do components communicate? How are they exposed to other applications? Have all security implications been addressed?

☐ Have future extensions and modifications been considered?

☐ What impact does the solution have on the existing maintenance schedule? Disaster recovery planning?

☐ Has this architecture solution been shared with development, project, and operational teams? Vendors? Third parties we will rely on?

☐ Where does this solution fall in the risk management horizon? Would it be considered risky given the existing environment, experience, staffing, and budgets?

Zoom Out—Big-Picture Concepts

Can't see the forest for the trees? It can describe the situation when an architect focuses too much on specific problems and misses the big point. Try these dress rehearsals to get into the habit of practicing the Zoom Factor to reach higher levels.

☐ Does this solution seem familiar? What has my company done like this before? What's new? What was my experience?

☐ What have I done like this as an architect?

☐ Do I know any real-life examples of this solution in operation today? Would real-life examples be available for the business to use to imagine how this solution would work for us?

☐ How accurate do the time estimates seem? How are the budget estimates?

☐ Could I imagine this solution working live today in the existing infrastructure? Could I imagine the operations and technology teams supporting it?

☐ How would customer service work for this solution? Would I need to hire more? How would I train existing teams?

☐ How difficult is deployment of this solution? How costly? How time sensitive would it be? How could I practice?

☐ How would a solution like this fit into the IT asset portfolio? Would it replace several gaps? Would it require special exceptions to the enterprise architecture road map? Our strategic plan?

☐ How comfortable would I be promoting this solution to upper management? Stakeholders? IT teams?

☐ How could I envision vendor and supplier relations for this solution? Does it conjure up bad memories? Is it uncharted territory?

☐ Would I need a skill upgrade to make this solution work? How far is it from what I already can do?

☐ What does the speed and ease of development look like? Would this feel comfortable, or does it conjure up feelings of risk and uncertainty?

☐ Are there best practices available? Successful peer and vendor experiences and case studies?

☐ What would the customer experience be like using this solution? Would it make their lives simpler? Our employees' lives simpler? IT simpler?

☐ What would stakeholders' expectations and comfort be with a solution like this? What would they be when they are first aware of it? Do I have a champion on my side already?

☐ What would it be like to test a solution like this? Would the QA cycle be normal, or would it require additional expertise and long-term dedicated business resources?

CHAPTER 8:
FINDING YOUR FRAMEWORK

I would observe that chaos happens by chance, by accident.
Order happens by intelligent design, and "intelligent design" presumes a
designer who is externally consistent and benevolent.
–John Zachman

Your architecture team will require architects with various skills, such as the whiteboarder, the wordsmith, the prototyper, the technician, and the politician, to formulate solutions. The team also needs an organizer, which is usually the EA. As the organizer, you will foster advancement in stages or chunks and know how to organize the deliverables. You are able to pull structures into place to organize the work and to allocate the appropriate processes to the architecture to complete the deliverables. In other words, as a skilled practitioner, you will understand and will have mastered how to use the architecture framework. Using the right framework, you will have the uncanny ability to organize and sort through concepts and components. Below, you'll find details on various types of frameworks and how you might employ them in your work.

The Basics about Frameworks

All IT architects should know the basic elements of a framework. Frameworks foster understanding and definition of the organization and the architecture. Conceptual in nature, frameworks use viewpoints to create views that represent different perspectives of an enterprise or system model. The most basic architecture frameworks used for enterprise architecture are organized in a manner of domain architectures. Business, applications (or solutions), data (or information), and technology are the main domain architectures or views included in the simplest examples.

The framework that is right for your organization will foster the evolution of your architecture. It will allow you to create a set of viewpoints that will enable your team to deliver the analysis and perspective for making sound architecture choices. Architects use many frameworks for dividing or organizing artifacts. The columns of the framework organize one perspective within the enterprise, and the rows categorize another. Using the Zachman framework as an example, a cell in the matrix will yield a model or artifact that visually represents the information or response to the question at the intersection.

In addition, the multidimensional nature of a framework enables you to make design trade-offs and validate your choices. The consistency of its organizational method will provide a solid decision base and repository for your models and information. The framework's structure, as well as your organization's understanding of the framework's role and purpose, will simplify your review and verification processes. It will provide a base for the transitional design of your enterprise as well as the development life cycle of your architecture.

Types of Frameworks

Various types of frameworks exist, as they are created for many reasons. Taxonomies or hierarchical frameworks are an organizational method for completing architecture activities. They are classified in a super type-subtype relationship. Architecture reference models are abstract representations of things in an environment used to educate and communicate with the teams that must work within the architecture. They include entities and relationships of the objects used within the enterprise and are typically technology-agnostic while providing standards for the teams that use them.

Commercial frameworks are those created by companies and are proprietary. The Zachman framework is included in this category, as John Zachman created it when he was with IBM. Government-created frameworks are those created specifically for use within the government or defense environments. Examples include the FEAF, the Department of Defense Architecture Framework (DODAF), and the

British Ministry of Defense Architecture Framework (MODAF). Open source frameworks are those created by consortiums or community groups. Examples of open source frameworks include the Gartner framework and TOGAF. Some frameworks are purely a classification framework, such as the Zachman framework, while others are wrapped up with the associated methodology of their creator, such as TOGAF. These frameworks will also indicate or include process descriptions, such as inputs or outputs, in each step. Examples of this variety are the TOGAF and the Gartner Group's method or process model. Deeper explanations of these frameworks follow.

The Zachman Framework

The first framework you need to recognize as a core part of your architecture knowledge is the Zachman framework. This framework has stood the test of time since the 1970s with one version alone: only recently has a second version been released. John Zachman himself describes his framework as a schema and classification structure. It is arranged as a six-by-six grid with viewpoints arranged in columns or slices and aligned with the big six questions:

1. Data–What?
2. Function–How?
3. Network–Where?
4. People–Who?
5. Time–When?
6. Motivation–Why?

The horizontal view begins with the most abstract and progresses downward with more detail. The layers include rows aligned with target contributors and their perspectives, such as:

1. Scope (Contextual)–Strategist
2. Business Model (Conceptual)–Executive Leaders and Business
3. System (Logical)–Architect
4. Technology (Physical)–Engineer and Technology
5. Detailed Representations (Out-of-Context)–Technician
6. Functioning Enterprise–Operations

Within each cell or at an intersection in the grid, usually a type of model or list should be collected and compiled at the level of detail equal to the perspective of those requiring the information. Zachman's grid is also known as a model-driven framework. Typically, you collect the information in a top-down order of progression, and ideally, as is needed by priority in the business and the architecture. A more recent perspective or directive is to create models at the intersections when they are needed. It is believed that all organizations need the most strategic levels completed at the top, and then choices are made as you progress into levels of detail where you may achieve value by modeling and analysis.

The results should produce a detailed description of what your enterprise architecture is defined as with respect to your business, data, solutions, and technology. When the Zachman framework is complete, it truly represents the enterprise and that is its biggest strength. In an orderly structure, it shows how the organization fits together. In addition, as the most popular and well-used framework, there is more software tool support than for other frameworks and methods. Many practitioners have studied and understand the Zachman framework.

Its weaknesses are thought to include the time it would take to complete the framework and the lack of process surrounding its use. Many look at the framework and without guidance deem the process to be to complete the models for each cell. However, consider the length of time it would take to create models in the current state for every one of the cells and then to also model a future state. Some inexperienced architects might head down this path unless steered appropriately. Unless properly guided, it is easy to do too much or too little in a specific area of the framework. The work needs to align with the architecture program's goal and purpose. There is no order or requirement to complete any of the cells.

Keep in mind that these single-cell models are often primitive versus composite or combined models. Each solves an underlying question and reduces ambiguity in the forces that beg for change within the organization. Organizations that want a streamlined process are rarely suited to use this specific framework.

What about TOGAF?

The other popular framework is TOGAF, cared for and created by a community consortium run by the Open Group. At the time of writing, Version 9 was the most recent version, released in 2009. This architectural framework has many components and is wrapped up with the architecture development method (ADM). It is complete with a diagram shaped like a spoke and wheel, with the requirements in the center and the *a* to *h* spokes representing sequenced steps in the process. This framework also aligns with the four major architecture domains: business, application, information, and technology.

Double-headed arrows indicate there should be bidirectional advancement within the requirements at each of the stages from vision all the way through the various architectures. What is strong about this approach is that each of the steps from *a* to *h* have some sort of matching to a very simplistic domain-oriented framework. Another strength is its inclusion of an enterprise continuum that prescribes the architecture life cycle, including architecture governance.

TOGAF's other strengths include its future-oriented nature and practicality in modeling the current state. In addition, information on the approach is readily available from multiple sources. Its weaknesses include the amount of detail required for its use and a description that is complex to read and understand. It also can lead to lengthy start-up efforts that include a cumbersome amount of detail. For these reasons, many feel this framework is better suited for solution architecture than for enterprise architecture and believe the multitude of contributors take away from its clarity.

Frameworks Used by Government Agencies

There are various versions and flavors of architecture that governments and their agencies commonly use. These include the Canadian Government Service Reference Model (GSRM), primarily used in government and municipal areas in Canada for business transformation, as well as the DODAF. DODAF, on which TOGAF is based, is an example of a very specific-use framework the U.S. government and its suppliers use.

The FEAF is another government architecture framework worth mentioning. It is simpler to understand and includes the most commonly used set of reference models.

What about Reference Models?

Reference models are representative examples of taxonomies or hierarchies described for each of the main architecture domains within a specific framework. The FEAF uses such reference models as the PRM, BRM, SRM, DRM, and TRM.

Planning-Oriented Frameworks

The aforementioned examples are some of the many versions that have evolved over time, and many other architecture frameworks are based on Zachman and DODAF. Some of the easiest to understand are the Enterprise Architecture Process Cycle (E2AF) and Steven Spewak's enterprise architecture planning model. E2AF is supported by the Institute for Enterprise Architecture Developments (IFEAD), a group founded by Jaap Schekkerman. Both of these frameworks are organized by domain architectures. They were both designed or intended to be used for enterprise architecture. In fact, the FEAF evolved from Steven Spewak's work.

You can read up on both of these frameworks either in white paper format or in book form. See the reference section at www.zoomfactorbook.com/bookshelf, where I list books that will give you further information on these topics.

Other Frameworks

Various other frameworks exist within the realm of IT architecture. They vary from the conceptual to the logical and physical, detailed in the area of software or solution-oriented architecture (SOA) frameworks. These detailed frameworks are more like designs or libraries that hold the various components together.

Apply Organization and Compartmentalization Skills

Beyond the knowledge of the frameworks, you'll need organizational skills. The organizer can group problems, components, and patterns together. You will need to be especially skilled in understanding business strategies and requirements and have the ability to group like ones together. You will need to be able to distill masses of information and discard the unnecessary. Some architects have an uncanny knack to do this on the fly and know when rat holes need not be explored. You'll also need the ability to simplify. Being able to express or document concepts in a clear manner is a very highly regarded skill among your peers. Making the complicated and technical look simple is a skill that is underrated.

EAs often simplify complex ideas through the process of compartmentalization, which is separating things into distinct parts or categories. By chunking or carving off the problem in stages, you'll advance in stages. You will group problems and solutions and select from a variety of solution parts depending on the situation you face. In documenting solutions, you'll accumulate several templates and methods by which you document, map, and model your architectures.

You'll put structures such as these and others in place to organize your work and the deliverables you'll produce. One of the most familiar structures for the architecture documentation is the framework. I mentioned many versions of such a structure earlier. You'll start with a basic knowledge of what a framework is, then layer on what you need it for and what you'll do with it to organize your work and its outcome.

Choosing a Framework

Why Use a Framework?

So why would you use a framework? You'll need one to organize and present a simplified version of your architecture. You'll need to store artifacts and deliverables and to chart your progress in modeling the organization. Generally, frameworks are enterprise encompassing and visually oriented. You'll use simplified versions of the framework you choose for each of the domain areas in your organization. In addition, when you create an architecture road map, you can use the framework as a taxonomy and guide for the work you plan. You'll find that frameworks such as Zachman are the most widely used for enterprise architecture; TOGAF is more widely used when it comes to application or system architecture.

Do You Really Need a Framework?

Possibly not, but you'd better be sure of at least one conscious decision: put the process you use to do architecture ahead of choosing a framework on your priority list. Many organizations put framework selection at top of their list when it comes to starting architecture programs. However, remember that how you'll do your architecture work is far more important than the way you organize it.

Once you have determined the methods and approaches you're going to employ to do the architecture, then you should figure out which framework suits that process. When you have a framework that best matches your process, and you have some experience and hours logged with the process and framework, then and only then should you consider picking a tool. Most architects will use tools such as presentation software, word processors, and drawing tools. If you are looking at vendors, one who is worthy will tell you that it is never a good idea to pick a tool and let it drive the processes you use.

Drive out Your Goals and Objectives

Your goals and objectives, not the framework, must drive what you do and what you model. You want to do only the amount of architecture that you need to meet your business goals. Creating models just for the sake of drawing them is a waste of your time and a surefire way to have your program or funding cancelled. So which framework do you choose? Well, that depends on what are you trying to do, what your scope is, and how experienced and ready your organization is for architecture.

If you choose a framework that is described in one to two inches worth of paper and you are just starting out, you may find its complexity overwhelming. You might consider the industry or organization you are in and find out which framework your peers most commonly use. By doing so, you'll enable yourself to communicate with colleagues and share information and experience that more accurately supports your current position. Ideally, your selection efforts will result in the framework that is the closest match for your organization based on all of these considerations.

The Selection Process

Let's go through a very simple and condensed version of the information you need to know. This information will be handy and something to keep in mind if you are ever responsible for choosing the framework for your work. Choosing the best framework for your organization is like picking out the best television at the electronics store. Which one is best depends on your budget, your intended use, the complexity in which you tend to use it, and the competency of the user to get the value out of its features.

You need know the framework's features, the general types of available frameworks, and some information about your intended use. You'll also need to know which framework a company of your type generally selects and the known benefits and drawbacks of using that framework. You should organize your considerations in this order:

1. Which process will your organization use for architecture?
2. What type of organization are you—government or corporate? What frameworks do other enterprises like yours use?
3. What size team will you have to use and complete the framework?
4. What is your budget? Will models be a critical component within the framework?
5. Where will you store the information your framework prescribes?
6. Will you be using tools with your framework? Which ones are available for the framework you are considering?

Zoom In—Action Steps You Need to Succeed

There is much hype and discussion about frameworks, but little about how to choose and use one. Here are some quick steps you may consider to accelerate the process:

1. Decide on your framework. My favorites are ones that allow me to organize, capture, and guide my work, more commonly known as taxonomies. I use my own version that collects business, information, solution, and technology categories. Within each, I collect an inventory of the functions or major components, principles that apply to that category, models or diagrams, and standards. There are a few well-known frameworks very close to the one I use or adapt to most often: the FEAF framework as well as the Index framework Bernard H. Boar refers to in his book, Constructing Blueprints for Enterprise IT Architectures. A variation on this step may be to take the Zachman framework and choose some of the top inner cells to tackle first. This option works well for those who are more traditional and may wish to complete the other cells.

INTERROGATIV PERSPECTIVES	What	How	Where	Who	When	Why	TARGET CONTRIBUTORS
SCOPE							STRATEGISTS
BUSINESS							EXECUTIVE LEADERS
SYSTEM							ARCHITECTS
TECHNOL- OGIES							ENGINEERS
COMPONENT							TECHNICIANS
OPERATIONS							WORKERS
AUDIENCE PERSPECTIVES							TARGET DOMAINS

Figure 4. Variation Using Shaded Zachman Framework

2. Decide on the versions of the framework you'll complete. Many can visualize current and target versions, but consider interim versions if you cannot make it to target in one fell swoop. The diagram in Figure 4 works very well for organizing and compartmentalizing multiple versions of the framework, such as current, target, current, and some interim version.

3. Set up your buckets in a repository and determine what the contents of the cells should be. Create a combination of lists, diagrams, and models, paying close attention to which shall provide value. If you can realize your goals with a list, choose it before creating models for sake of brevity.

4. Scavenge your organization for existing models and delegate the hunt to your team. Even better, ask external team members to provide you with this information and get them involved.

5. Prioritize your need for the cells. Get moving, start the work, and plan a status update every few weeks to ensure you are on track, consistent with other team members, and still feel there is value in completing the cell. Your first cut should use a fixed time method for completion, which will get you to 80 percent completion with 20 percent of the effort.

6. Assimilate what you've got in the current state and plan for areas of research, analysis, and design to determine a focus for the target state.

7. Decide whether you need interim versions and use for your transition planning.

8. Govern the content of the models and determine which, if any, should be updated.

Zoom Out—Big-Picture Concepts

Here is a great exercise if you want to evaluate what your real framework needs are.

1. Project an image of the Zachman framework on a whiteboard.

2. Hand out four colored whiteboard markers to your team.

3. Ask them to rank and prioritize the cells from one to ten based on these criteria:

4. This cell gives us critical information about the business we know we need to know now.

5. Our stakeholders wish or have stated they wished we had this information.

6. By knowing the answers we'd arrive at in this intersection, we could solve a business problem we know we have today.

7. We would be able to use the information gained in this cell as a leverage point in our transition plan for the enterprise.

8. Design of our solutions would improve if we had the information in this cell.

9. Our technology department would function better if we had this information.

10. We would know what we don't know if we had the information in this cell as it would reveal our gaps.

You can also use a color-shading technique on a diagram if you want to save it digitally. A great trick might be to print the above questions on index cards and have them available for those who will have control of the markers!

CHAPTER 9:
CREATE BLUEPRINTS AND ROADMAPS

*Map out your future—but do it in pencil. The road ahead
is as long as you make it. Make it worth the trip.*
—Jon Bon Jovi

Architects should be ingrained in process, including documentation and articulation of plans. Throughout the various stages of the architecture life cycle, you'll create plans in varying levels of detail. This chapter is intended to introduce and describe two of the plans and documentation you will create that differ in the timing and stage of the architecture process, intended audience, and granularity: blueprints and road maps.

Domain architects habitually create blueprints to describe the logical, physical, and conceptual viewpoints of a system or solution. Blueprints contain a description of the problem, purpose, functions, parts, resources, and configuration order. They pictorially describe integration and blocks of diagrams in progressive levels of detail.

Enterprise architecture revolves around the transformation effort in your organization and is primarily comprised of the planning done in enterprise strategy and architecture, the realization of the enterprise architecture, and enterprise portfolio management (EPfM). EAs naturally create road maps as part of the strategic-planning process to describe transitions from the current state to the target state for a multiyear transition effort.

Now that you understand the basic differences[1] between these two documents, how do you actually create a blueprint or a road map?

---

[1] A tip to help you remember the difference between these two documents is to think "solution blueprint" and "enterprise architecture road map."

Laying Out the Blueprint

There are no industry standards for architecture documentation, but if there were, Bernard Boar, author of *Constructing Blueprints for Enterprise IT Architectures*, might get the nod as the first cut. His chapter covering the documentation of a system or solution matches my blueprint definition and includes detailed instructions for all of the textual and diagram components you may wish to add to your blueprints. A blueprint can be described as a document completed by using the engineering method based on his work.

My personal preference is to create blueprints for solution, system, and technology architectures and to create road maps for enterprise-wide architecture plans. Depending on the newness of the technology and the solution, I prefer to customize the level of detail in a blueprint and match it to the experience level of the resources that will be tasked with construction. When you hand off an architecture blueprint, its readers shouldn't have to know anything about what you are trying to achieve so long as they follow the steps.

Architecture blueprints are often known as diagram sets that identify components at design and construction levels to display a concept for those who are required to build from it. A good blueprint will show the roles, interactions, and relationships of components at each level or diagram view. A blueprint includes such details as sizing, platform operations, and manageability and capacity estimations. It may extend to include such considerations such as scalability planning, proposed solutions, and deployment. If you take the construction of a house as an example, many perspectives or layers of the building plans are given to various tradesmen to plan their construction.

In a blueprint set for a house, there is a layer for systems that includes electrical and house venting. A layer is included for framing the house, showing the exterior as well as an image and the sizing of the floor plan. Various views are intended for an assortment of trades for deployment and construction of the house, depending on their needs. Within IT, common areas to frame a blueprint for are the various development environments within your organization. If you've ever heard the terms "development," "quality assurance," "test," "stress test," "production environment," or "staging area," these are all examples of environments you may choose to build to support your application development efforts.

Depending on the size of your organization, you'll create one or many of these environments, and the architectural drawing should depict what these environments should look like. The blueprint you create will show the basic components that are the same or similar in all environments and call out the differences that exist for each of the environments on the various views. A final diagram in the environment example should show how the software migrates from one environment to the next.

However, diagrams aren't enough to tell the full story. To build from them step-by-step, you need a grid or list of components and the details with size, configuration, hardware models, and various other criteria to enable those in the technical area to build the environments. These diagrams and descriptions, along with the use of the environments, will allow the developers, designers, and quality assurance teams to understand where development work will be performed. It will allow management to understand why replication of infrastructure is required and enables managers to make the appropriate budget considerations. It will allow business users to understand the constraints and methods in which they will interact with the environment.

Blueprints may start logically from a template page of one logical model and progress to layers more physical in nature as they describe build specifications. As you near the construction phase, the information contained within the blueprint may be transferred to a configuration database as the architecture is built, and then it is unlikely that all layers of the blueprint details will be maintained over time.

Various types of blueprints exist for various domain architectures. For example, consider process decomposition diagrams and use case diagrams for the business architecture domain. Within the technical domain, you may see rack and stack diagrams, network diagrams, or the layouts for virtual operating systems. These examples are very common: they are the diagrams that depict both the logical and physical nature structurally.

For an organization that chooses to use a blueprint approach rather than the road map, maintenance of the blueprint will occur in a much more granular way. It will often occur in conjunction with or as a replacement of portfolio management. A blueprint will evolve when new or changing business capabilities are identified, thus requiring a change to the architecture. Sometimes a blueprint may be updated to reflect recognition of enhancements in the architecture that would benefit existing business operations. Finally, a blueprint may be updated when improvements can be made to the existing architecture, often due to reduction in cost or improved performance.

The Solution Blueprint

One of the most common documents produced by an architect is something called a system architecture document, software blueprint, or solution architecture document. Contained within it are the many layers or views that can be also termed as a blueprint set. One section will outline the business architecture. You will include things such as business goals, objectives, major functions, and process maps for the solution, just to name a few. This is where the business capabilities you plan to realize should reside. It may include a detailed description and mapping of the various business departments and the functions and processes for which they were responsible..

Another view incorporates a section known as the data view. You should list the data models at conceptual, logical, and physical levels. In the area of database design, you will include such things as logical and physical models, data warehouse models, and star schemas where applicable. Occasionally, you'll incorporate information on the metadata repository, metadata models, and data governance plans. The solution view will include component, service, and pattern levels and their required quality attributes. The main parts are the descriptions of the integration layers and approaches; the mappings between the business, the solution, and the technology; and the solution. Where applicable, you can add commentary on various solutions, such as security and history.

The technology view describes the physical components in terms of hardware and software and the specifications that make up the system infrastructure. It should be possible to assess the suitability of current products for construction of the solution. The intent is that the technology view will act as a blueprint to enable the construction of an environment for the system to be built upon.

The Technology Blueprint

As just mentioned, the technology blueprint may be a section within a solution or software blueprint. It also may be a stand-alone artifact created for infrastructure development and construction. It may include a security plan both from a solution perspective and an enterprise perspective. In a blueprint, one section usually depicts the alignment between a business function and the technology-enabling component. I have frequently been asked to complete a technology blueprint for companies when they were trying to get organized, analyze or rationalize their current situation, and plot their future paths. When the element of time was required, we were able to use the blueprint and morph it into a technology road map.

Technology blueprints can be massive in size. My preference is to create them using PowerPoint slides with embedded visual diagrams to maximize flexibility. It then becomes possible to include a number of formats and documents designed by various groups. Other artifacts you may wish to include are design diagrams and database models. You can embed models that have come from products such as Erwin, Power Designer, or other diagramming tools. As a sidenote, Power Designer produces a very nice document that generates a data dictionary, data listings, and data models in whichever format you fashion.

Blueprints can be intensely long booklets created with either word processing or presentation software that include some of the major architecture deliverables. Such documents can be digitally and hyperlinked in storage, file, or content systems but should be printable for physical transportation to meetings and for marking up. You might also want to produce all or parts of these documents to give specifics to vendors and management for various discussion purposes and estimates.

Relationships with Enterprise Portfolio Management

At this stage, you need to know a little bit about EPfM to fully appreciate the differences between blueprints and road maps. An enterprise portfolio is created as a means of planning programs and projects that an organization is going to undertake in the near term in a prioritized order. Programs are often planned within a budget cycle and characteristically grouped either by like capabilities or by combined efficiencies and cost savings when implemented together. EPfM is covered in greater detail in Chapter 15. For now, it's important to know the relationship between EPfM and the road map, as well as its relation to blueprints. Often a blueprint is created for an individual portfolio or grouping within the program at a level of detail from which a build can occur. The groupings may be called themes of a road map, and they should map directly to a business goal or driver.

Groupings and Timing—IT Assets

You'll need to justify your plans through your business resources and ensure that your groupings and plans will actually satisfy their needs. By laying this out, you need to review the entirety of the situation and take a look at the risks. Backtrack to ensure that you are not missing some lost opportunities based on the cycle or timing in which you select the initiatives. Review the sequence from a perspective of risk identification with respect to time. You'll need to ensure you have the infrastructure, budget, and build time available, which often proves to be the main timing cog in the road map mechanism.

At some point, you will want to move this exercise into a visual format. You might do this using a Gantt chart or flowchart drawings inserted in presentation software or word-processing documents. Whichever method you choose, keep in mind that your road map is not your project plan, and the amount of effort you expend on timing and estimates should not be great. At the early stages, coordinate with the SOA group if you have entered the SOA arena as part of your strategy. This provides a greater means of alignment between capabilities and planned services and mapping them over time.

If there are wholesale changes to your organization as part of the implementation, it would benefit you to prioritize the value and urgency of the capabilities the business needs most. You won't be able to do everything, and involving the business in the prioritization works best. While it may seem complex, try to integrate this activity with your portfolio management process. This requires your EPfM team to sequence the projects and initiatives by involving the input of the architecture team. To summarize, you are trying to create great big building blocks in a puzzle-like manner to get the big picture to look like your desired state.

The Road-Mapping Process

All you need is the plan, the road map, and the
courage to press on to your destination.
–Earl Nightingale, 1921–1989

A road map is one of the outputs of a high-level strategic plan. While it includes the element of time as phases in the migration toward a target state, it is not a project plan. The architecture road map is aligned with the dimension of "when" in the Zachman framework. It is prepared with a longer-term perspective as an action plan for the target state. There are many more details in a road map than those in the purely technical viewpoints. Most often, a road map summarizes the business capabilities that need to be created, the reason for creating them, and a mapping to the technology enabler plotted against a long-range timeline. It includes plans for the transformation at the enterprise architecture program level and does not itemize the specific steps at the project level. It is based on a high-level prioritized approach at sufficient detail with which you may validate the business strategic objectives, but not enough to put a budget forward or book resources.

The road map provides the information needed to plan and prescribe the enterprise portfolio progression. Consider it one of the inputs you need for the portfolio planning exercise. The portfolio plan will include the scope, team, and work plans for each business area within the program. It is an iterative process, as the grouping of the prescribed business changes from the program and the plans for implementation form the road map. You'll use the road map as a high-level guide to implement the enterprise transformation and to evaluate where to add new components.

Road maps differ from blueprints in that they show transitions over time for the current state to future state. They should form the basis of your architecture vision at the level of EPfM per grouping or product family. The time dimension is one of the main perspectives, and it constrains the grouping or product context. The views are primarily business-oriented, as they should be to align to the product families. You will include views on the market, product, process, technology, and people for each portfolio.

The Enterprise Architecture Road Map

One of the most common instances of road maps is what's called an enterprise architecture road map. This may also be titled the enterprise architecture plan when it is the combination of your high-level planning elements, your framework models, as well as the transition plan you use to realize the architecture. Another way to think about it is project plan meets strategic plan meets budget planning over a one- to three-year time span.

Typically, a road map will be a little bit lighter in weight than an enterprise architecture plan in terms of the current state. The road map will zero in on the future state and the transition included. You most often will see these types built in iterations with the planning, focusing on the current state and target state included initially. The transition plan will be added later, as this method is used to size or scope the work without much attention to the exact timing and order. I've seen many a company refer to the transition plan as the "operationalization" of the architecture.

The current state and inventory need to be included when you create an enterprise architecture road map to establish the time and scope element. A critical component will include versions built for each year in the road map, which makes things complex when you are trying to keep track of the various states visually. Imagine drawing a new picture after each phase in the transition has been completed. You may start to see why I find MS PowerPoint or some other presentation software of value here. "Duplicate slide" might become your best friend!

Using a slide deck makes it very easy to insert diagrams, insert and remove pages, and apply versions. You can also add other drawings, maps, and charts at any point in the process. Other road maps that I have worked on with various clients were created using word-processing software, which are more cumbersome as they less scalable because of the number of large images, tables, and charts. This further complicates reuse.

The enterprise architecture road map needs to be plotted over time for various reasons—most of the time it is for the sake of economic planning. Other reasons are in timing and view to the future. Even when planned components are timed correctly, actual build time may not be accurate, which may cause a ripple effect on the schedule. The architecture can be adjusted as the iterations evolve and as the business requests new capabilities. As technology progresses, new solutions may supersede planned solutions.

Ironically, don't get too far ahead of yourself in building the road map. It rarely happens, but when companies throw extra resources at the plan to build in parallel, there may be problems similar to doing years of analysis and then years of building. You might find out that big pieces don't work and you've wasted time on critical interdependent pieces. It is impossible to determine the exact amount of time it will take to construct the architecture, so the road map becomes a tool of layout and estimation with rough precision. With some skill and careful calculation, you might discern what the estimated time will be and the proper layout for the largest and most risky pieces.

The SOA Road Map

I won't try to develop what should be an entire chapter of another book, but I'll offer a word here on the SOA road map. If your team is considering an SOA approach to solution development, the mapping step of your architecture process will be either in whole or in part an exercise of matching business capabilities to services rather than systems or applications. You will use the same annual prioritization and assessment step when evaluating your services. Opportunities will be a rationalizing theme, as often the discovery or search for a service that is available to match a strategy or solve a business need is what drives its adoption at a company. Candidates often find these opportunities when evaluating the market for supplier channels and products and services your company uses, produces, or creates. You'll find potential value in the operational efficiencies, where service advancements could spell cost reduction for your firm.

As SOA is still a new approach for many companies, you will see many learning components added to an SOA road map. Included will be information regarding the governance processes, the fit within the current solution or software organization in your company, and the transition to this approach. It will resemble a blend between a true road map in which you have a current state (most likely you will be transitioning from the software application paradigm) to the target in which you are starting to pilot or develop a few new infrastructure services as a baseline for your environment. Topics will primarily focus on the underlying architecture, such as service capabilities, delivery, integration, interoperability, and management. It will be more granular than most road maps, as services by nature are much more independent. The emphasis will be on adoption and impact in using the services with respect to current business operations. The goal will be to minimize disruption to your company's activities. The rollout strategy, including release strategies, will be a key component in the SOA road map you create.

An organization that has become mature in the SOA environments will perform much like the enterprise architecture planning/road map blend presented above in which services are assessed annually, followed by a portfolio analysis. Both will feed the road map evaluated on an annual basis, including the rating and planning for existing services, with an emphasis on adding new services and infrastructure. The SOA road map will most likely be more heavily used during the governance practice of architecture in an organization as a means to curb the development or improvement of anything slated for the service-oriented approach. See www.zoomfactorbook.com/book-resources for more information.

When Can You Benefit from the Use of Road Maps?

A road map is not always done at the enterprise architecture level. One of the most typical uses of a road map after the enterprise architecture is in the area of the infrastructure, as highlighted in the section on blueprints earlier in this chapter. A technology architecture road map is probably the most common type, as many technology projects are undertaken over the span of more than one year. Typically, you are trying to systematically plot out infrastructure renewal. These blueprints are often reused and maintained, largely because of their nature as an asset and the desires of the business. Large components can commonly be categorized as a capital project.

Often infrastructure projects end up very low on a priority list when it comes to portfolio management, but if you see where they match the business capabilities that depend on them, they can be scheduled and included appropriately. In an optimal situation, they are grouped with the business capability portfolio. An operational plan is another example of one of these types of road maps as is the ever-growing process for your company's hardware of your servers, storage, and your computers. A road map features a graphical view of each technical project plotted against a timeline in which it is planned for implementation over a three- to five-year period.

When Do You Create a Road Map?

Road maps differ from blueprints in that they show transitions over time for the current state or the future state. Road mapping is an activity on which an architect should spend a fair chunk of his or her time each year. It should form part of your yearly IT strategic-planning exercise. You should create it at a very high level during your initial enterprise architecture planning exercise. Where possible, create it in conjunction with business strategic planning, but often it follows as soon after the process as possible. Road maps should form the basis of your architecture vision, and they show the time dimension for each grouping or product context. Thus, road mapping should occur prior to and feed the release planning of your portfolio planning exercise and the budget cycle.

At the EPfM level, your portfolio team will evaluate the road map, filter it, and determine the achievable project list for the year. They will apply a resource-planning layer and an evaluation of IT budgets and determine whether all targets are still in alignment. High-level projects will be mapped out using prioritized initiatives and then will be governed through your project management office or process. As the EA, it is critical that the road map always be in your crosshairs, and that you evaluate and maintain its continual alignment both on an annual basis and as you consider adjustments to the components and capabilities.

Why Use Road Maps?

Reflect again to the EA's goals. The business wants to know what kinds of capabilities are possible, in what time frame they might receive them, their cost, and estimated changes to the portfolio or the assets required. Everyone should want to know about the risks involved with any change to the portfolio. The IT managers want to know about the resources they need to allocate and the details about the planned solution. You want to know what is needed to ensure the highest quality possible in the shortest amount of time for the lowest costs possible. These elements of time and program details are laid out best in the format of a road map.

Road maps form a part of the strategic-planning cycle that most are interested in, as they represent the intersection of vision and reality. It is by no means a blueprint; rather, this is a higher-level strategic plan. Ideally, the whole process of creating the road map is done in conjunction with portfolio management planning for the purpose of seeing how the transition to the target state maps out in a high-level timeline.

Who Needs Road Maps?

The business wants to know which capabilities are possible to automate, when to expect them, and the costs, savings, and business risks involved in making them real. The technical staff will want to know what they should build, how they should build it, and when they should expect the projects to occur. IT managers want to know the details around the risks, the resources required, and the methods for construction. They'll want to know about similar solutions already in place and how to measure for success.

How Are Road Maps Created?

Your analysis will include a market survey, evaluation of current trends and competitor behavior, and the opportunities that exist because of technology. You will include views on your products, process, and people. You will use your current state analysis and models as input, and you will detail the gaps between your current activities and the desired capabilities of your business and necessary matching to competitors to stay in the game. Your gap analysis will fuel the migration plan and the road map. As you become skilled and experienced in the area of enterprise architecture, you will readily create themes and initiatives in which you can better prioritize the plans for business components to be built. See the Zoom In section of this chapter for a detailed step-by-step process to create your road map.

Many clients I've worked with in the past have merged their enterprise architecture planning activities with road-mapping activity, producing instead the enterprise architecture road map. They include main events as a means of establishing the priorities, sequence, and timelines that are planned. Another example is the SOA road map, which might include planning things such as the types of services and infrastructure you will construct to design an SOA environment and the types of services, order, and timeline in which you will construct them.

You can create road maps in various levels of detail. You may create multiple road maps for various initiatives or one for the enterprise as described earlier. Some organizations may create a top-level road map as a single page and display it as a poster to guide them through their program. Those organizations would typically create many supporting road maps, either by domain area, time period, or even by business grouping to include the details needed to understand the big-picture road map. These same organizations may go further by housing many supporting documents in their architecture repositories to detail the decisions and plans behind the transition plans. A distinguishing feature of a road map will always be an intentional ambiguity so that planning is not crippled by the need to keep advancing the plan forward.

Your Career Road Map

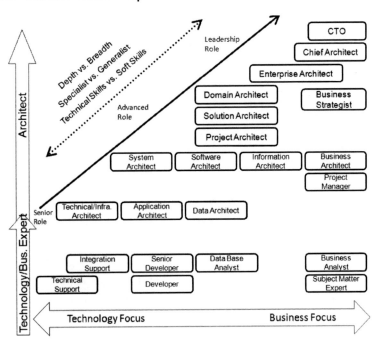

Figure 5. Your Career Road Map

Note: detailed version with checklists available at
www.zoomfactorbook.com/book-resources

Zoom In—Action Steps You Need to Succeed

While the road-mapping process may seem like a daunting process, the sequence and steps are quite logical. A high-level strategy as per volume and perspective levels required within the framework should take place before undertaking the road map. Here are the basic steps:

1. Decide on the approach and the amount of current and future state modeling and documentation you wish to collect/create.
2. Identify the gaps between current and future in the areas of:

    a. Business capabilities

    b. Changes to organization, processes, information, and technology

    c. Analyze and reconcile your IT asset portfolio. Consider retirement, replacement, upgrades, elimination, and addition. Review existing solutions and give each a utility score. You may want to set a standard naming categorization such as maintain, optimize, limit, consolidate, and strategic.

3. Group assets and new items into initiatives.
4. Prioritize the initiatives.
5. Justify and estimate all required new and modified initiatives.
6. Measure risk using your architecture and level. Set the planned initiatives according to the corporation's appetite.
7. Determine a sequence for initiatives using business priorities, costs, budgets, and risk.
8. Lay out the road map by initiative on the vertical axis and year on the horizontal axis.
9. Rinse and repeat as new considerations come up that would significantly affect the road map.

If your organization moves to a service-oriented approach, it means that business capabilities may be mapped to services, not necessarily systems or applications.

☐ Services will be retired, rehabilitated, rearchitected, or removed.

☐ Road maps may have to become more granular to address the impact to services.

☐ Service-level road maps will be especially important during governance of implementation projects.

Zoom Out—Big-Picture Concepts

Get it done faster! If you just can't get started, there has got to be a better way. I'd love to see more agile EA get done, so today I'll share the most common and critical parts of an enterprise architecture plan. Here is the checklist I use when creating plans for my clients and customers.

The enterprise architecture plan is a process as well as a document set or repository that contains the written plans for the vision and development of the enterprise architecture.

There are many recommended components, many of which are included here. I recommend that you consider creating a shell document or presentation with the following titles to set up your taxonomy. As well, it can act as a quick guidepost for your endeavors.

1. Vision statement including strategy
2. Business drivers and goals for the enterprise
3. Participants/contributors in the planning process
4. Leadership and sponsorship
5. Guiding principles
6. Approach and strategy to the enterprise architecture plan
7. Current state section
8. Target state section
9. Transition plan/road map
10. Next steps/issues/outstanding

If you include all of these sections in your shell document, the rest is fill-in-the-blank. Even if you have to go through and fill in what you know for sure or simply list what your team can collect, you can always go back and validate your additions.

Don't spend a lot of time on the sections that you are surmising. Put a few key points down and find a stakeholder to validate. It's easier to throw darts at the wall than start with a blank page.

PART III:
REALIZE YOUR SOFT SKILLS

In this part

- Chapter 10: Assess Your Skills and Abilities
- Chapter 11: Who's Leading Whom?
- Chapter 12: Get Politically Savvy
- Chapter 13: Consult Without a Suitcase
- Chapter 14: Make Diligent Decisions

Part III shares a description of the critical knowledge areas as well as the ways in which you may gain experience in these areas from various project assignments. This part will review some of the most prevalent soft-skill areas you must master to negotiate the curves and turns of the EA career.

CHAPTER 10:
ASSESS YOUR SKILLS AND ABILITIES

I never teach my pupils. I only attempt to provide the conditions in which they can learn.
—Albert Einstein

It is time for a pit stop on your journey to architecture excellence. Here, you'll need to do some work toward deciding what your career path might be. After a few years of experience as a technical architect, application architect, data architect, or system architect, the door may be open toward a place in the team of EAs at your organization. Consider the training you have had as an EA practitioner so far. Have you contributed to activities and deliverables most related to enterprise architecture? Or were they solution, data, or technology architecture-driven? See the link at www.zoomfactorbook.com/book-resources to see whether you are headed in that direction.

Now it's time to reflect on what architects might need as human resource skills, specifically soft skills. Even though architects must possess soft skills, few books and educational seminars address these specific skills. Let's go through each skill to briefly highlight its relation to your career as an EA:

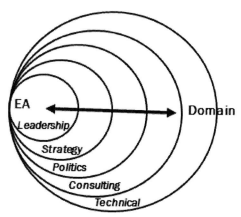

Figure 6: EA Skills Continuum

The crux of this continuum is that the EA needs to be a soft-skill artist more than a technical genius. You relied on your technical skills to become an architect, and now you need to release that focus if your goal is working on the enterprise. To illustrate this point, consider an example where an enterprise and domain architect both meet with stakeholders to mull over a potential solution.

If you are an architect strong in the most important soft skills, you are able to phrase the business problem and strategy at hand in business terms. You can present and discuss a potential solution in layman's terms. You can hold a strategy meeting and agree to move forward. You'll know when you should mention certain aspects and will have done your homework in advance to know who will support and oppose you. Your presentation will be at the appropriate level of detail for your audience, minimizing the technical terms and instead focusing on the value your solution has for the business.

If you are still relying on your technical strengths, you will discuss the various technical solutions and their benefits as they pop into your head. You'll list various technical risks, configuration implementation problems, and strong personal reasons why the company should implement this solution. You'll be sure to include some talk around the doom and gloom of not doing the project and its various impacts on the IT department and perhaps even you personally.

Is the difference fairly clear here?

This step will examine some traits that will allow you to focus on advancing your career as an architect and to gain ground toward becoming an EA. The architect's critical spheres of activity span from the domain architect all the way into the center core of the EA, across these major skills: these skills gain importance as you reach higher levels of leadership. If you can master these traits, a spot as the chief architect is in your future.

The Domain Architect

The architect who specializes in one of the domains such as business, data, solutions, or technology will bring strong technical skills to the enterprise architecture team. You may excel in the area of consulting to your business stakeholders, but this skill still might be relatively new to you. You may be learning the architecture process, but it too may still be quite fresh. You will have dabbled in organizational politics and have limited leadership and team skills. As time goes on and you gain skills, you will become stronger with managing politics and cultural issues as well as strategic planning. As you build your core and become a strong EA, you will excel in the area of leadership.

You've got a lot of expertise, especially in the detailed or the technical skills in one of the domains. You pay an awful lot of attention to detail, but you have a lesser understanding at the broader, big-picture level. You have a vague idea of where the enterprise can go, and you are able to focus on it and also right back out.

The Project Architect

Comparatively speaking, project architects will typically have narrow business knowledge. They are primarily motivated on a short-term basis toward fixing a problem in their solution space or domains or for a specific, time-constrained project. Project architects are typically either domain architects or technical specialists. Most architecture assignments for projects are consulting architect roles and are not full time. Technical architects and specialists will advise and design, contributing to the infrastructure and environments required for the project solution. The solution architecture projects are the exception.

As a project architect, you tend to turn the abstract into the concrete; otherwise, you are not satisfied. You really try to sell, champion, and promote solutions, but you take pride of ownership in their design. Your focus primarily centers on solutions and implementation or execution of the architectures. You are typically very goal- and task-oriented in getting your projects to a completed state.

The Enterprise Architect

The EA role places a premium on soft skills. You have broader subject knowledge and a large diversity of experience. You will build proficiencies from many areas in your life. Increased entrepreneurial knowledge will come from your dealings in business events, such as mergers and acquisitions, expansions, cost-cutting measures, and the like. Experience gained working as a volunteer cannot be overlooked either. As you work at various companies and multiple vertical domains, your experience will add to your maturity as an EA.

The soft skills you need to acquire and excel at are in the areas of facilitation, communication, and cultural and political sensitivity. As an EA, you will tend to put the big picture first but understand the need for details. No matter what kind of conversation you are having, you will always be thinking, "How does this fit into the enterprise strategy at hand?" You will have wide perspective in business knowledge in more than just the domain area of your base expertise. You will be able to easily grasp abstract concepts and typically will be long-term motivated.

As an EA, one of the key roles you will have to play is that of a leader. Some of the other roles you'll play are those of the relater or those making relationship management decisions with various people within your organization as well as with external people. You'll play the politician, consultant, marketing specialist, and public speaker. In addition to playing the leader, each skill highlighted earlier, including process, modeling, patterns, and analysis, should now be embedded within you.

After you learn to be technically excellent, you must acquire great people skills. You can learn some of these skills, and others will come naturally. If some of the noted skills are in areas where you feel weak, never fear. You can gain this knowledge, and this book will suggest activities to make you better at them.

Comparisons Between Architect Types

If you were to compare traits, skills, and focuses between domain architects, project architects, and EAs, you would notice a few distinct differences. Career paths and the skills required for each of these types of architects mainly vary in the area in which they have their primary focus. EAs are focused on the big picture and enterprise strategy and vision, while project architects are focused on the technology, the finer-grained details, and their integration with the rest of the parts. Domain architects fall somewhere in the middle, as they have both strategic vision for their domain and the domain's role within the enterprise. They also focus on their technical expertise within the domain as subject matter experts.

Skills in common that all types must share with an EA include consulting with both the business area and the other technical specialists with whom they work. All architects need to strive for reuse of patterns and applications as well as previously created components and solutions. All architects are strong in the area of analysis and tend to be solution-oriented.

From the career perspective, as an EA, you will have some skills to build over a longer period. You'll concentrate on developing skills and traits such as strong leadership and mentoring. Your focus and perspective will shift toward the business, the entrepreneurial vision, and the strategic moves you must make to advance your company. As an EA, you converge on what the company needs to transform from its current state to the target state as well as advance the enterprise program portfolio at the organization to make strategic gains. You are very typically process-oriented rather than purely task-oriented.

Domain and project architects will concentrate more on individual solutions, where they will base strategies on either the solution or the improvement of the domain. They will be somewhat less process-focused and study details at a lower level.

Assess Yourself

At this point, return to your self-assessment. Do you really have the skills or the desire to engage yourself as an EA? If not, that's okay—there is plenty of room in the world for project architects and contributors as domain architects on an EA program. You have to be honest as to where you are so that you can zero in on the skills you need to work on for your career road map.

For an EA, leadership skills are much more critical than technical skills. When you formalize a team to work on the enterprise architecture program, you'll need to select team members who span the critical spheres of your planned activity. The members composing the team will be very strong technically and will also have strengths in consulting, politics, strategy, and leadership.

Team members need to engage at all layers. Though each architect will have core strength in all of these skill areas, the responsibility for activities requiring these various skills will be distributed across the team. Each architect will need to possess these skills to some degree. Therefore, at this stage in your career, you need to emphasize soft-skills development, as you've reached a milestone. Make room for development in the specific skill areas where you feel you are weakest.

If your desire is truly to become an excellent architect, soft skills are critical, and not just in architecture and IT: you'll need these key skills to advance in any organization in any career. Some of the things you may need to work on are political and cultural sensitivity and communication skills, both written and oral. You'll have to excel at giving and preparing presentations, drafting documents, and delivering artifacts.

You'll also have to work on your negotiation and persuasion skills, as an architect is typically a change agent, and change is always a hard sell. Additionally, you have to become very good at facilitation because you will work with numerous groups of people, and you'll need to gather many ideas as a synthesizer and consolidator. Ultimately, you are the champion of the vision of the solution.

The EA leads mainly by influence and example and very often has no authority whatsoever. Thus, you will use leadership through vision, motivating your team and demonstrating the types of things you are doing in strategy and team building. Some organizations structure enterprise architecture teams a little differently, where the team leader also has direct responsibility for ranking, rating, and appraising employees. This is a little different situation in which you will have staff authority.

Zoom In—Action Steps You Need to Succeed

Are you qualified to be an EA? You did a self-assessment in Chapter 1. Here is a skills checklist that matches that of many successful EAs:

- ☐ Abstract thinking
- ☐ Analysis
- ☐ Big-picture thinking
- ☐ Budgeting
- ☐ Business knowledge
- ☐ Communication
- ☐ Diplomacy
- ☐ Effecting change
- ☐ Expressing technical concepts with non-technical descriptions
- ☐ Facilitation
- ☐ Leadership
- ☐ Modeling
- ☐ Pattern thinking
- ☐ Persuasion
- ☐ Political awareness
- ☐ Presentation
- ☐ Procurement
- ☐ Project, program, asset, and portfolio management
- ☐ Relationship management
- ☐ Risk management
- ☐ Self-development
- ☐ Self-awareness
- ☐ Strategy
- ☐ Time management
- ☐ Vendor relations
- ☐ Writing/documentation

Zoom Out—Big-Picture Concepts

Using the self-assessment back in Chapter 1, match to the areas in which you just checked in Zoom In. Where are there matches? Where are there gaps?

Now—the most important part—where do your passions, interests, and desires lie for your career? Are these all aligned with the EA role? For example, if you checked leadership in Zoom In, and your self-assessment labeled leadership as a strength but you really dislike leading people, you've got a gap. Since this is a major strength needed as an EA, you might want to question your career decision. On the other hand, if you also checked communication as a strength, and this is also a match in your strength area, this is a strong indication that you will do well as an EA, perhaps just not as the chief architect. Here are a few other things you might want to assess in determining your fitness for the EA role:

- ☐ I have created my personal career vision or road map.
- ☐ I have created an elevator speech about our EA program and have practiced it at least twenty times.
- ☐ I am comfortable getting up before a whiteboard and drawing while sharing a potential solution.
- ☐ I am comfortable speaking before those who are above me in position at my company using non-technical terms.
- ☐ I have the technical skills to become an EA.
- ☐ I have the soft skills to become an EA or plan to improve them.
- ☐ I have the desire to become an EA.
- ☐ I am motivated to practice to become an excellent EA.
- ☐ I am interested in our business at this company and want to learn more to improve my knowledge and create value for my company.

CHAPTER 11:
WHO'S LEADING WHOM?

Management is doing things right;
leadership is doing the right things.
—Peter F. Drucker

The EA is the most difficult IT job to define today, primarily because it is all about change and driving strategic consistency in an organization. At their core, architects are leaders who make things happen. People identify these leaders either explicitly by reviewing the organization's structure or implicitly by observing their behavior. As the EA or lead architect on a project or in an enterprise architecture program, you will need to establish a clear leadership style to direct change and make the enterprise architecture program work at your company. You need to validate and share your unified vision and strategy with your team: to lead, you cannot work alone. Others need to know where you are going so they can help you get where you need to go. Believe that the development of your leadership skills is a mission-critical activity.

As an excellent EA, you must possess various leadership traits. You express modesty and avoid public glorification. You are honest with your team, maintaining your moral convictions and personal integrity at all times. You maintain a calm demeanor and demonstrate actions by principles most of the time. You set ambitious goals aimed at improving the organization, and you try to channel your team members' efforts to help themselves and the company succeed. You lead conversations with questions rather than answers, as you want to promote dialogue, not a dictatorship. Finally, you follow one of Dr. Stephen Covey's most esteemed behaviors—you seek to understand first. You always keenly look out for risk, but you obtain data before waving any red flags.

As a leader, you may recruit members for your enterprise architecture team. You will build the team by sharing your vision and creating a charter for the team, then setting down some basic rules or principles for participation. As team members strive to effect change in the organization, they must believe in your solution or they won't be willing to galvanize support for implementing it or transitioning toward it. In other words, you will have opportunities to motivate your team and negotiate the barriers that will expose themselves. These are not easy tasks, and they will be some of the biggest obstacles the enterprise architecture team will face. You'll need to negotiate for various trade-offs in the architecture and try to influence many in the organization to buy into the multitude of decisions you have been asked to make.

Implementation groups will need to understand the architecture, its values, and its reasons. If they understand why you are doing something and the background leading to the decisions or the solution, they will be able to see its value and the reasoning behind it. To obtain the critical buy-in, you'll need the adaptability trait because you'll need to shape your leadership and communication style in a way that suits the specific audience. In doing so, you'll use your Zoom Factor to move from very technical to high-level business-oriented matters. You'll inspire others with your strong belief in the potential good of the solutions, but you won't push so hard as to offend your stakeholders.

Leading Your Team

As part of your responsibility as a leader and in conjunction with management, you will need to establish the structure of your team. As the team leader and builder, you'll require many people to contribute to the architecture. Your team will be composed of many individuals with various levels of soft skills. It is vital that you give the architects test assignments so you are able to assess and improve their skills and efficiently allocate your work. In Chapter 17, you'll find more information on virtual teams and building the skill level within your team.

Your objective should be to take good ideas from everyone and everywhere and make them part of the coherent whole. You may adapt ideas originating from many places without losing the team's sense of ownership in the solution. Leaders frequently have a wider area of expertise and expanse of knowledge than many of their team members and may understand how to take a solution found in a completely different vertical or industry domain and adapt it for what their organization needs.

You must also play to your team's personnel strengths. The critical spheres of activity demand that people on your team may have to assume various roles. Critical roles such as visionaries—those who clearly see what needs to be done and are somewhat innovative and entrepreneurial in nature—must be present. Use the politicians who are naturally gifted at weaving their way through the organization. Get contributions from and collaborate with the communicators who have the gift of gab or of the pen. You are all analysts, strategists, and facilitators. Your team needs personnel who fill all of these roles.

To lead, you must learn to use all of your strengths and connections with the stakeholders and business contacts to influence, consult, and educate. Continually ask yourself whether you've covered all of your bases from both the enterprise and the domain perspectives. You need to take the reins when required but know when to step aside and allow team members to do their thing and take the lead when it will advance the cause. These steps help build ownership in the end product and strong faith in you as the leader.

Make it your goal to bring team members together. Often you can achieve this by having your team set up a team charter as a building exercise. Typically, solution or application architects also help all team members contribute to the architecture. They take ideas from everyone and make them part of a coherent whole. They will listen and integrate the opinions of all who are involved and make sure they apply them to the other domain architectures to come up with the best solution. Architects may also adapt ideas originating elsewhere but without losing the team's ownership of the solution.

Externally, your virtual team should be careful not to convey the impression to your IT organization that you are an elite group preaching from an ivory tower, busy figuring out what everybody else's future will look like. From experience, a new architectural organization that brings architecture to a company for the first time faces certain types of challenges. Others are used to making decisions with respect to new products, tools, and direction. Now that your architectural team has this responsibility, imagine their reaction. Most technologists would prefer to be playing what-if, doing research, and prototyping potential solutions. You'll meet resistance, if not sabotage, to the new architectural leaders' efforts because they just don't want to let that responsibility and power go.

Sharing Your Vision

You need a strategic vision for your enterprise architecture program, IT program, or whatever architecture project is at hand. You should create it near the beginning of the team's existence, and then articulate it clearly. You might be a gifted writer; in that case, words may best communicate your vision. If you are well versed in public speaking, you might use the combination of pictures, words, or speech to create a skillful presentation. Your vision is the big picture and should match the business context that the business goals were set within. Your job will be to rein in groups that go off on tangents because they are not concerned about or aware of the big picture. You'll need to filter information to get the gems that they need most to construct the best solution possible.

Getting buy-in to the architectural approach you plan to take will aid in growing a functional team. Consensus by committee might be the path you choose, but you definitely have to take the lead on the approach. You will need to install and communicate collaboration and decision models for the team. The team will need to be quite clear on how you will make decisions and document artifacts.

As a sidenote, it is critical that your team documents decision results, processes used, meeting minutes, and all identified action items. If your team demonstrates accountability, it will be more likely to become bound within in an organization that hungers for a governance process.

Alignment and Your Elevator Speech

You will need to develop an elevator speech on your architecture vision. This means you will need to prepare a short, well-rehearsed speech you can give in an elevator when somebody asks you, "How is the enterprise architecture project progressing?" You also need to know what keeps key players up at night—for example, your company's CIO, IT manager, and other executives.

If you have an idea about what your organization's greatest problems are, you can more skillfully weave them into your plans. Take what it is that would help the executives sleep better at night combined with the solutions you are crafting for some other purpose, and you obtain extraordinary value. Just be sure your target architecture matches program portfolios.

How will you recognize a match between your enterprise portfolio with respect to IT projects and assets? Does your enterprise architecture match? Do you have some metrics for the vice presidents or executives at your company? Start very simply and collect a handful of metrics absolutely critical to the organization. Examples of such metrics are:

➤ How many new customers do you have?
➤ What is your current investment value?
➤ What are the returns made today by product line xyz?
➤ What are your defect counts in the biggest application development project?
➤ What are your quality ratios or executive scoreboards?

Knowing this information for meetings with executives builds relationships and demonstrates alignment. Witnessing your knowledge, they will understand you truly care about the business. Try to escalate the relationship to such a level that you are able to have comfortable one-on-one conversations with the executive team.

Artfully try to gain influence, get buy-in on your objectives, and use the buy-in to further your architecture initiatives.

Strive to get a good understanding of what each executive's priorities and personal objectives are. Very often unwritten and unspoken issues exist. If you can understand where the executive or leader is coming from, you'll better understand why that person is either resisting or trying to advance your cause.

Mentoring Your Team

Architects often act as mentors to other architects, members of their team, or IT staff within the organization. You can show leadership by example. Remember that simple is best, and the architecture you try to share with those you are mentoring should be simple. It takes an extreme amount of talent and skill to make architecture look uncomplicated.

Be a good role model and walk the talk by applying process to decisions and governance. In addition to setting good examples, you will often need to develop your team members' skills, perhaps in modeling or political and cultural sensitivity in their communication. Architecture mentors are usually good at giving examples and showing an architect what they mean by aligning new information with something they already know. Mentors should be able to categorize technologies and be able to demonstrate various imagery and solution scenarios.

In addition, you'll often be tasked with transition road map facilitation. You need to assist your team in understanding what their roles will be in transitioning but mentor them to make real change happen. Show your mentee how to standardize complicated processes in your organization, such as change management and the technology solution documentation process.

Take the time you need to illustrate examples when using some soft skills, such as communication and consulting. You must be able to mentor team members with respect to creating artifacts, understanding and learning the architectural process, and dealing with the politics and the situations that arise to advance the vision and the architecture.

Break Down Leadership Barriers

Leadership barriers will arise in any organization and are not bound by architecture teams. The architect leader often carries the burden of repairing a weak IT or business relationship. Typically, there is no clear support for the enterprise architectural program or architecture program in an organization. Oftentimes as the lead architect, project architect, or EA, you must take the lead in gaining support and winning support.

Soft skills are commonly weak in the enterprise architecture team members, which isn't surprising as you were likely nominated to the team because of your technical and project skills. It is also likely you were named as a contributor rather than as a volunteer. It is not unusual for an enterprise architectural team to have no clear mandate for the EA program, and it is unlikely that your team has been able to state goals also supported by stakeholders. Here are a few suggestions and ways you, as the leader, may break down some of the decision barriers facing you.

Openly Declare Your Decision Path

EAs are typically given the responsibility for large architecture decisions, most of which drive the direction in which an IT organization moves. Because you will be responsible for such duties, show leadership by publicly sharing the process in which you will collect the information required, analyze and evaluate it, and document findings and decisions.

Build Consensus

An organization that is very consensus-oriented in its style and culture makes life more difficult for the enterprise architecture team because its membership won't accept leadership easily if it emerges. You will also face some challenges with respect to a changing workforce: today, you have an aging workforce with the cycle leaning toward retirement. Many individuals will share common motivations and strategies in this respect. The mature work population may be more apt to resist change and protect projects and existing technology they relied on and built in the past. The younger and ambitious team members will be trying to move to a better place higher in the organizational hierarchy and encourage innovation and change.

Companies have such big expectations of the new, young, incoming workforce. You are more technically aware and increasingly business savvy at a younger age. Many young or budding architects gain experience through smaller businesses in school or as an initial position. Enthusiasm replaces experience in many cases; this phenomenon makes the aged and more senior workforce very uncomfortable and agitated, especially when you are playing a lead role.

The changing demographics due to the global nature of workforces have also played a considerable role in the barriers you face. It now becomes necessary for you to understand the communication differences in the cultural roots of team members, stakeholders, consumers, partners, vendors, and suppliers. It becomes critical to foresee misunderstandings that could occur due to cultural differences in language and motivation of all affected by your plans.

Dealing with Program Skepticism

If an organization has a prior history of failed enterprise architecture programs, there may be a history of program restarts. An atmosphere of skepticism can also create barriers inside the organization near architecture. The team may also have human resource organizational barriers. For example, you may not be part of a dedicated team assigned exclusively to the enterprise architecture program. Just trying to get enough time from the team to contribute may be very difficult in itself. Most often, there are not enough resources, and you have to mine for others to help when you have trouble finding architects and you really wish to grow your own. See Chapter 17 for more on this topic.

Value and Support Your Virtual Teams

Virtual teams are one of the most common structures for enterprise architecture programs today. However, because of the online nature of the communication on these teams, considerable barriers exist—including socialization of the enterprise architecture program. Time barriers and lack of face-to-face reading of personal gestures and gauging of personal reactions to some of the proposed strategies gets lost, creating additional obstacles to progress. Furthermore, you focus on task execution versus social behavior, which makes interacting more difficult. Finally, virtual teams commonly have a great deal of difficulty reaching consensus.

Limit Team Growth in Numbers

Additional barriers might exist when the team grows too large. Often large enterprise architecture teams are very cumbersome and ineffective. One of my experiences in trying to create a virtual team was that each organization, department, or team thought it was entitled to have somebody allocated to the team, feeling it was the way to get its say while making a statement by having someone on the team. It was very difficult to point out that only a certain number of people had the absolute right to be on the team because of their skills, experience, and knowledge.

Today, typical standards and best practices suggest that a core team should consist of five to seven individuals. The team should be derived from various domain areas with individuals having strengths in diverse soft-skill areas. Often architectural teams are pulled in many directions because their members are not 100 percent allocated to the team. In addition, with large teams, everybody tries to dominate yet nobody wants to lead, which brings the issue of too many agendas to the program. One hundred percent dedication time helps to alleviate these problems.

Limit the Geographic Distribution of Your Team

A common concern is the geographic separation of your team. Many organizations try to create virtual teams across many territories, such as provinces, states, or possibly even countries. This adds extra friction with respect to time zones as well as shuttling information back and forth. Add face-to-face meeting time factors, conference call time, and actually getting on each other's schedule, and the net result is overcomplication of an already complex exercise.

Develop Mitigation Strategies

As an excellent architect, you acknowledge the existing culture and processes to enable change and acceptance. You identify the viable options and the issues affecting IT and business alignment. You assess the credibility of IT in the eyes of the business and assess the CIO's impact in the boardroom, and you do your best to surface business concerns early.

A key to this component of mitigation is to look at the business operating model, capabilities, services, processes, and views and make sure you are apprised early. You identify the organization's appetite for standardization and uniformity and take a structural view with key roles and responsibilities of the business and the IT organizations. You also examine the culture and identify the organizational structures, your factors, and what you can and cannot change.

Let's glance at the human resources view and then try to build cultural awareness and leadership skills within the architectural team. To overcome culture and leadership barriers, you have to look at the different operational departments:

> ➢ What is your composition?
> ➢ Are you purely reactive?
> ➢ Are you a gunslinger?
> ➢ Can you handle rigor, structure, process, and standards?
> ➢ Do you need architectural-readiness preparation?

Many things are going to become barriers to your architectural program, and acknowledging that barriers exist is a start to successfully getting past them or working within their boundaries. Knowing who you are as a person through your personal assessment helps you to set a solid foundation first. If you know your strengths, skills, passions, and values, you are able to set your internal compass and personal game plan. Weigh these against your weaknesses and fears, and utilize a mentor to help you combine your personal plan with the goals and strategic plan you strive to implement at your company. Make the study of leadership a personal project and ongoing commitment to personal growth.

Some other strategies you can undertake are building awareness of the roles and responsibilities as well as making sure each team member understands your role and place in the architecture team. We all want to try to find leaders who are most adept at reducing the confrontation and opening dialogues. These good listeners are going to be champions for the program. If possible, try to create a decision responsibility matrix early so that you know who's responsible for what and when.

Ensure that critical skills exist within the team. Having variations in role strengths within the team, such as the visionary, leader, contributors, communicators, analysts, strategists, and facilitators is your risk avoidance. It will allow you to mitigate and manage the risk in using too many people from the same strength areas and not having enough of those you truly need. Recognize when your team needs direction and share your strategies. Putting people first while establishing clear leadership will help you strive to build and develop leaders to take your team to the highest level.

Ensure that team members share knowledge of the common vision with the individual business units. Ensure they have the game plan in helping you to assist the organization cope with the change you are driving. Identify consistent decision models, and each member will accept and embrace team recommendations. This way, you can all be champions of your program decisions. Drive collaboration to bring each team member's creativity and experience into all recommendations. It is absolutely critical that the team shares a unified vision toward championing a target state architecture throughout the organization and each member takes an active role in selling it.

Zoom In—Action Steps You Need to Succeed

To make a great impression, you need to do several things to come across as a professional and demonstrate leadership to your team. Gaining credibility is a big part of the hurdle facing the new EA. Here are some things you can do to act and appear more professional:

- ☐ Speak clearly, precisely, and persuasively.
- ☐ Listen carefully and skillfully; make eye contact with stakeholders and others with whom you communicate.
- ☐ Demonstrate empathy to those who have something at stake that comes with architectural change.
- ☐ Project and exhibit an extreme poise and confidence.
- ☐ Ensure your appearance is impeccable with respect to your grooming, gait, and self-assurance. Possess a neat and orderly workspace.
- ☐ Utilize professional communication with first-class written deliverables and e-mail.
- ☐ Self-assess your own speaking style and meeting behavior; monitor the satisfaction level of your client and audience while delivering your message.
- ☐ Watch for recurring themes in briefings written for the CIO exchanged between your boss, the leader at the top of your IT organization, and the executives.

Zoom Out—Big-Picture Concepts

As an excellent architect, you acknowledge the existing culture and processes to enable change and acceptance. Use these strategies to do your best to surface business concerns early:

- ☐ Fully understand your business operating model, capabilities, services, processes, and views.
- ☐ Understand the key roles and responsibilities of the business and the IT organizations.

☐ Acknowledge the barriers to your architectural program.

☐ Use your personal assessment to set your internal compass and personal game plan.

☐ Utilize a mentor to help you combine your personal plan with the goals and strategic architecture plan you strive to implement at your company.

☐ Make the study of leadership a personal project and ongoing commitment to personal growth.

☐ Ensure that critical skills exist within your team such as the visionary, leader, contributors, communicators, analysts, strategists, and facilitators.

☐ Recognize when your team needs direction and share your strategies.

☐ Make certain your team shares a unified vision toward championing a target state architecture throughout the organization and each member takes an active role in selling it.

☐ Put people first while establishing clear leadership: it helps you to build and develop leaders to take your team to the highest level.

☐ Create a decision responsibility matrix early to track activity and task responsibility; you can all be champions of your program decisions.

☐ Ensure your team has the game plan and is unified to assist the organization cope with the change you are driving.

CHAPTER 12:
GET POLITICALLY SAVVY

Man is by nature a political animal.
—Aristotle

Corporate politics flourish in every organization, and for the architect, there is no exception. The first step in learning how to survive in the political jungle is to take on the role of the cultural anthropologist. Study company customs, the players in existence, and how they came into being. Carefully gauge the type of company, its style, and the cultural politics it operates with. Learn everything you can about the key stakeholders who influence architecture decisions.

As an architect, taking on the role of leader in making change is an immensely difficult job, and any investment you make in reading the culture of the organization and your specific work group will be time well spent. You will gain big benefits by studying the relationship between the business and the executives within the inner circle, HR, and the employees as well as between HR and the executives. Also, look at the relationship between IT and the executives. When the opportunity presents itself, take the time to network and try to be a little bit closer to the people in positions of authority. Figure out when it is time to lay low and observe.

The Political Dance

Be well aware of issues and political hotbeds that exist in your organization. Have a good understanding and knowledge of the key stakeholder positions and the goals and alliances they hold with each other. Understand their personal and business objectives and how they intermingle. Sometimes solutions are not viable because of the politics involved—for example, business executives who have already determined which vendor they wish to use or which solution they prefer.

As an excellent architect, you know how to wordsmith critical conversations. Delicately word your messages and make sure you present opinions as your viewpoints rather than as facts. It is imperative that your spoken thoughts be objective and fact-based regarding actions that have taken place in the past. You never know who in the room was instrumental in their fruition or made strategic choices that didn't have a positive impact on the current state architecture. Learn when you should take things offline or respond later in a less public place.

Politics and Culture Are Larger Than They Appear

You will need to master several central knowledge areas. An architect must be able to carefully wordsmith statements and articulate descriptions, solutions, and responses to persuade and convince stakeholders. Explain limits on solutions when you present them and state their intended usage and shelf life. You will be required to carefully protect the information as it is disseminated so that it is not inflammatory to any group. Remember—your objective is to achieve buy-in for your vision and solutions. By thoroughly understanding the business objectives behind each solution, you establish the best possible political position in rallying support for a particular solution.

Be sensitive to your surroundings. In general, each person who is positioning for a specific solution has some personal motivation. For example, a team may strive to continue with a particularly bad solution because it has a personal stake in it. Perhaps it wants to avoid personal blame or to avoid similar events in its past by starting fresh with new technologies or solutions. Architects should keep their eye on which product the executive team wishes to push forward, sell more of, or eliminate. This will shape the solutions available to the architect.

Negotiate the Speed Bumps

Some of the architectural political speed bumps you may encounter at your organization are included in the following examples. At the top of the list of architectural problems is having no support or sponsorship for the architecture program in the first place. A lack of program or business vision to lead enterprise architecture activities causes difficulties in getting input or information regarding the business vision from executives. This is followed by a lack of consensus on the required capabilities. You may have sought out and interviewed people in various business organizations with little agreement on definition, responsibilities, and how the business processes work. This is common not only inside a department but among and across departments as well.

Another speed bump you may encounter is the lack of consensus on the principles on which you guide the architecture program. Within the business, constituents may disagree about whether there are too many or too few principles and even which principles should be followed. A common architectural political speed bump encountered early in the process is one of current state analysis paralysis. Sometimes you just can't get enough access to the subject matter experts to create a current state architecture. They may not understand why they should participate in current state architecture activity. Their reason may be that they believe they know how they do their business and fail to see what could be gained by contributing and having something documented from their own perspective. Ensure that you are striving for only what is truly important to achieve the end result of a target state, and then keep trying.

The Architect, the Negotiator

An architect acts as a negotiator from a legal requirement perspective, as the cost of noncompliance can be such a high price to pay. Sometimes you need to be the legal perspective champion in reasoning why something may not work or whether something should be done. Your company's reputation, cessation of operation, and legal costs are some of the factors a company may have to face. You may need to negotiate with some of the technology and application development resources in the organization to show them the importance of such factors in the solutions you build.

From a revenue and financial perspective, you'll need to evaluate the investment costs in a new technology or solution and articulate whether they will yield an enhanced revenue stream. From the cost side, you may need to negotiate for cost avoidance and calculate direct and indirect savings. Sometimes it is necessary to propose architecture or infrastructure changes that don't necessarily have a strategic advantage but simply allow you to avoid future costs.

Classically, architects will negotiate for positioning of their vision for the reason of risk management. You'll take a position from the standpoint of what would happen if you didn't take action, such as a threat to the company or even bad publicity. Companies are typically exposure-averse, so you might take these types of positions to advance the architecture cause.

As well, you might negotiate in terms of lost opportunity. What value is to be gained in being first to the market? This only may be relevant if you have good knowledge of your competitive standing in the marketplace. Consider your overall innovation perspective as an organization. Do you typically try to be a leader or a close competitor in second place? What do making educated decisions for the future mean for the organization as a whole?

Corporate Cultural Barriers

Multiple cultural barriers exist in an organization, and multiple cultural personalities often naturally exist. People generally have biases and habits in the general area of finance. Items such as price, efficiency, and costs may be top priority to some. If this is their attention locus, they'll oppose solutions that support excellence and quality. For example, the operations area will often butt heads with the marketing or sales areas.

You may have opposing forces in your organization, such as those that are innovation-driven versus ones that are customer-focused and for growth. Other favorites may be speed to market or general urgency for delivery. People will vary from having a can-do attitude or being methodical tortoises. These types of oppositions within a company invite friction, as some may want to jump in and get it done, while others may want to take a more theoretical and thoughtful approach. Risk tolerance and the awareness of such are also going to exist in an organization. Conflicting forces will include the risk adverse versus the high-wire act teams.

Size and complexity of the organization can also be an issue, as well as the following concerns:

- ➤ Are processes too numerous, too rigid?
- ➤ Are there terminology differences across business units?
- ➤ Do categorization methods and business definitions vary greatly?
- ➤ Are you inconsistent in your treatment of customers and suppliers across business events?
- ➤ Do your business units treat IT consistently?
- ➤ Do some units demand quality and consistency while others demand speed and efficiencies?
- ➤ Is strategy shared outside the boardroom in some areas or sometimes communicated in parts or ineffectively?

Another cultural barrier may be conflicting reward mechanisms. Internal competition and distrust can lead to communication barriers and information hoarding. This incredible distraction in many organizations will often exist at some point in the company lifetime. Some businesses lack access to technology or value it differently across departments. Some feel it is a privilege where one stands in line to get it. Business units have different definitions of business value. You may also observe large variances in business goals, priorities, and context from unit to unit.

As I have spent many a day architecting at insurance organizations, many of my war stories come from these experiences. An example of conflicting units might be claims with the policy organization. Since the policy team generates the policy revenue, it feels it should get more attention. However, the claims department might believe IT should work on its projects most of the time because it is trying to reduce claims history. These examples are all too real, and the message here should be that you must recognize and manage each behavior.

Lack of Clarity or Priority

Another bump in the road can be lack of clarity or priority in the future state. It is one thing for the architect to state what he or she believes the future state to be, but it is yet another to get agreement and support for the organization to forge ahead with these priorities. Include gap analysis paralysis on your list of speed bumps. Often there are just too many gaping holes in the architecture when comparing the current state to the target, or it is plainly a massive project to collect the current state to compare it to the target. It might continue for far too long and jeopardize the life expectancy of the enterprise architecture program.

Lack of Time and Budget

Some of the principal things almost every organization complains about are the lack of time, budget, and effort for the transformation road map. Often all you require is the true business need and support to create a few models in the beginning of your program to get moving. You need momentum to sustain your program. At the beginning, it takes a dedicated team effort and program support from influential stakeholders.

The road map is a living target, and it takes understanding and support for those around it to comprehend it and to keep it on track. You may encounter focus problems because architectural projects are taking too long to demonstrate tangible value. It is easy for you to lose your perspective because of project constraints and emergencies from other emerging and conflicting strategies.

Lack of Leadership

One of the biggest bumps on the political highway to architecture is the lack of solid leadership. Take into account the kind of politics you encounter internally within your own IT organization: there are all kinds of sources of resistance. If you happen to be a new architect to your organization, the old guard will be among the first to resist. Internal IT and the business have an uncanny knack in resisting change. They will be quite resistant to somebody stating that he or she understands what the organization should do as a strategy or moving things forward within your IT organization.

Internal IT Power Struggles

From within the trenches, there are unpleasant power struggles. You may face an IT middle management who feels a loss of control and power of influence to the architect team. Occasionally, even the CIO will feel a loss of power with the construction of the enterprise architecture team due to their increased visibility among the senior management or executives. Sometimes the CIO likes to be the trusted advisor and face of all IT within the executive team. If this is the case, your team's increased traction for strategic influence and involvement may get a little uncomfortable.

Understand your feelings about power and the part it plays in your work. Great architects understand how to use power to their advantage and for the company's best interests. Adequate or mediocre architects use it as a personal badge of honor.

The technical staff will be another source of resistance, as specialists and generalists alike have a hard time believing you understand enough about what they have spent their whole career becoming an expert in. They may believe they know best, but you understand the big picture and strategy and they may not. It will take effort, understanding, and communication to get everyone onside. Another political issue inside IT is the varying perspectives in the area of approach or method. The bottom-up club might have a hard time believing there is value in what is driven from the business perspective. They don't understand the top-down team. Different groups will believe their different perspectives, so you will need to facilitate a meeting of the minds and foster buy-in to the approach.

There are also the reactive versus the proactive camps. Typically, those who work within the infrastructure groups tend to behave in a more reactive manner. It is not necessarily by choice but by need. The proactive group wants to make sure it plans changes, avoids specific negative events, and manages the unexpected. The reactive camp can prove combative against the proactive individuals. Finally, we have the biggest conflict of all—the change embracers versus the change averse. These two groups will always be in opposition until the end of time. This is a perspective you will have to manage through politics and internal management, and hopefully the introduction of an architecture approach will allow all to see the benefits they may reap from the change.

Plot Your Political Survival

Your survival kit will require credibility and respect. Be prepared by being known as one who keeps your word. This will mean you'll need to be on top of your game when others are around, which means really knowing your stuff. Use subtle tactics to ensure those around you know about the results you provided in the past. Make sure there is a reason for you to be heard. Your track record should stand for itself. Natural selection will keep only those who are giving, gaining, and earning respect in the political game.

Remain professional and display a courteous and respectful manner at all times no matter what the conflict. It is quite easy to lose your cool when some absurd statements are made around the planning of technology and priorities, but level heads will keep in mind that statements are often made out of ignorance. Knowing your stuff includes being the subject matter expert. When architecture is your subject, ensure you are not fumbling with definitions of terms and methodologies. Too many architects will be cited for not knowing what they are talking about if they use jargon and complex terms not delivered in appropriate terms for their audience.

Influence Without Authority

You will need to be able to explain concepts and approach in a rather simplistic manner. This skill makes the politically astute architect incredibly valuable: with it, you can use influence without authority. To do this, you are going to need to keep relevant people in the loop, build a network around yourself and your team, and gather support from certain individuals. Consider a strategy of shopping your solutions around to key onside stakeholders to gain advance support and acceptance before trying to present them to the masses.

Achieve your vision by making your solution compelling to a broad base of people. Use your amazing listening and networking skills to pick up the minutest details. When you sit in the corner of the room, listen to what's being said, the way people are saying it, who is present, and everyone's reactions. You will learn an incredible amount about the organization and how you will go about winning with your specific objectives.

The architect who is a good politician possesses a trait of self-adjustment. If you are able to manage up and invest in both lateral and downward relationships, you will thrive. You will need to be unselfish and communicate habitually through questions. The person who poses questions to draw a point or conclusion from the listeners is often deemed a genius, intelligent, or politically savvy. As well, the person asking the questions controls the conversation that takes place in the room. In reverse, when somebody starts asking some pointed questions that cause people to feel embarrassed, uncomfortable, or combative, notice how they do not succeed nearly as well.

Great architects will be great at drawing others into the conversation. When you are able to ask open-ended questions, it allows others to feel comfortable in sharing their opinions and to get their recommendations, requirements, and objections out in the open. You will have multiple viewpoints and be incredibly influencing in the way you speak. It will take an awful lot of patience, especially when trying to forward your goals and further your initiative. You'll need great resilience and sensitivity to the power in your organization.

One word about the politics of architectural governance is worthy to note in this part. It is typical that the architect is forced to sit in a pass or fail role with respect to standards compliance in solutions. It is best that you avoid saying that things cannot be done but instead explain that they don't align with the architecture unless done in a specific manner or under certain standards. You must influence those who do not agree with certain positions you take. Allow them to see the context from which you speak, so that the persons who disagree may see the other side to the solution.

Build Personal Resilience

Resilience will be of one of your survival mainstays. You'll need to be able to take a good figurative beating—this can mean you'll be able to stand up and give a presentation on one of your views and be able to withstand the pot shots and rock throwing that goes on immediately during and afterward. Some circumstances may foster this type of behavior: typically, people who throw rocks feel "we weren't consulted," "we don't do it that way here," or "we didn't do it."

Often some consulting and communication skills can help you avoid these episodes—things such as trying to float solutions through some champions beforehand to defuse potential situations. One tactic is to find people known to support your cause who can be present in the room. Whatever the result, resilient architects don't take lost projects, promotions, or ideas personally. You need to learn to understand that everything you recommend is a change, and all changes aren't accepted. Changes almost always have budgets attached, and not all budgets are going to be passed.

Resilience is especially important when much is at stake in architecture decisions and governance. Resilience in psychological terms refers to a person's positive capacity to cope with stress and catastrophe. Well, most of your architecture feats will not end in disasters, but the nature of architects is to be passionate about their cause, and so some may go home with the feeling that they have encountered a catastrophe. It is the luck of the draw, and it is human nature to see both the positive and negative side of such a worthy character trait as passion in work. A lack of resilience may lead to an architect's tendency to avoid future negative events, which could lead to the architect shrinking away from voicing his or her opinions, fearing taking calculated risks in proposing solutions, or avoiding change entirely. If you find you have difficulty bouncing back from work setbacks, you must find a way to handle this problem.

You will also need to be able to easily accept the unknown. This relates to your ability to create and present half-baked ideas and proposals. In some of my past travels in working with customers, I found that an all–too-common trait in an EA is being unwilling to share an architecture program or approach until it is far into completion. Then, it is often too late to get buy-in.

The reason for holding back is that you are concerned with reactions from your peers and the rest of the organization. You may worry about the mudslinging that might occur when you assert things that will make up the standard and the intended direction. This architect needs the ability to brainstorm and work with groups to complete the ideas while there is opportunity for group ownership. An excellent architect won't fear being judged or shot down when ideas are proposed and understand that it's just a part of the role.

Nurture Relationships and Sponsors

EAs must have good working relationships with the executive management team, the IT management team, and the project management team. Ideally, they have good working relationships with the project team, but realistically one or two will oppose what the architect is trying to do because people will always have personal reasons for their solutions.

To sustain these relationships, two-way communication is critical. You need to keep the relevant people informed. You must know what is being done to support the IT strategy mandate, the standards, and governance within the organization. You must build a network among peers and colleagues both inside and outside the organization. As well, you must build a network of executives who are willing to stand for your proposals as well as a management team who supports your activities. You must be involved in the political activities of achieving visions compelling to a broad base of supporters. You must hear and listen to as many of the requirements and discussions around potential solutions as possible.

You must be able to influence various parties from executive and IT teams to external vendors. You should provide several or multiple viewpoints both in documentation as well as descriptions at the highest levels. Include a coarse-grained architecture perspective for executives down to the lowest levels of detail for technology and application resources. You'll need patience as you work in the abstract and conceptual matter until you have compiled all of the pieces. Show resilience and sensitivity to the power struggles you face, as you will usually be the one in the middle trying to persuade without authority. Even though some of the solutions you put forward will not be approved, at some point in the future, your efforts may be recognized.

You can survive if you keep a few key points in mind. The name of the game is increasing IT's credibility. You are the ambassador, and it is up to you to foster acceptance and trust through your competency and leadership. You'll learn when to back down and take things offline. You also know when not to raise risks to hypersensitive levels with the intent of increasing fear and forcing action.

Manage Your Relationships

If it hasn't become obvious by now, the EA must take on several roles. You must be the mediator, the mentor, the negotiator, and the facilitator, and it is critical that you learn soft skills pertinent to each of these roles. One of the key relationships you must build is one with stakeholders, and you also must act as one of their trusted advisors. Keep their confidence.

The relating architect will stay aware of each stakeholder's position on each issue and carefully and intentionally shape beliefs and manage expectations for the realization of your shared vision. After you've spent time earning and building the trust of business stakeholders, they will call on you for advice on these issues; if you haven't made this investment, you likely won't be invited into the circle. To debate issues, the architect must have knowledge of positions from both sides. Views from the architect to the business, the business to the architect, and perhaps even the IT management to the architect and vice versa are all critical vantage points necessary for you to ponder possible solutions.

You must spend some amount of your time working on your relationships to further your efforts in requirement analysis modeling and in decision making. You will use influence and persuasion to gently advance your vision while taking great care to understand your stakeholders' underlying desires and goals.

Zoom In—Action Steps You Need to Succeed

Common roadblocks within IT are the relationships and alignment between the multiple methodologies your organization chooses to use. Various groups may choose to study the newest methodologies in parallel, unbeknownst to each other. It is typical for IT leaders to lack the understanding of the relationship between the cast of prevalent methodologies, approaches, and their acronyms.

It is critical that you are on top of this potential methodology conflict, as it will burn many hours and energy if it is not handled. You should understand the definition and appropriate use of each of these, as well as their relationship to the enterprise architecture program:

- ☐ Systems Development Life Cycle (SDLC)
- ☐ Project Management Book of Knowledge (PMBOK)
- ☐ Enterprise Architecture–Framework, Reference Library, Approach
- ☐ Architecture and IT Governance
- ☐ Information Technology Infrastructure Library (ITIL)
- ☐ Control Objectives for Information and related Technology (COBIT)
- ☐ UML
- ☐ Agile Process

☐ Rational Unified Process

☐ Numerous other frameworks, standards, and approaches

Zoom Out—Big-Picture Concepts

As an EA, you are also the change maker. This role carries the weight of some fully charged political situations. If possible, avoid these political landmines:

☐ Technology holy wars that are not based on pure fact and economics

☐ Making statements or judgments on business processes and decisions that are not entirely fact- or impact-based

☐ Taking decisions to a higher level than necessary: deal with them at the lowest organizational level possible

☐ Taking sides opposite previous decisions without knowing the full history of the sponsors and originators of the decisions or solutions

☐ Fighting battles on behalf of another party—it's pure lose-lose as you will lose without the proper facts and underlying substance

☐ Fighting battles you aren't willing or able to back with facts, statistics, or a written business case

☐ Proposing a solution that adds unnecessary risk to the culture, technology, products, clients, customer relationships, execution, or capital

☐ Getting into a reactive battle that you weren't aware you needed to fight. Take the time to understand each party's position and motive for the situation

☐ Taking a position with facts that may insult or surprise your audience. Find ways to delicately introduce this information to supporters so they may support you

☐ Proposing big-ticket solutions with large change impact implications when you are a new EA or have a new enterprise architecture program

CHAPTER 13
CONSULT WITHOUT A SUITCASE

Strive for excellence, not perfection.
–H. Jackson Brown Jr.

As an architect, you need to acquire consulting skills and act as a consulting architect to both the IT organization as well as the business. Your enterprise-level knowledge in the areas of modeling, technology, strategy, and planning is of great aid to others in these groups. Your strengths in effective communications allow you to operate in many situations at levels uncommon to others in IT. For you, some of the most beneficial attributes of the consultant are the abilities to negotiate, persuade, listen, and support. Your ability to influence people rather than using authority allows you to demonstrate value and accomplishment in the enterprise architecture program.

Your Consulting Role

You will play several consulting roles, including those of expert, advisor, collaborator, and facilitator, to advance the causes of the enterprise.

Acting as the Expert or Trusted Advisor

You will act as a consultant providing expert advice on a regular basis. You will build trusted advisor-type relationships with various business executives as well as the organization's CIO, managers, directors, and project managers. As an EA, your responsibility will be to explain complex situations and subjects to non-technical people. You will use every opportunity to present to continually higher levels of management until you become proficient. When before executives and various vendors, you will find ways to explain requirements and technology in layman's terms and in varying levels of detail. Your sixth sense will tell you when to speak up in front of executives.

Examples of the advice you'll give might be guidance to the CIO, various other architects, and project teams with respect to the areas of application and technology solution design. You understand what the developers want and require from the architecture, and you provide clear visual documentation around decisions and solutions so everybody involved understands what is to be done. Your solid understanding of the strategy and business problem acts as a gateway between those areas and technology, and you are adept at imparting such knowledge within the various IT groups.

Acting as the Facilitator or Collaborator

A consultant strives toward getting commitment to decisions from stakeholders and their customers. You are characteristically focused on the specific goal at hand and are able to keep an especially streamlined approach in relation to the target state objectives. Many activities you participate in establish collaborative relationships with both the business and IT. Within IT, you bridge groups in software development, technology, and operational teams through support of prototyping and testing. As a cohesive force between IT management, project management, and the project technical leaders, you bring the core strategy perspective on various projects and initiatives.

You'll need to act as an effective facilitator in various group sessions so that you bring out the best from attendees while minimizing the time and effort required by all. Ensure that you have the appropriate number and blend of individuals in proportion to the host or the facilitator. Agreed-upon facilitation rules will guide you to successful sessions. Adequate preparation will include a strategy for discussion, whiteboarding, and pre-meeting documentation, scribing, and minute taking. Meetings will be your primary platform for decision making, but be well prepared to guard your calendar and allow for time blocks to debrief, file appropriate information, and complete required documentation.

Contribute as a Consulting Architect

Your primary contributions as a consulting EA will be that of confirming the feasibility of the architecture, aligning the business and strategy, and setting expectations regarding the architecture's value for the enterprise.

Confirm Architecture Feasibility

You'll determine the feasibility of an implementation or technology first by understanding the context in which the solution will be used for best results. A broad-level understanding of the requirements and technology to be used will build upon your deep knowledge of the vision and business strategy drivers. Your experiences with similar patterns or technology solutions will prove invaluable. Teams may ask you for assistance with feasibility studies as an expert advisor or as a conduit between the teams and the business. Project teams may also request to work with you for your elicitation skills, as they may not have your techniques or relationships with upper-level executives. Your abilities to filter background details and focus on the critical components are what set you apart from others in qualification for this role.

Focus on Value and Business Alignment

You will track core objectives and business goals in all issues related to requirements. You continually seek the points where value is achieved and keep in mind the purpose of solution alignment with business goals. To successfully implement a solution, the business and IT need a solution they are both happy with and can commit to participating in. For the work to be deemed a success, you need to fully understand what the executive needs to take place.

You should map business drivers to IT initiatives, drivers, enablers, and key technologies. You need to ensure any proposed solution meets the strategic focus areas and goals. Strategic focus areas are usually broad in nature and aligned with some business project initiative or driver. You need to understand the goals of the individual sponsor executive so that they can be the primary drivers throughout a project. You should use an up-to-date business conceptual model to view the areas of impact and to get confirmation from the business that everyone understands the target state.

With a keen awareness of the application inventory and the SOA strategies, you hold a unique perspective of all planned initiatives within the organization. Knowing which services and solutions are in flight, planned, and slated for replacement are significant points of insight for you. Your involvement and familiarity with the enterprise portfolio of solutions, applications, data, and technology are critical to ensure alignment.

Setting Expectations

One of the EA's roles is setting expectations with business users and project teams as they work together. You may use a high-level expectation-setting exercise to ensure stakeholders understand any differences between the requirements they are provided and the functionality or solution they'll receive. You also need to set expectations within the IT organization with respect to the solution's place on the future enterprise architecture road map. Each year, you should engage in a health or status check of each application to determine whether your team should do work in the upcoming year to determine its rightful place in consideration of any changes in the enterprise portfolio. Typically, new requests are stored in a log program teams manage until they begin the annual review and planning process. You may see patterns in the types of maintenance requests being made, and you can use them to set the direction for major changes in the component libraries.

Communicate Like a Consultant

A consulting architect will show supportiveness, empathy for both the business and technology resources, and a good understanding of how people express themselves. You'll understand technical constraints and pressures the infrastructure and systems areas undergo and the difficulty imposed on the development groups. You will appreciate the frustration and angst of business resources in getting the tools they need to do their work and to see their strategies come to fruition.

Your solid solicitation techniques will allow you to extract the appropriate levels of information from various parties. Business executives won't feel like they are being interviewed or hounded for information when you ask. Negotiation and feedback will allow you to bring opposing parties into closer levels of agreement. You appreciate the critical nature of getting stakeholders to commit to decisions: you think in terms of agreements, tasks, and statements of work, and you ensure the information you provide adds context to the business problem or opportunity at hand at all times.

In addition, you need to develop a solid basis in communication. Your approach will be that of an expert, and you must be fully prepared for conversations with both the person and the subject. You'll employ strong active listening techniques where you strain to hear the words, their meaning, and their emotion. You'll know what you are going to say in advance and say it in a reasonable and respectful manner. You'll be confident in your message and initiate the conversation by alluding to the benefits you wish to share. From experience, you'll realize you will need to build trust with your audience in advance and develop common beliefs to bridge the alignment between the architecture and business goals. You'll know that the best way to communicate with individuals or small groups is by specifically tailoring and customizing your messages.

Manage Your Messages

Excellent architects also concentrate their efforts on powerfully delivering one laser-focused message at a time. You usually act like a salesperson as you continually nudge people toward change while moving them closer to their own goals. Clear and concise diagrams and documentation are your main means of communicating your message. To succeed, you will need to provide clear and concise documentation both before meetings and afterward. The messages you send should be educational and informational and should lead to clear decision making.

You will construct messages to the top floor, or to executives, differently than those going to the CIO and to the rest of the IT department. For executives, your messages are short, laser-focused, targeted to one topic or decision, and intended for the non-technical reader. You would appropriately add slightly more detail for the CIO but still continue along the theme of being concise and somewhat non-technical.

Messages to IT management will be unique in that they should recognize individual motivation. Managers oversee resources, and each time an architect proposes a solution (read "change"), management immediately considers the resource impact and asks, "What does this mean for me?" Consider the same effect for corporate executives— they will wonder how much your proposal will cost and what impact they will feel in their personal agendas they actively promote. Include details on timeline, budget, and resources as well as specific impacts and acknowledgement of their current projects.

You will steer messages to the architects toward deliverables, artifacts, models, images, and proposals: architects are going to detail the basis of decisions, requirements, and timelines. In sharing solutions with your team, use effective labels such as draft or interim so they can understand that ideas are still up for debate and you are able to provide input or clarification if needed.

When you speak to large groups, carefully phrase your messages. Consider the audience for messages that go to IT staff in general. Each person who reads these messages is thinking "What is this in for me?" and wondering about the effect on them and their careers. Realize they will be somewhat resentful that someone else is creating the strategy and planning for their work. They may resist any messages that might affect them personally, whether the message touches upon their role, technology, responsibility, schedule, or vacation. Take the time to recognize whether the change you impart will cause their favorite technology to be phased out or whether there is new opportunity for them.

Deliver messages to vendors in a limited fashion. Understand that the rate of information flow will increase when you start sending questions to vendors. Tell them specifically what it is that you are looking for whenever you ask questions and send them messages. Note whether you are just looking for information, the type you expect, and your purpose and timeline for getting this information. However, be stingy when you divulge information surrounding budget, stakeholders, and organizational change.

Your messages to business resources or subject matter experts should be non-technical and non-objectionable. They also care about what's in it for them and may feel that change is threatening. Be empathetic to those having difficulties with the technology or the solutions put forward. Recall that there are no perfect solutions and there will be challenges with architecture. In showing empathy, demonstrate that you hear their problems and will consider all of their information when trying to arrive at new solutions.

Communicating Bad News

Inevitably, you will have to communicate bad news at some time in your career. Architecture should never be last minute, so early communication on this subject is the best strategy. Be well aware of the audience you have to communicate with, as some may have been responsible for making the solution necessary or what it is today. Speak about risk and drawbacks in a constructive and objective rather than a subjective manner. Focus on the process and not the people, and try to provide solutions, alternatives, options, and next steps where possible. If there are no potential solutions, you must suggest areas of research or investigation.

Communicating Risk

Through your research and work with those contributing to a potential solution, you will see many associated risks. It is your primary responsibility to understand the risks involved and the pros and the cons of each. Help others understand in both quantitative and qualitative terms what the contributing factors are to the risk, such as the methods, locations, or technologies used to do business, and how they influence the architecture. Show cause and effect diagrams to various business individuals where possible. They might be able to dispute a cause or restate effects and offer up some potential solutions.

Communicating the Architecture

One of your main jobs is to communicate, share, and promote the architecture. You are obliged to become the solutions champion within the organization. This involves selling the vision and keeping it alive in the face of challenges and opposition. You'll need to explain each component and back it up with supporting information that sets the context for the solution and clarifies the decisions you made. Each group of stakeholders needs to understand how the architecture meets their requirements. It might require multiple representations or views of the architecture specialized for the target audience.

Examples might include high-level context diagrams showing flow from the capabilities and functions the business requires in terms they understand. In drilling down, include visual representations of lower-level detailed technical information. Any architect must be able to model to communicate. Drawing pictures on whiteboards, in side-by-side meeting sessions, and in your notes is necessary to capture good ideas and transfer them to digital modeling tools. You will insert models into various decision and specification documents, share them through presentations, or store them in repositories. These models may be versioned as the evolution of the solution changes over time.

Choose the communication you need to be effective. You might wish to carry a notebook consisting of graph paper to sketch models in your notes. Whiteboard communication is great for small- to medium-sized groups, and presentations are great for medium to larger groups. You might want to keep in mind the effort required for everything from models to presentations and use the appropriate medium and level of detail for each. Further details regarding the power of one-page diagrams and whiteboard skills are discussed in Chapter 14 on Decisions.

Communication via E-mail

A good understanding of what constitutes professional e-mail is necessary for everyone in today's digital world. As an architect, consciously decide what types of things should go into e-mails, documents, templates, or face-to-face conversations. Typically, e-mails, particularly long threads and especially those that have touched an architect's hands, can be passed on to various parties. You must take care of sensitive information and consciously know that what you are doing is primarily change. You should consider the impact of your note when passed on to others.

Consider also that typical e-mail conversations start as a note, but as the thread grows, the information may be better placed in decision documents. Ensure your e-mail is objective and to the point. Also keep in mind that your time is even more valuable now, as modeling and getting yet another cell of a framework populated is most often better spent than typing long conversations. Also, be specific if you are asking someone to do something and schedule your desired response and promises of your effort into a calendar so that you are sure to follow up, and keep your word. Be sure to cite sources for your information if you are stating opinions or research. Finally, consider whether you are wasting anyone's time by requiring them to read what you are sending, and review carefully before your final send off.

Artifacts, Deliverables, and Documents

EAs will spend a great deal of their time creating architecture artifacts and documents. It is your "deliverable" or output to an architecture initiative or project. Many types of artifacts exist, ranging from models, lists, and diagrams to full documents and presentations. The artifacts and deliverables are primarily diagrams and documents stakeholders use to review and base decisions upon. The more detailed varieties will support the various processes and activities the team will undertake. Many, if not all, should be housed in a repository and most will be accessible to most people in a company. Architects will create a variety of document sets; this chapter will mention a few.

Architecture Specifications

A common deliverable architects spend a lion's share of their time on is architecture specifications. Commonly, it will be some sort of document that describes an architecture solution, position, review, or plan. The document set will include many pages or views and various components. It should start with the business strategy or driver on which it is based, include architecture patterns or styles being prescribed, and include such things as components, services, connectors, and constraints. A unifying or simplifying theme should be evident throughout the specification, including reasoning behind choices.

If the specification is used as a decision guide and description of the background that led to it, it may include some models, principles, deliverables, the business context, and a description of the various views. Generically speaking, each spec is some sort of architecture view or set of views that can also be named or deemed a layer within a collection or perspectives. The purpose is primarily for understanding for either approval or construction, depending on the detail level. A specific example is a solution or system architecture specification. You create this whenever you wish to communicate a solution to a group of people. You'll create the specification in an iterative manner and will present various levels of your perspective to varying audiences as you create iterations.

The typical solution architecture specification will include many of the above-mentioned sections and parts. It should also include details on the business context and major business components of the architecture within functional views. If you have selected the Zachman framework as a standard within your organization, this would be at the scope and business layers from the perspectives of strategists and executive leaders. From the classification perspective of the framework, this would be at the context and concept layers. For more information, I highly recommend visiting Mr. Zachman's most recent work at www.zachmaninternational.us/index.php/ , which clarifies his relationship with external parties and offers the official definitions and an opportunity to print the framework or buy the framework standards. If you choose to use the TOGAF for solution architectures, version 9 is ably laid out at www.opengroup.org/togaf/.

An architecture specification can vary from organization to organization. It might take the shape of a road map or blueprint when it takes enough iterations and the intended audience includes layers as deep as those responsible for the infrastructure. A technique I like to use before applying any of the previously mentioned frameworks is to use the basic process described in Chapter 5. Lay out your document or presentation file with titles and placeholders. Decide in advance what you would like to include, and then you can collect and categorize the data as it appears. This works well in iterations, as you can replicate the sections for each iteration or view. Near the beginning of my architecture career, I used this technique and divided the spec in half—purely by logical and physical.

Take the time as an architecture group and decide what you want to include. Other views I've used or seen are integration and deployment views, especially when the solution has many moving parts. Blueprints are especially helpful when the components of the infrastructure are onerous and brand-new purchases. The spec should be built in layers, keeping in mind that the business layer is most important to the stakeholders who will approve and keep the project moving. Ensuring you have that right is probably the single biggest piece of advice to offer. For more information on the models based on the Zachman framework you might include in your solution, see www.zoomfactorbook.com/book-resources .

Solution Review

A spin on the architecture specification might be something termed a solution review. When a solution is being brought forward to the architecture team or stakeholders for review, a presentation is crafted from the solution specification itself. It is most often used for approval of the architecture, and then through governance process as more layers and details are added. It should include a description of the business problem, the context or business environment to which the problem applies, and potentially a business model or conceptual or functional model of the business components the solution addresses. It should highlight responsibilities for each of the business functions and a list or description of the high-level functional requirements included within the review or the solution.

Details as to how the solution will be provided through subcontractors or business partners leading to budget discussions, costs, and current solution portfolio impact is common, especially when there are integration points with existing systems. If these solutions include various products, they will be described, documented, and possibly modeled at a high level. If there are services to be created or provided, they will be described. If the review is for the purpose of acceptance or approval, there typically will be a set of milestones and timeline included. It might offer the skills and resources required to get information from the business to provide the technology solution and the description of the business areas.

Solution Impact Analysis

A solution impact analysis may provide documentation or communication around the impact of a proposed solution on a specific architecture. It might be separate from the architecture specification or review process. New solution proposals may oppose an in-flight enterprise architecture plan along with its known target state and transition plan. Impacts will have to be handled because of the time required to implement the enterprise architecture plan. An example might be if an organization has an enterprise architecture that includes a data warehouse and marketing applications, and a portal or customer resource management solution is prescribed. You need to understand where the overlaps and gaps arise with the current and target enterprise architecture states, describe these gaps and overlaps, and then potentially alter the target state for transition.

An additional type of architecture analysis document is a decision request. Such a document should include information on the background of the decision, the reasons behind the decision within the context, and the requirements and needs for the decision. It should also reflect the current state and potential issues or problems with the status quo. The prescribed architecture change should include a diagram that depicts the impact and a section that describes the strategic or tactical nature of the request. Often there should be a record of pros and cons for the decision and the results of any decision made along with the reasons. Decision requests are most often used as part of the project management process when architecture impacts are discovered or when standard solutions must be reconsidered within the infrastructure departments of IT.

The Enterprise Architecture Plan

If you haven't guessed it by now, the enterprise architecture plan is an entirely separate documentation set and the largest piece of work an architect will produce. The plan is typically produced by a team led by the chief architect or EAs. At the highest levels, the plan will include an executive summary that sets context for the enterprise architecture plan and versioning information. It will include a description of the strategy and the basis for creating the strategy. It will include a set of guiding principles for the enterprise and for individual domains. More details are included in Chapter 18 on Strategy.

It will describe the current state architecture for the individual domain architectures based on the framework you selected at your organization. The target state architecture will mirror the layout, and a gap analysis section will describe the distance between the current and the target. A transition plan that articulates the road map from getting to the target state will become the focal point for later iterations and may or may not include timelines or specific goals for retirement or creation of the new technologies or components. Many organizations choose to forgo the portion pertaining to the current state. When this route is selected, it is important that various inventory documents are created and referred to by the plan.

The Architecture Decision

To differentiate slightly from the architecture decision request, architects use a decision document to present options for addressing issues and opportunities. Details of each option must be defined in succinct detail to support the selection of a preferred alternative. It should clearly communicate where uncertainties exist, how those uncertainties affect the implementation of an option, and how they will be managed. Contingencies should be identified and detailed wherever it is appropriate.

When a decision is finally made, you should revise the document to include a short description of the decision, the reasons for making it, the date, references to any documents or research material, and the people involved in making the decision. Do not forget that part! The use of the decision document is not limited to a specific phase in the IT definition and delivery methodology. You can use it at any point in the methodology where you need to document options to facilitate a decision. It may include a collection of decisions made throughout the life of a project, made in advance of the project, or made in the past that are driving a specific architecture specification. Realize that the value in the documentation is most often for the future, as reflection may cause us to rethink decisions later. Documentation is also helpful to paint a picture for those whose work and lives may be affected.

Your Architecture Artifact Toolkit

You may create artifacts using a variety of tools, the most common being the WEPV suite—MS Word (W), MS Excel (E), MS PowerPoint (P), MS Visio (V). Many artifacts are created using a master template set the enterprise architecture team chooses near the beginning of its program. Others are provided by mentors, coaches, vendors, and consultants as they contribute their efforts to your program.

To expand this list, it is worthy to note the upcoming variety of open source tools available to the architect. The open source equivalents of these products are StarWriter, StarCalc, StarImpress, and StarDraw produced by Sun Systems. The savvy architect will create a community and forum to support the collaborative nature of these activities at the company. Forums, wikis, and blogs are just a few of the ways the enterprise architecture team enables contributors and team members to share and publish their work for many to share and see. Recently, teams have also used content management tools to capture these architecture outputs.

Proprietary tools are a category of their own, with examples such as modeling tools and repository and indexing software, as well as full-blown, real-time enterprise architecture solutions. Some may consider the various methods and frameworks such as TOGAF and the Zachman, FEAF, and reference models to be tools themselves. Nevertheless, it behooves you to know what is available and to know your requirements cold before selecting such tools. Never select tools to drive the process. Modeling, frameworks, blueprints, and road maps were addressed in earlier chapters.[2]

Consider the use of an architecture coach or consultant to help you advance your programs. The benefits of using a coach are many, including helping you solidify the roles and skills you'll need to communicate your vision. Experienced coaches can share many methods and techniques to help you prevent rough starts and marring valued relationships. Consultants may guide you to develop specific deliverables, but you should not use them to outsource your entire enterprise architecture program.

Zoom In—Action Steps You Need to Succeed

As an architect, you will likely be called upon to create a presentation or present a solution. You will develop a presentation style as you learn and grow as an orator. Public speaking is part of the job as an EA, but you'll get to start with small projects and practice on your own group. Some of the most critical of any advice I can offer is probably around presentations. Here it is:

- ☐ Have a good reason for creating the presentation.
- ☐ Take the same care as with written or spoken communication: do not slap together a slide.

---

[2] Modeling, frameworks, blueprints, and road maps were addressed in earlier chapters.

☐ Presentations have a way of living forever, so take care to follow best practices with font size, quantity and style of text per slide, color, and graphics.

☐ Determine whether it will be also used as a takeaway document or purely for viewing.

☐ On average, it takes about five minutes to cover a slide unless you are flipping through quickly and people question the value of the presentation.

☐ Consider creating multiple versions if you have a diverse group of people who have different reasons for attending. Create a shorter version (or deck) for executives and a detailed edition for architects and technical staff.

☐ Small things such as including a date and context details will protect your reputation in future—trust me on this one!

☐ If you are nervous, remember that the most important details are your rate of speech and keeping it at a casual level with your audience.

☐ Your pitch will expose your attitude, so you will want to keep it firm and assured to appear mature.

☐ Vary your speaking voice so that the audience makes it through your entire message.

☐ Keep your tone in check to avoid anything that might be construed as sarcasm, defensiveness, or aggression.

☐ Avoid offensive, defensive, and negative words.

☐ Be as specific as possible, removing vague words such as "lots" and "often" and absolute words such as "always" and "never."

☐ Make your presentation pleasant to listen to, carefully including pauses for emphasis and appropriate humor if your corporate culture permits.

☐ Ensure your filler words are absent (remember that "ah" and "um" counter from Toastmasters?).

☐ Keep the outcome you want in mind.

☐ Practice if need be, and you'll be fine.

Zoom Out—Big-Picture Concepts

You'll want a different strategy for communicating to executives and to upper levels. Here is a quick checklist to ensure you are headed for success:

- ☐ Consider your executives' time and get to the point quickly.
- ☐ If senior executives will attend your presentation, limit it to fifteen pages in length at most, including a title and a call for questions.
- ☐ Include an executive summary right at the beginning, and write this slide last.
- ☐ Point to appendices to replace wordy detail slides.
- ☐ Avoid hype and keep things short and focused.
- ☐ Avoid words that imply demand and avoid technical jargon.
- ☐ Summarize key recommendations and include items that would be of the most interest to the executives.
- ☐ Ensure that you weave the executives' number-one request or concern as the main theme throughout your presentation.
- ☐ Be sure to feature one or two killer slides that give a strong message on one page. It becomes a takeaway sheet that should scream, "If you can't remember anything else, remember this page."

If the presentation is to be used as a document, here are a few other messages you might want to include:

- ☐ Assumptions you've made
- ☐ Description of the current situation and the exact business goals your solution will align to
- ☐ Description of business impacts, especially in the areas of cost and effort
- ☐ Scope and context for the presentation/document
- ☐ Groupings by area, perspective, department, or technology you are focusing on
- ☐ List of people involved in creating it
- ☐ List of areas out of scope for this consideration

☐ Next steps or action items
☐ An outline of risks and methods for mitigation
☐ Appendices of research areas
☐ Decisions remaining to be made
☐ Conclusions or recommendation

CHAPTER 14:
MAKE DILIGENT DECISIONS

Stay committed to your decisions, but stay flexible in your approach
—Anthony Robbins

In your background as an IT architect, you will likely have covered the subject of decision making. From the generic perspective, the process of decision making is about evaluating alternatives according to a specified set of criteria. This is presumably evaluating which alternatives best fit a current set of business requirements. You can consider the type of solution required and then determine a desired approach. A common method of problem definition is to clarify the description of the problem, analyze the causes, identify alternatives, and then assess each alternative. You might choose one option, implement it, and then evaluate whether it solved the problem. In training, typical examples include decisions about restaurants to visit for dinner as a group or selecting a car or college.

Architects Require a Rigorous Decision Process

With IT architecture, the decision-making process gets far more complicated. In the solution design process, you are required to make various trade-off architecture decisions. You consider different possibilities and combinations of methods and patterns to satisfy the requirements of the intended system. Some may be conflicting or inconsistent in nature. Keep in mind that hard decisions you must make are most often very expensive to change later. You'll typically make decisions around quality attributes as dictated by solution requirements. The final selection may be a combination of components derived from the needs and opinions of multiple stakeholders with inconsistent preferences. See how tricky this gets? It is not as easy as evaluating whether the problem was solved. Trial and error are recipes for disaster, and other than learning from past mistakes, the process must be more exhaustive.

Escalate to ten thousand feet and consider the decisions needed at the enterprise level. You will need to make judgements on a wider scale from a system-wide perspective. Making sound decisions results in "good" or "great" architecture. The cost and impact of incorrect decisions multiplies, and the level of stakeholders with whom you communicate also increases. Politics plays an even more significant role. Research and validation take even longer. The big picture must be in sight and decision making at this level must consider multiple groupings of systems, data, and the infrastructure at the enterprise level.

The EA can't afford to choose a solution, then test and evaluate. Some basic decision-making steps are just not appropriate for IT or enterprise architecture alone. Trying out technology without a specific and predicted method can be risky, expensive, and hazardous to one's career. Pray and hope is not a best practice, and a full risk analysis is most often required before settling on an alternative. If you revisit the topic of process, recall the discussion on prototyping and controlled methods of the trial and error method. Enterprise architectural decisions are those made in areas of high visibility, impact, and risk to the business. You'll have to take all the necessary steps and afford the due diligence as set out by the framework you choose for the process.

Use a Decision Framework

It is easy to prevent these problems by evaluating the architecture choices early and selecting an appropriate method. Architects are familiar with frameworks, so why not use this familiar tool? You can use a decision framework to determine what steps will be required to gather the information and which kinds of decisions will be acceptable. Depending on the level of architecture decision (software, system, solution, or enterprise), a standard or proprietary methodology may be available. For example, the Architecture Tradeoff Analysis Model (ATAM) is an option available specifically for software. Many organizations, including IBM, use an approach customized for their offerings, generically called Architecture Design Review (ADR) for multiple solutions, including the enterprise architecture. Whatever the review process, the steps are basically the same.

The architect collects and analyzes the data and selects the alternatives that are still appropriate. The architect synthesizes the data, evaluates it based on the decision criteria, and discards unviable options. Determine the final option and test it using prototypes and various models against multiple scenarios. You'll need to obtain commitment to implement the decisions, and you'll need strong negotiation skills if the decision being made will need to overcome organizational resistance. Look at the decision framework developed over years of my experience in consulting on architecture. It appears simple, but it includes the feedback mechanisms necessary to avoid failure:

- At stage one of your model, you have tried to clarify and define the decision in as simple terms as possible and establish a set of objectives. Use this work to identify drivers and the key resource team, and use the current state as your context.

- At stage two, evaluate specific alternatives. In between stages one and two, gather data and analyze it, creating alternatives and considering their impacts.

- In stage three, you'll evaluate the match and potential impact to people, process, and technology. Drill down to create a solution and architectural context. Summarize the ramifications of decisions, shortfalls, and redundancies. This is where you'll do some risk analysis and management and study the architecture trade-offs.

At stage four, you will analyze, interpret, and present consequences. You may think you are done, and in a normal decision-making process for a simple situation, this might be true. However, for an architecture decision, this framework dictates a method called backward chaining to double-check that what you are considering is what you really should do. It consists of the scenario analysis, gut checks, and various other checklist gates. You want to ensure that your architecture has integrity.

Stepping backward from stage four to stage three, review the decision in context of all of the organized data you have collected—do you really know that the solution you've selected will match your requirements? If so, step back to validate between stages three and two. Use the architecture you selected and prove your work. You may create some prototypes to test the concepts.

Between stages two and one, you can backward chain again to look at the architecture at a higher level to test it against your original objectives. Consider again the resources you would need to enable the decision.

This is fairly straightforward, but it should simplify almost every other method you find in existence that gets you to good with your architecture and your decision.

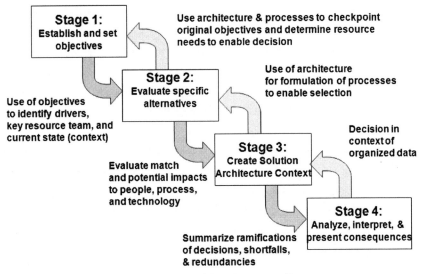

Figure 7. Decision Framework

You may consider each of these stages as steps or gates. What is different from a traditional gated decision is the use of the feedback loop to check your work. The EA effectively uses different decision styles as appropriate for the situation. To get more information on decision styles, models, and processes, visit my decision-making sites at www.decide-guide.com/models/ and www.decide-guide.com/process/, where you'll find many other more complicated models that may better suit your needs.

Your contribution to the decision-making process may include a role in creating a transition plan to implement the decision. You'll want to outline the areas of risk and prioritize the components and steps needed in the process to make the transition.

Tactical vs. Strategic Decision?

Time pressure will add a different element to your approach. It will be different than when your decision criteria require the intense need for a quality decision, when you are in a high-risk situation, or when your decision is riddled with an innovative or competitive urgency. Tactical versus strategic decision styles should be a consideration. If the study of alternatives points to the right thing to do, it should be noted as the strategic decision. If time pressures force your hand, you might want to show a tactical decision alternative and include the timelines in which both would reach implementation.

You must be willing to make the decision even when it isn't popular and especially when it is critical to the enterprise's vision and strategy. You cannot be concerned with pleasing everyone. These choices usually end in disaster for the organization and your career. You must be strong-willed and be able to set forth a direction that is best for all. Be sure to consider and integrate diverse views of the team members and the project stakeholders in both the alternative list and the final decision.

Assess the Risk

Part of your decision-making process should include an element of risk assessment of the potential alternatives you have decided to include on your short list. With each alternative, identify, analyze, and then prioritize any risks. Create your risk list for each individual alternative. What might not work as planned, and which alternatives are so new that your organization has little experience with them?

What assumptions have you made that have risk attached to them? Do some scenario analysis on the uses of your alternatives and see what unknowns pop up.

With each risk, you will need to address and measure the magnitude and likelihood of the risk occurring. Determine your exposure to the risk by calculating its probability times the magnitude of the risk. You might choose a probability ranking as broad as "highly likely," "likely," "even," "not likely," and "very unlikely," and magnitudes in the range from 0 to 100 percent loss. Try to attach a cost to the loss. Estimate the cost of the solution, and calculate the losses for each risk situation, multiplying by the probability. A clear picture should emerge and quantify your choices.

Finally, review the methods you could use to mitigate risks with your alternatives. You can choose to avoid the risk (skip this alternative from your decision process altogether), control it by monitoring it and employing some mitigation tactics, assume the risk, transfer the risk elsewhere (perhaps to a vendor on a solution you purchase during contract negotiation), or reduce it by modeling, testing, and prototyping. In any event, these tactics all take effort, and you will want to employ all of them when you narrow your decision alternatives.

Decision Trade-offs

With any architecture decision, you must consider trade-offs. Some are quite common, and as you have gained experience as an architect, you will recognize most of this cast of characters:

> ➤ Performance vs. Accuracy
> ➤ Speed vs. Detail
> ➤ Exact fit (functional) vs. Best practice forcing business change
> ➤ Time vs. Completeness
> ➤ Cost vs. Speed
> ➤ Robustness vs. Cost
> ➤ Availability vs. Cost
> ➤ Reliability vs. Cost

These are just a few examples, but notice that most pit quality or speed against cost. Most are a measure of quality attributes against the means in which solutions are implemented. In any event, know which trade-offs you face and make calculated and documented decisions about which you choose to accept. In some cases where the stakes are high, you will need to do some calculated measures and studies such as return on investment to confidently make your decision and choose the acceptable trade-offs. Ensure that everyone responsible for funding your decisions has all the data available on your decision before they recognize and back it.

Your Decision Instinct

The architect who has a diverse background and a vast range of experience will have great instincts about the architectural decisions needed. Study your own experiences and those of other great architects, as well as those of parallel organizations in your industry, to help you see more natural selections from the start. Be sure to tap other people's experience to produce an improved outcome, incorporating other people's feedback. If you feel you are lacking in this area, try to find relevant case studies, join associations, and meet others who are in your situation when you are trying to reach decisions.

Validation is still required, as the mentioned framework heavily alludes to. You must take care not to align yourself with your first gut instinct. An intuitive nature is learnable; it is a concept or perception formed from associations with similar models, contexts, or scenarios. Have faith that you have learned to see patterns and that the decision-making process is no different. You are typically unconscious of such a skill, but when you have seen and recognized many patterns in the past, your instincts in making the right decision will become innate.

Documenting the Decision

Decision Repository

Make one of your early decisions around the construction of an architecture decision repository. If you understand why you made the decisions in the first place, it will allow you and your team to understand and not spend time revisiting decisions. As well, if you understand why decisions were made, it will allow you to see some of the barriers and the adaptable points in each of these decisions. If you can gain value from the work you have previously done, your architecture will enable you to grow and learn from it. Decisions and the governance of them from both an architecture and IT position are considered part of a far larger topic called architecture governance. We will cover this topic in somewhat more detail in Part Four on Perspectives.

Give Good Whiteboard

Giving good whiteboard is a term that has been given to people who effectively articulate and share concepts and ideas using the whiteboard as their medium. Oftentimes, the whiteboard is used in offering various alternatives in a decision-making process or in communicating the architecture. It is a skill observed and attributed to nearly all good and excellent architects. You should be able to stand up and enlighten a group on the subject of architecture, whether to expand on or demonstrate a concept, belief, or potential solution. You can leverage this skill when creating great single-page diagrams as part of architecture documentation.

Let me dive into a little analogy. Several years back, I was involved in a long journey in choosing a technology and solution for a large financial organization that encompassed several huge corporations. We were near the end of a multi-month project riddled with far too much political pain. We created several pages of presentations to summarize several views of what we had done and our final recommendations. When far too many hours of presentation creation had passed and many dreary eyes emerged, the presentation was deemed far too lengthy to present to the executive.

We went back and shortened the sixty-page monolith to just over ten pages, retaining only critical information the executives and voting shareholders might care about. We included a one-page visual that seemed to have oversimplified the turmoil we'd been through. In the end, that page proved invaluable. It showed all of the components included in the multimillion-dollar solution. It encompassed geographical and logical distribution of both infrastructure and users who would benefit from the solution and use the technology.

This one little page also showed the scope of the project and the advantages and benefits with each component using what are termed "call-outs" in presentation language. Now consider the strength of this single page when given to executives. It was one of the first things they saw early in the presentation and then they could refer back to it with the adequate amount of supporting documentation. It greatly reduced the amount of page flipping in the presentation, and we better spent the time explaining how things fit together and exploring the issues.

Please use this example for yourself and realize you will, of course, need all of those extra pages to support the diagram and back you up. This single page is something your sponsors could come back to over and over again. The single message you want to impart should be contained within one powerful image. In this specific example, the president of the company, who was non-technical at best, was able to walk around with this diagram and use it to communicate with various other executives and shareholders. He was proud that this was "his own" and that he understood.

Would you believe this simple idea came from the whiteboard diagram we used to start many meetings and discussions with vendors and team members when we were trying to decide what the solution would be? It was our context and landscape for those decision-making discussions. Our ability to communicate using the whiteboard was crucial in taking our work right from analysis and research through to delivery and acceptance at the highest levels.

What Constitutes Good Whiteboard?

Dan Roam, author of *The Back of the Napkin*, has an excellent process for solving problems with pictures. The book is included in the suggested reading at www.zoomfactorbook.com/bookshelf. He too uses a framework to suggest various types of diagrams to address various ways of expressing your visual thoughts. To extrapolate his intent into architecture terms, he would use the following methods to diagram architecture solutions:

1. Pictures to show roles or people
2. Charts to depict quantity and metrics
3. Maps to illustrate proximity or location
4. Timelines to express when an event occurs, timing and sequences
5. Flowcharts to confirm a process, and
6. Grids to compare products, components, or variables to support strategy and decision making

As an exercise for yourself, pull out an architecture solution document and consider how you could have used the list above in a meeting with you in control of the pen at the whiteboard. Knowing how and *when* to express your ideas visually will advance your credibility at the board.

Adding visual components has proven to dramatically increase the effectiveness of endeavors. You might use this for a pre-planned presentation on the whiteboard in the boardroom. Good diagrams seem to evoke questions and reduce confusion in strategies and plans. Why not bring clarity in leading your team as well as simplifying your complex problems? You'll also get the opportunity to inspire and motivate those around you and shine a light on subjects that may have perplexed many.

Consider what you are trying to tell your audience, what would be lost on them, how you will convince them, and what final action you want them to take. Consider who will be attending your meeting and contemplate in advance what diagrams would be most valuable. For example,

> ➢ Strategists and planners will want to know *why*
> ➢ Accountants and analysts will want to know *what*
> ➢ Sales and marketing people will want to know *who*

Cross this information with the specific types of diagrams needed for all of these types of people based on their type and purpose, and you may fulfill their needs. When moving this to a presentation you arrive with, consider the other aspects that will make you a master presenter.

Use color to focus the eye's attention on that which is most important, using contrast as your tool. Arrangement of the objects in the diagram may be important if you want the attendee to view things in a specific order. Larger arrows can also direct interest toward main themes or objects. Contrast should be appropriate for your setting, for the light available, and for printing hard copies. Consider the size and shapes you use to indicate significance.

I should add a final note on that great single-page diagram. Never, ever, ever use blinking or distracting and "cute"-style graphics with your architecture. You are the serious, intelligent type, right? You are asking for serious commitment and funding, aren't you? Having those great blasting sounds as your images appear is not likely to persuade your audience. One exception to flashing graphics is the custom animation available in presentations. Having series of diagrams "appear" if your discussion lends itself to stages of implementation or timeline for delivery can be very powerful.

Zoom In—Action Steps You Need to Succeed

Consider and practice the following standard sample diagrams you can use on whiteboards to express thoughts quickly and clearly when trying to make decisions:

- ☐ Use case diagrams
- ☐ Block diagrams
- ☐ Context diagrams using timelines, arrows, and flow between components and their audiences
- ☐ Scatter diagrams

- ☐ Venn diagrams
- ☐ Stack diagrams
- ☐ Matrices
- ☐ Network diagrams
- ☐ Gantt charts

Make sure you have a good purpose for getting up to draw. There always seems to be someone in the room who demands control of the whiteboard pens. If you are uncomfortable with the pressure to stand up and draw, consider the things you learned in grade school. Answering the six key questions—who, what, when, where, why, and how—follows not only best practices in whiteboarding but also aligns with John Zachman's framework. Consider this the best way to clarify your idea or approach and to ensure you are heard while being seen. Always consider the decision you are trying to get agreement on, and use visual elements to bring the group to a common understanding.

Zoom Out—Big-Picture Concepts

There are many decision models available to help the architect use what is most appropriate for the problem or issue. For a detailed review, see www.decide-guide.com/models/. Your main concern should be driving decisions, having an agreed-upon process for arriving at them, and documenting both the issues and the results. The route you take to arrive at a decision should be a direct function of the cause and impact of your decision. Here are a few tools you may wish to use. Choose one that is most appropriate your issue at hand:

- ☐ Cost-Benefit Analysis Model
- ☐ Boston Consulting Group (BCG) Matrix
- ☐ Weighted Matrix
- ☐ Decision Support System
- ☐ Decision Trees
- ☐ SWOT
- ☐ PEST

- ☐ Pluses, Minuses, and Interesting Points (PMI)
- ☐ Pareto Analysis
- ☐ Six Thinking Hats
- ☐ Mind Mapping

Part IV:
Propel Your Perspective

In this part

- Chapter 15: Your Various Perspectives
- Chapter 16: Tune Into the Big Picture
- Chapter 17: Build Your Architecture Dream Team

Part IV introduces architecture perspectives such as vision and big-picture thinking. It also addresses the concept of using road maps to broach the subject of moving from current to future state from both project architecture and enterprise viewpoints.

This part also includes a way of using realist filters to test recommended solutions, and it provides a checklist method that will help budding architects ensure solution integrity, demonstrate their skills, and gain credibility as an expert. It concludes with team design, construction, and leadership, as they are typically the key areas for enterprise architecture coaching.

.

CHAPTER 15:
YOUR VARIOUS PERSPECTIVES

*If I have seen farther than others, it is because
I was standing on the shoulders of giants.*
—Isaac Newton

Your experience in diverse areas, such as training, projects, politics, and corporate culture, has enhanced your ability to determine the optimum solution. You improve the problem-solving and solution-design process because you bring various perspectives and a vast variety of viewpoints to the team with the intention of constructing great architecture solutions. Your skill in considering and knitting these various perspectives together in the architecture will prove paramount to the solution quality and value you deliver to the business. Team collaboration on these perspectives dramatically increases the likelihood you will find a high-quality solution.

Perspective Through Diversity and Collaboration

Your most trusted resource will be your own experience, as you will use it to frame what you offer with respect to patterns and what your team and peers offer. Your skills and contributions at various points in your career will play a role in how you see the requirements and how they match the multitude of options you see before you. To predict your success, keep your eye on the key performance indicators (KPIs): stakeholders, who provide the highest priority value points; budgets; and future plans.

Balance should be a concern to you as you seek out the various perspectives from others. You create an enterprise architecture team because collaboration is key when you are trying to take on multiple roles, numerous skill sets, strengths, and subject matter expertise to convey and project perspectives on the architectures. Those who get crippled in decision traps in analysis paralysis and excess research are usually victim to either group-think problems or seeking full consensus from too many players.

It may be tough as the leader, but deliberate limitations should determine the number of opinions you'll need, ranking them by perceived value and the value your key stakeholders will place on them. Choose the right mix of technical and functional capabilities and problem-solving and decision-making techniques. You will choose best by seeking patterns and technology that closely match your alternative set, recent experience, and references by peers who have used similar components.

Visions via Internal and External Forces

Internal and external forces play big roles when it comes to transitioning toward the target state. As you expand your range of perspectives, take a look at the business strategy and the forces that it places on each group. What kinds of things does this change in strategy cause people to do? At the outskirts, you are looking to leaders—what do they want you to do? And where do you want to lead the organization? A little different perspective is perception: you will want to look at how you separate people from the problem. You are looking at the reality—it will always be subjective for each group.

Review the situation the way all other sides see it. Your perspective needs to be from all angles, and seeing the others' vantage point helps you to understand that you can't always induce or deduce their fears from your intentions. You shouldn't blame the other side for the problems you incur along the way toward transition; you need to understand this fully when you are trying to stay in the middle and prescribe your architecture.

The Business Perspective

It is critical that you understand what the business most wants from enterprise architecture. The perspectives of your business resources control the life expectancy of the program from acceptance to its longevity. Learn what you can about their perspectives before crafting solutions and direction. The business resources want you to help them and tell them where they can find efficiencies. Most of all, they want you to outline the options and identify the risks associated with them. They want you to listen and be their partner in their strategies. They want you to be an advisor and give them technology investment advice by learning what would be valuable to them, keeping up with innovation, and being mindful of opportunities right before you. Usually, the business will want the architecture team to spend less and do their work faster. On the other hand, EAs tend to want to spend more and do things slower, with higher quality, and in a prioritized fashion.

The business always wants to add more capability where the architect or the architecture group is considering potentially combining functions or is questioning whether more functionality can be added. The business will always want the solution as quickly and as inexpensively as possible. Architecture is typically concerned with addressing quality and designing the solution to have quality built in. An architecture capability can:

> Align business and IT
> Speed decision making
> Improve investment decisions
> Speed time to market
> Reduce integration problems
> Reduce costs
> Establish a foundation
> Transform organizations

You will need to review all perspectives to determine which capabilities the business should add now and which it should pencil in for a later date.

The View Through Enterprise Portfolio Management

The EPfM or portfolio program is one of the critical perspectives you should consider. It is an enormous topic—one too large to cover adequately here as we could easily spend a full day of education on it (see www.zoomfactorbook.com/education). A portfolio is the collection of individual investments planned and jointly overseen to optimize the total financial return on IT endeavors to your corporation while maintaining acceptable resource levels, risk, and schedules. It is an approach that considers solution, data, and technology investments currently existing at your enterprise and those that are suggested for inclusion in the future as assets.

The EPfM is driven by enterprise architecture planning. You will evaluate gaps between current and target states and initiate methodical decision making for those programs that will make up the next steps in transitioning toward the target state. You will group projects logically by programs and review them strategically and financially to determine whether the business should pursue them over the next year and often over a longer period. This perspective allows you to uncover many situations in which business areas are proposing overlapping projects and allows IT planning to have a perspective of redundancies. Using EPfM, you are able to proactively assess the fit of proposed projects in the grand scheme.

You can subdivide the vast array of available perspectives by architecture domain. Your enterprise technology and solution architects are often those most involved in the portfolio management activities, although most of your team and peripheral contributors would assist in this activity. It is typically conducted in conjunction with budget and annual planning activities: at this time, large infrastructure projects are paired with solutions and applications. Often, it is the only time when technology programs receive adequate corporate attention, as few stakeholders put them high on their priority lists until they can see the benefits of implementation. The biggest reason for this lack of attention is that it is difficult to prove tangible business value for pure technology upgrades.

The benefits of portfolio management are plentiful and include the following:

- Total cash outlay for projects is reduced
- Cash flow is planned and managed from a big-picture vantage point
- Visibility of actual spend is increased

- Bottom line is increased; budget is prioritized for the right projects, not wasted on the wrong ones
- Projects are better aligned with strategy and business objectives
- Proportion of innovation, growth, and improvement projects alongside those needed to run and sustain the organization is optimized
- Focus and chance for success, return on investment, and risk management for all projects in the portfolio are increased
- Architecture is better aligned with infrastructure projects required to run the enterprise
- Linkage to the enterprise architecture program is established

Portfolio management and program activities are also ways for the SOA programs and enterprise architecture programs to double-check their business alignment. The initiative allows an organization to keep its portfolio current by evaluating new additions against the technical condition of older ones. Decisions are made on retirement, modernizing, repositioning, and maintaining or evolving the assets based on their life cycle and quality. While it is important that this is done continually, it allows a corporate perspective on the services and solutions planned and prioritized for the upcoming period. The general focus of the EA will be on the strategic matters. You will take a bird's eye view or the big-picture perspective of the enterprise in everything being evaluated as an asset. You will examine from a vantage point of transformation, as the team attempts to take its world from the current state to the target state. Here is the typical order and context for the EPfM activities:

1. Strategic planning + budget
2. Enterprise architecture planning + budget
3. Enterprise portfolio management planning + budget
4. Project/program management + budget
5. Operational management + budget

Each step is reviewed from a budgetary perspective. Upward or backward steps are needed until the annual budget comes into balance and all planning initiatives and programs are approved.

The Architecture Perspective

Depending on your architecture approach, method, and framework, your perspectives will differ. If you take a purely domain-type perspective, you will see architecture through the eyes of the various architecture domains, including:

1. Business architecture
2. Information architecture and data views
3. Application, solution, and integration views
4. Technology and infrastructure views

Within each domain, you will take a conceptual, logical, and physical view. This may seem daunting, but it aligns well with most architecture methodologies and sets up against various cells in the Zachman framework. Your view of the business architecture will include high-level requirements and business process models showing the change from the current processes to the new. You should describe the changes in business capability requirements, such as business volumetrics and other forecasts and changes to nonfunctional requirement needs. Within the information perspective, you will gather changes in needs for data and the business, application, and technology impacts on the architecture.

Within the application and solution area, you will look at all existing integration perspectives and upcoming changes. You need to see functional requirements as well as the logical services and components to be provided. Taking a physical view, you will see any changes or needs in the development landscape and map specific physical components to their logical components, functionality, and services. You must decide whether they will be bought, reused, or built, as well as decide on their key nonfunctional characteristics, and you must describe any conciliations made.

A view of integration will allow you to see the sequenced links between conceptual applications and the business activities to be supported. We should see how the applications interact and exchange data. It is here that gaps between the business process and IT solution will become apparent. You'll review and see the end-to-end business solution at the conceptual level and through to the logical level.

You'll determine the physical implementation of interfaces and technology choices in the areas of application methods and service solutions. You'll have to determine the interface patterns to be used, the data content of interfaces, and which patterns you can reuse. We'll double-check this against our conceptual and logical views as validation points.

Your technology and infrastructure view will occur against both data and application views. You will derive specifications from all physical views provided thus far. Here, you may have to circle back to change some of your specifications to match budget, standards, and the operability of all selected solutions. Incremental changes to the technology architecture will dictate the work to be done, the perspective taken with the infrastructure, and finally the operational view. You'll review installation models and highlight any red flags or needed adjustments.

It takes great skill as the EA to coordinate and guide these various viewpoints. You can and should use templates to guide the process and allow for the structure of the descriptions and the separation of concerns with the architecture. All should provide communication with the stakeholders with respect to budget, impact, and risk. These perspectives often don't include the element of quality, except where a step is taken to validate all back to the conceptual models in each domain and right back to the business requirements. Cross-viewpoints are needed to ensure that all has been included and accounted for.

The Zachman Perspective

A noteworthy viewpoint should be one contained and prescribed by the work of John Zachman. He intentionally created this framework to consider the enterprise from various perspectives appropriate for your needs. He originally kept it simple by having several columns aligned by the 5W and H questions. He brought the perspectives he felt any organization should take with the rows in the framework. Each row adds continual value to the enterprise, and you should view it as adding more detailed views as you progress deeper vertically through the matrix and need to answer more questions.

The first row in the Zachman framework is comprised of the visionary lists that recognize the enterprise's scope and boundaries. This perspective gives you a baseline as to what the business sees as its future. The second row encompasses the perspectives of executive leaders and subject matter experts with semantic models showing actual business context or concepts. This view shows an extended vision using business terms. The third row from an architect's perspective includes schematic models that characterize enterprise-level systems logic. The architect drives out concepts at the logical level, drilling down on the detail presented and viewed by the business.

The fourth row is the viewpoint of the engineers or the designers and the blueprint models they need to specify enterprise technology constructs. Think of this in the same manner as you think of building a house. If you have an architect and you develop the concepts and a very abstract view, it takes the draftsmen to create the blueprints of the various layers and models for you to build the house. The fifth row depicts what the implementer needs to see and includes specifications for the component instructions used to build the solutions. Finally, the sixth row shows an operational view for workers, including instances for deployment.

These are the pure models required for you to build and realize the vision of the architecture. In a nutshell, this perspective was what John Zachman was trying to achieve from his models and his framework. He tried his best to give everyone the view they needed to see the enterprise, to afford understanding, and finally, to provide the detail needed to make reality happen. Imagine the greatness that could be exploited with respect to all of these perspectives and also in thinking. You will use multiple modes of thinking to gain different perspectives to ensure that you understand the entire concept as well as possible before spending on construction. Carefully pick and choose the artifacts needed from the perspectives most likely to be accurate.

Use your skills to articulate and communicate the architecture as we previously covered in communication and whiteboard skills. Use them to share your different perspectives with different audiences for an assortment of purposes. Use caution in selecting the number of perspectives you take with modeling work, keeping a realistic view with the resources you have on your team to explore the many perspectives with models. Demonstrate your great instinct and visions while remaining the realist. While it is great to act as a visionary in seeing the gaps in the current and target state architecture and creating creative ways to fill them, maintaining a sense of reality will allow you to stay aligned with the business. You are an opportunity seeker, but you will have to make trade-offs in determining where your organization can gain a competitive advantage and where you may achieve the benefits of efficiencies in cost of savings.

Your Aspect Through Governance

The focus and perspective of the domain or project architects is on execution and implementation of specific tasks. Often, the meeting point with enterprise architecture and the business will be through an enterprise architecture governance perspective. Similar to EPfM, architecture governance is a huge topic that deserves a full text to adequately explain the knowledge you will need as an EA. You'll find more information on this topic in Chapter 19. Be sure to review the resource section at the end of this book for a list of great references on the subject. Architecture governance will be your means of applying a consistent method or process to control and manage standards and systems in your organization. You will define the perspective of audit and control as it should apply to those who affect the architecture of the enterprise with their projects and technology solutions.

Your Risk Perspective

Each architecture perspective brings an element of risk whenever new technologies are selected and architectural decisions are born out of compromises. It is critical that you review, quantify, qualify, and articulate all risks to stakeholders. Any risks to solutions proposed should come with mitigation strategies and constraints known by all. You need to evaluate any changes to the architecture against the risk perspective and account for them through established change and risk management practices. You must make difficult decisions regarding changes to architecture and re-engineering as early as possible. The architect is almost always involved in monitoring this perspective, as hard as it may be.

Success with Perspectives

Business is driven by financial objectives, not just strategic plans. You must account for the various perspectives of all players in architecture to craft workable, acceptable solutions. Reality is always subjective, and you'll need to look at the situation from perspectives that are mainly not your own. You will be more successful if you don't deduce others' needs and wants, but instead try to understand their intentions. You will succeed by searching for opportunities consistent with their needs and perceptions. To enjoy your greatest success, create architecture most consistent with the values of your primary stakeholders.

Zoom In—Action Steps You Need to Succeed

Your broad experience affords you the ability to maintain multiple perspectives in the best interest of your organization. Consider using a checklist such as this when beginning new activities as the EA or when evaluating ones before presentation to others:

☐ How does this solution match the value and vision statements of my company? Does it make or keep us profitable while allowing us to grow? Will we offer great products and services to customers by using this solution?

☐ Where does this solution fit into our corporate strategy? Our IT strategy? How does it match the investments we already have made and are planning to make? Would most consider it a good investment? From the perspective of our existing IT asset portfolio, is it a good fit?

☐ What effect would this solution have on our collection of business capabilities? Would it strengthen it? Weaken it? What happens to the processes surrounding existing capabilities by using this solution? Which new processes would have to be created?

☐ How does this solution match the objectives we had for our IT plan? Can it be made possible using the functions we already produce, or is it brand new? What services do we provide that can be leveraged? Will this add or take away from our existing service catalog? Are there service catalogs that exist that contain a version we can use as-is or with little change?

☐ What issues will this solution bring? How will we handle change management in implementing this solution? How are existing standards, applications, and solution life cycles affected by choosing this solution? What services require updates to implement this solution? Where does it fit on our EA road map? Are there any industry models that use this solution? Is it outside of the original transition plan, or does it help us move closer to our target?

☐ How can we plan, coordinate, and facilitate implementation of this solution? How will our operations team manage it? What extra training will be required? What impact will it have on our "run" capacity? Does it trigger any cyclical events that will draw on our resources (extra hardware, contracts, leasing, capacity)? How will we track incidents and problems? How will it fit within our change management systems?

Zoom Out—Big-Picture Concepts

You've learned the process to do a gap analysis. What is the basis for defining a gap? Usually this includes missing business capabilities, expired or tired systems, and innovative improvements. You can use various perspectives to find most of these gaps. You will excel when you catch what others in your organization usually don't.

Where are your blind spots? Here are some examples of possible lapses:

- ☐ Timing of various projects and expectations about the stability or static nature of existing data or interfaces. Will the data you believed you would leverage be in the state needed to achieve value, or are there plans to make changes others aren't aware of?
- ☐ Strategies believed to match organizational goals are only good focal points when everyone agrees upon and supports those strategies. Who opposes the strategies, and what effects will this have on your enterprise architecture? Will audits and controls squash these plans?
- ☐ Will you still achieve your strategy's value if your project were to overrun by 120 percent of budget? 130 percent? Have you accounted for all of the necessary states to be met, such as data consolidation or user training?
- ☐ For projects with incredibly long build cycles, have you accounted for the impacts of various software and hardware upgrades? Large enterprise applications can take years to build or implement. During that time, versions of databases, operating systems, and other infrastructure will need patches and upgrades.
- ☐ Are the strategies and decisions you have planned going to meet the needs of those who leverage or reuse the solutions?

☐ Are the components you plan to use stable enough to rely on?

☐ Are your strategies limited in their use in any way? Can you visualize repurposing or expanding them in the future to serve broader needs?

☐ Are you planning to recreate or design something that is scheduled to be commercially available as a product? If so, have you researched future release horizons?

☐ Is there anything you don't know about the vendor you've chosen to supply technology or components that could come as a rude surprise?

☐ Does any component rely on a stable pricing model that could cause questions surrounding value if the model is changed, e.g., per processor to per seat? Per user? Per online user when taken to the web?

☐ Will all departments get the expected value in the planned form of deployment of the solution? For example, will marketing expect benefits that your new customer service application cannot possibly provide? Do they know that?

☐ Will the architecture be pleasing to the executive and stakeholders but abhorrent to the operations and development teams?

CHAPTER 16:
TUNE INTO THE BIG PICTURE

All architecture is design, but not all design is architecture.
—Grady Booch

Grady Booch maintained that significant design decisions build the basis of the system and measured significance by the cost of changes. As an EA, step back from time to time and ask yourself, "What am I trying to achieve with the enterprise architecture?" Architecting in flexibility and architecting out the magnitude of design decisions should be your personal guiding principles. If your enterprise architecture really hinges in significant design decisions, have you got the big picture in mind?

As architects mature in experience and choose the path of EAs, their skill set will slant less toward the technical end of the spectrum and more toward a strategic innovator or visionary. Big-picture perspectives focus more on the strategic enterprise level and the enterprise portfolio level and less on specific operational concerns. Your experience across many domains will help you view all architecture from an enterprise perspective. Your ability to zoom ahead, seeing the architecture vision you created for the enterprise architecture, allows you to skillfully guide IT business projects.

What Are You Really Trying to Achieve?

It is time for internal reflection and consideration as to why you are trying to advance this specific enterprise architecture. Is there any personal gain to be had? What would it mean to you if it were accepted, and what would it do to you if it weren't? In other words, you should follow the words of Zen master Lao Tzu, who said, "Knowing others' wisdom is wisdom; knowing yourself is enlightenment." Great EAs will take time for careful evaluation of both their internal and external mirrors. How well was your vision accepted? What reactions do you get when presenting your architecture perspectives? Consider the reaction to and the success of your work, both in acceptance and in final delivery. Do you need personal adjustment?

EAs need to have the trait of humility. You shouldn't need to own anything, as the company owns what is done. You should just take pride and satisfaction in the vision that takes your organization in transition.

Instead of focusing inwardly, focus outwardly on the organizational perspective. There are three big-picture perspectives the organization will have, and the enterprise architecture should answer these questions:

1. From the business perspective: What capabilities are possible and when can they have them? How much will they cost to implement, and how much will they save by doing so? What risks must you bear by taking these transitions, and what must you forgo to do so?

2. From the IT management perspective: How will you implement this project? Is there any resource risk? Do you have any experience implementing something like this? How will teams make sure the project is done right? What is it possible to achieve within this time frame? Which technology projects relate to these business projects?

3. From the EA's perspective: What needs to go in your road map? What should you build? What should you buy? What should you integrate? What should you build it with, and when should you do it? In what order should you build it? What are the risks involved with this plan, these technologies, and these projects?

From the big-picture perspective, you can take many views from various levels of detail. From a dimensional view, certain decisions intersect with the architecture domain's business, information, applications or solutions, and technology. There will be those decisions made at the enterprise level that apply to organizational goals and the business strategic objectives. At the domain level, decisions will apply more to the departments and the strategies they have for the products and services they offer. At the system level, your decisions should be strategic in nature and focus on the implementation of solutions.

Your role as EA is to create an architecture vision and work with your team and IT to analyze the gaps to get to the future state. Great architects are able to think abstractly and visualize that which is complex. Your ability to think conceptually allows you to see the big picture on the horizon. You think in terms of the entire system or solution and make trade-offs to address intersections between goals and domains. You are skilled at analyzing the whole landscape and evaluating and prioritizing stakeholder goals, missions, values, and concerns. You are cognizant of the business capabilities that emerge as primary in the architecture itself, over and above all of the technical requirements. You choose components that will make up the solutions that will enable business capabilities, and you make yourself aware of the effects your solutions have on existing components and processes for business users.

Sharing Your Vision

As an EA, you will become known as a change agent, and characteristically, your personality will have a slight competitive edge. You are driven with a passion to see the realization of the mental picture you have designed. You are tenacious and know that if you focus on a vision long enough, it will become reality. You'll be heavily involved in future shaping a solution or realizing an opportunity within the enterprise architecture plans you have in flight. You use the architecture visioning process for insight into a problem, determining core causes as well as the requirements for realizing it.

One of your core responsibilities and activities as an EA will be to share your vision with your team, IT, and stakeholders. Imaginative and creative architects exhibit results time after time. You will need to articulate the vision that is so clear to you well enough for your team to see it vividly enough to motivate them to elaborate on and design it. Strive to make the vision as simple as it needs to be to reach your target audience.

Make Your Visual Image Compelling

A compelling vision is the key to architecture success: it is what kick-starts the modeling process as well as your enterprise architecture plan. Vision is the key to making a goal or desire reality. To create a persuasive vision, it is helpful to understand your company's past experiences while layering them upon the architecture's current context. Thus, your enterprise-wide understanding of the big picture, its principles, and its mechanisms is critical.

You can derive future context from a detailed technology blue-print of various solutions or an intricately complex strategic plan. Future state interviews, stakeholder values and profiles, and a great picture will drive and contour the visioning process. Use the desired capabilities you obtain from the interviews for your overall vision.

The vision serves to build management commitment for support-ing the architecture and financial and moral realizations. The visual experience also helps organize and streamline stakeholder input. It aligns the architecture team and guides individual architects in scoping and structuring decisions. This core centralizing feature will allow your team to streamline their analysis and create a conceptual prototype with system-wide capabilities. Remember that what the shareholder most wants is of primary importance. As an architect, you are the shareholder advocate—you want to help the shareholder tell you exactly what it is you should see as the definition of success.

Trends, political factors, the economic climate, customer needs, and technology factors are typical criteria that help shape the vision. In keeping aligned with economic and business views, you see your future state by comparing your company to other industries and watching the trends. Seeing the next big thing and determining how to adapt it and exploit it within your company landscape forms the realization of the vision.

Seeing the Future

The visionary architect should be able to take the company's goals, vision, and mission and map them to current capabilities as well as those identified in gaps. You will begin to see the future state architecture in relative chunks or components. Let all of this percolate in your mind as the chunks become pieces and the pieces become solutions.

Use your inherent ability to get started by seeing the future in patterns, and realize the business drivers as you visualize the future architecture. Start with scenario planning, which will allow you to see major components, systems, and resources that will form solutions. As you play out various scenarios, determine the various results and impacts to the architecture. You should be able to foresee risk, ramifications, and outcomes: this is a practice of those who are exceptional architects. You should be able to envision the planned architecture as effective, while efficient and clean in its design.

A strategic framework should guide the evolution of enterprise systems matching the growth and direction of the business. As an instinctive architect, your focus will be on business and environmental trends that bubble to the surface while you question the peril and risks that lurk beneath. Further effort will allow you to visualize a road map and bring in the details, then articulate and sell your idea so it will become reality.

Prioritize Your Priorities Through Planning

Your big-picture insight most likely started with the business drivers and key business initiatives. Continued thinking in this manner should frame, guide, and prioritize your actions through the enterprise architecture planning process. Your focus must be in providing value to the business by acting on necessary initiatives. If you also use the enterprise architecture plan as a guide for which projects should emerge from IT, the chief architect will have a better chance at crafting the best possible mix.

Your perception and vision will shape all of your smaller decisions as the architecture is realized. Why does business demand change? This fundamental question should drive your architecture. As part of your EA program, an assessment step should precede project planning and be built into your governance and portfolio management process. Many IT projects focus on the wrong problems at the wrong time, omitting appropriate and prescribed methods to determine whether a project should commence, continue, or cease. To compile your list, you should rank projects against their counterparts for pure business value, drivers, and need.

Often, the chief architect or CIO knows where technology can be leveraged to gain competitive advantage. Vendors often market solutions to the business directly without IT involvement: then, misalignment occurs because the business strives to add technology for single or isolated needs. The converse is true when technology solutions are driven from IT only for the sake of technology alone. Instead, if you align the IT strategy with the business strategy and map business projects to the necessary infrastructure changes with timelines that fit within the enterprise architecture transition plan, you can better achieve value.

You will still need to architect in the ability to proactively act on opportunities for change. Architect out everything that inhibits change. Be cautious when you compromise solutions and ensure everything has passed your own litmus test before suggesting solutions to the business resources, as they could fall in love with something that will wreak nothing but havoc in the future. Is there a need for enterprise clarity on the value of IT to business? Absolutely. Our best opportunities arise when the business understands the value of bringing EAs and leaders together before making business decisions so that technology can be appropriately applied.

Gain Value from the Big-Picture Perspective

Technology may be used to enable more business capabilities, facilitated by choices that provide true business strategic value. One activity to explore is analysis of the value chain in our business, which will appear in more detail in Chapter 19. For now, know that information is the primary driver for IT value to the business and it is the architecture process that drives information value. The business wants better information to manage the enterprise and operate more efficiently. Agility around implementation of business change is realized through your architecture programs.

How can you express solutions to business resources so that they will understand? When you promote reuse, you gain financial efficiency. Often, if you use a term like "software component reuse" or "reduced redundancy," their eyes will glaze over. Instead, state you will be building a function that allows users to log in once to access multiple applications and a single dashboard view of their most important client data; in response, you will see a more engaged audience.

If you discuss the process in which you manage the enterprise program, business resources will understand alignment and portfolio management. They will embrace the financial efficiencies gained from a shortened budget and planning cycle, not to mention the reduced risk when using a controlled and repeatable process. As you target systems for retirement and consolidation and rationalize our systems, you become leaner and save the effort and costs of maintaining too many complex, inflexible older systems. To the business, this operational efficiency is seen as value and is understood.

Drive Value Through Innovation

Some companies will drive value in enterprise architecture through innovation. Through reviews of business processes, your fresh perspective may uncover innovative ways to shorten business processes. Architects add value through innovation when evaluating industry competition. See the resource section in the back of this book for readings that will spark your innovative juices. Some of your best ideas will come from researching different markets and applying solutions from different markets to your own. A valuable category of opportunities is in modernization. How might you become better organized to make better use of your resources?

Consider the knowledge capital, not just the physical capital or assets, in your organization. How can your organization become aware of what knowledge exists? What methods can you use to achieve excellence, profitability, and greater efficiency? You might revisit some past ideas and see whether some previously discarded solutions that may have been attempted too early might work now. In searching for replacement ideas, options that were remnants of these failed solutions should likely be included. Rather than throwing out the baby with the bath water, be creative, benefit from past mistakes, salvage the good components, and find a better solution.

The matter of how your business operates will most likely bring you the biggest gain. There are six levers of innovation that you can explore. In the area of business model innovation, there is the value proposition, the supply chain, and a target customer. On the other side, specifically in the areas of technology innovation, products, and services, process technologies and enabling technologies spark innovation. When you look at these levels, you will have to investigate each one individually and in groupings and look for ways you can bring beneficial advantages to your organization.

Traditionally, your architecture focus is moved into action through a design, development, and implementation cycle. Following its activation, you'll find ways to enhance it. Alternatively, consider the process of continuous improvement through architecture as evolutionary change. Try to see ways of reducing your expenses within the existing cost structures your company has and find efficiencies in your operation and its energy. Other ways to use technical innovation to drive business growth may come from using technology to find new customers, markets, and products. New processes, organizations, partners, and suppliers you find through innovative channels may yield cost savings.

Your most highly profitable ideas may come through discovery. You may have unpredictable eureka moments, and ideas may occur to you entirely by accident. From a bottom-up perspective, brainstorm ideas with your team. From the top-down, create a point of view and evaluate the interaction with other parts of your business. Evaluate requested capabilities for the business while scanning newly available technology. Manage the resulting knowledge capital as you interact with business resources during these explorations. Your findings may not be useful now, but your research may prove fruitful in the future. Build your portfolio of innovation right into your architecture program. Encourage the testing of ideas and try to apply a little bit of what you learn. Start now and start small, and you may find something that exudes excellence later on.

Align and Right Size Your Architecture

By now, it should be second nature for you to articulate and diagram how enterprise architecture and EPfM fit within your organization. The careful selection of technologies that truly advance the core initiatives your business cares most about will allow you to right size the architecture. Reflect for a moment on portfolios, projects, and architecture. Even though you should first define enterprise architecture from a big-picture perspective, you must realize it at a project level. So you can ensure that you are realizing your transition map, you should identify proper checkpoints and criteria across the program.

Review larger projects with architectural impact at the early stages to ensure that projects are being planned to meet the portfolio, strategic drivers, and the big picture. The enterprise portfolio and enterprise architecture plan should directly align with targeted results within the IT infrastructure and solution catalog. In most organizations, having an EA dedicated 100 percent to a large project for its duration is ineffective. Involving an EA merely to ensure that plans and standards are being followed is overkill, as the governance process you have in place should allow deviations to be explained and approved.

Each major business goal has a strategy and tactic that you will employ to achieve it. You may deploy projects and tactics as a separate system or solution. If possible, try to group and combine various goals and strategies. Consider that upgrades, enhancements, or packaged solutions may be a response to a major business goal. Notice how enterprise architecture spans the goals and forms the big picture.

Another cross cut depicts program and project management. Think of it as one layer deeper in detail. Throughout both our enterprise architecture planning exercises and our portfolio planning tightly aligned with architecture, each year we will address the primary goals of the business. Goals may include projects driven by legislative change, innovation, or emergency maintenance to our infrastructure. Choice of an appropriate systems development life cycle and methodology will ensure a repeatable and predictable manner in which we deliver our projects. Finally, there should be alignment with the infrastructure that we house in our IT departments and a direct line to at least one strategic goal.

In his best-selling book *Good to Great*, Jim Collins identified several facets of great companies. Some of these things that make companies great also ring true in great architects. Collins advocates that technology should be used as an accelerator, not an initiator. Consider this position first and foremost when fitting solutions together, rationalizing your priorities, and reconciling your vision. Understand that new technology should not be introduced for the sake of the technology itself. Use it instead as a leverage point for competitive advantage or increased productivity, efficiency, and profitability. The architecture has to be the right fit for the business at the right time. Thoughtful decisions that convert potential capabilities into bottom-line benefits signal excellence within the enterprise program.

Companies that carefully select technology and right size the architecture in their organizations are often those who steer clear of trendy technology. Recall past experiences you encountered with various operating system releases. If you stand back and watch others take their cuts and bruises, this is an opportune time for you to observe the technology take its first breaths. Your ability to carefully plan how you will take advantage of opportunities and new potential in technological advances will script your success. You won't gain advantages by using the same productivity tools everyone else does.

As the architect, your responsibility is to work with the business to determine whether new technology and the potential competitive advantage are worth the related risks in being first. Most often, differentiating your company from your competition is one of the biggest reasons to make that leap of faith. You'll realize benefits when you know exactly how you will utilize technology to calculate the risks and know how to turn unrealized potential into results or leverage. To me, leverage is one of the key features or tactics behind architecture. The greatest value is not gained by documenting information and models within the domains; rather, you gain the most value when you begin to look at the linkages and interactions between the domains and you see patterns that expose advantages. By looking at these types of relationships, big pictures emerge.

One of the things *Good to Great* specifies is using something called a "stop doing list" to simplify things. A few years back, I wrote and presented a paper called "Win Often, Win Early." At the time, I was describing some of the new things a chief architect might do to catapult an architecture program into forward motion. I recommended that the EA distill inventory lists across architectures and try to simplify them. It makes sense now more than ever to eliminate unused technologies or those with little benefit. Review the processes and steps you take in your architecture activities and evaluate whether they remain efficient. Ones that eat up support time should turn on the red lights. The idea is to avoid keeping unnecessary license expenses for tools and services you are no longer using. Distill and simplify that which you have, and you'll have a strategy that will provide value to your stakeholders.

Return to the "stop doing" list to trim more fat. Architects come to recognize patterns in solutions that usually end badly. Generally, you need to avoid these solutions and skillfully dissuade those aligned with them when they are up for consideration. A prime example is buying software from large technology companies that continually swallow others and then leave users hanging with abandoned support or a lack of complete integration. Large enterprise resource planning software upgrade nightmares are another good example of bad enterprise architecture memories.

These potential bumps in your plans are easier to recognize when you measure potential value versus costs. These experiences form your landscape, and you learn that new silver bullets are just that— shiny objects for those in search of such. As a broad category, I would call these initiatives big, hairy Enterprise Resource Planning (ERP) solutions. Good architects should not be right fighters. You don't know that you are right; you just learn to predict risk and danger through skilled hypotheses, pattern visualization, prototyping, and research. Within the culture of discipline in great companies is a high element of architecture practice. Use a disciplined and repeatable process as you architect processes and seek to find value before selecting large packaged solutions.

The Zen of Self-awareness

Self-awareness is the self-conscious state in which attention turns toward oneself. It makes people more sensitive to their own attitudes and dispositions. Self-consciousness plays a large role in behavior that is especially important for the EA. You need to continually monitor your motivation and be able to self-adjust. Self-awareness is a basis for human traits such as accountability and the consciousness, which are critical for the excellent architect.

Self-consciousness affects people in varying degrees, as some are able to self-monitor or scrutinize themselves more than others. This becomes incredibly important when you are visually or verbally communicating with others. If you notice others are tuning out or acquiring a blank stare, you need to understand that your message is not being conveyed and you need to either wrap it up or break things down into simpler parts. Also, you may need to interject and engage your audience more in the conversation rather than assuming a teaching or mentoring role. The self-monitoring individual is a very skilled communicator who can adjust a speech, conversation, or even a presentation based on an audience's perception and reception.

Self-awareness is the very advanced architecture soft skill used to present a concept to a non-technical audience. Evaluate the reception as you are delivering a concept and adjust your tone, verbiage, and the level of detail based on the nonverbal reception you are getting from the audience. Awareness is the first step in the creation process, and as you grow in self-awareness, you are better able to understand why you feel the way you feel and why you behave the way you behave. That understanding gives you the opportunity and freedom to change the things you want to change about yourself and create the life you want. Without fully knowing who you are, self-acceptance and change become impossible.

Let me repeat the purpose for this book—I have been highlighting the ability to adjust as if on auto-focus and create the road map for the career of your dreams. You will want to focus on what's really critical and important to survive as the EA or chief architect. When the business does not accept your proposals and architectures, you'll need self-awareness to analyze how you feel.

You may feel frustrated, go home feeling beaten, and begin to question your career. If, instead, you are able to adjust your mindset, consider that you are trying to be the change master, and acknowledge that this is difficult, you will be in a better position. Having clarity about who you are, what you want, and why you want it empowers you to consciously and actively make those goals a reality. Otherwise, you are going to continue to get caught up in your own internal dramas and unknown beliefs, allowing mysterious thought processes to determine your feelings and actions.

Drive Yourself

I must confess to you that the reason that I eventually stumbled upon architecture is because I was not fulfilled with my career and I explored opportunities on my own. I picked up books and searched for ways to take this approach into a large organization. I finally sought employment with a company that proactively promoted or sold architecture services. Become self-aware and find other ways to propel your career. Take the initiative to follow whatever activities and steps it will take to become excellent. If you face the reality about the things you don't like to do or aren't skilled in doing, you are taking a proactive step to becoming excellent.

Decide on your personal mission or strategy. As an EA, it is usually a shared meaning for the organization. You are trying to make sure that everybody understands what the target state is and what the enterprise will become. You also want to share how you are you going to achieve it. Think about how you're going to get there and your personal and corporate values. Is your company a good match for your innovative nature? If your organization is not change averse, innovation often comes in even the most normal or everyday companies within processes and products. You are signing up for some of the most exciting and innovative work available. You are seeking more change than almost anybody else in the IT profession, and typically, with it will come a lot more of the responsibility and compensation.

Decide what type of compensation you want, whether it is monetary or freedom from detailed busy work, and envision your ideal career path. It might be the freedom to do more research, make more decisions, and work on projects you believe you will enjoy. Consider some of the rewards available to you as an IT architect. Informal relationships tend to be some of the most fulfilling aspects as you get to know people in the business and as you strive to give them what they want.

Decide how much challenge you want to accept. Are you willing to be proactive, have the end in mind, and manage risk versus avoid it? Many incredibly brilliant technical architects will do whatever they can to avoid risk. If you take the path of an EA, you'll have many sleepless nights and be a tense and stressed individual. However, managing risk allows you to work with the challenges that you're presented and find the best solutions and trade-offs. Put people first and seek to understand others, and your career will flourish as an EA. You will have moved yourself out of the backroom—away from being a head-down IT professional and toward the humanistic side of the business.

A fulfilling career in architecture involves being proactive and acting less as a problem solver constantly fighting fires. If being a problem solver makes you happy, architecture is still an option for you, but perhaps in a different way. Either way, you will want to consider using a road map for your career as well as for the work you do to get from the current state to the future state, and consider carefully the bends in the road along the way.

Passion, business strength, and entrepreneurial nature are detailed in the last sstep of this book. For now, focus on what you do best in the world at your company. Think about the company's core competency, what you want to hang on to, and your competitive advantages. Shine the spotlight on your strengths and how they align with your goals: they should be at center stage within the frame of your big picture.

Zoom In—Action Steps You Need to Succeed

Notice how we were focused at the highest enterprise level and now we've turned to you. You are at the center of the big picture, as the program radiates from you. Most often, there are very few architects in comparison to the number of IT staff. If you are continually being begged to attend meetings and help people make decisions, you become unable to advance your own projects and initiatives. You'll feel overwhelmed at times, and sharing a few specific tips on time management for the EA is appropriate. You likely feel overstressed and overbooked most of the time. Here are some suggestions for how you can better manage your schedule:

- ☐ Consider proven techniques such as time blocking in your monthly or weekly calendar. This is especially valuable if you use shared calendars and others may book your time.
- ☐ Block specific periods of time in which you can make gains toward your own projects during your personal peak periods. If you're like me, the best times are mornings; coincidently, it seems that most people like to book meetings during the same time.
- ☐ Book at least two good time blocks each week for you to work on your projects.

☐ Promptly schedule a replacement block when your CIO infringes upon your blocked time that you must allow.

☐ Block time at least once a week for research. Fridays seem to be a good fit for this task. Be aware of the trends in your area, your vertical industry, and architecture trends.

☐ Follow a few blogs and other current sources of information.

☐ In addition, make calendar entries for recurring meetings, such as team or governance meetings.

☐ Use a proven method to prioritize your activities and tasks. For example, use Steven Covey's *7 Habits* quadrants, ranking each as a I, II, III, and IV. Quadrant II contains the most valuable activities to do, and as an architect, most of your team's activities will fall into this quadrant. Very little of what hits our radar is stuff from I and IV.

☐ Add a twist and further rank each with a's, b's, and c's. In reality, you are only going to get to work on the a's, and other people's I and IVs shouldn't make your list for blocked time.

You will definitely become or feel like you've become a victim of the system unless you apply some of these techniques. It won't always work—people will ask you to make exceptions—but eighty percent control is better than zero. An incredibly powerful suggestion one of my coaches recently made to me is to have a current to-do list of six—and no more than six—items. If you have more than that, you will become overwhelmed and your head will feel completely crowded. If you have more than six, keep the others in an overflow.

Zoom Out—Big-Picture Concepts

How can you express value to the business? Adding new capabilities and efficiencies tops the business value list. The business wants better return on investment for IT assets. How might you achieve this? You could take steps to implement the following actions:

➢ Reduce redundancy
➢ Reuse software components
➢ Reduce licensing costs

- ➢ Reduce support costs
- ➢ Reduce hardware and software acquisition costs
- ➢ Consolidate resources
- ➢ Retire equipment and software that is of little use or benefit
- ➢ Rationalize software and equipment
- ➢ Consolidate solutions and infrastructure

The business wants improved quality of goods and services. Ways the architecture can provide this include the following:

- ➢ Provide better information.
- ➢ Reduce the effort required to access data.
- ➢ Make the system more available.
- ➢ Reduce risk.
- ➢ Be more responsive and adaptable to business change.
- ➢ Use repeatable processes to develop systems, thereby increasing quality and reducing risks, integration time, and support time.
- ➢ Standardize platforms to better the user experience and cut down repair time.
- ➢ Use an architecture process to reduce design risks.

CHAPTER 17:
BUILD YOUR ARCHITECTURE DREAM TEAM

He, who wished to secure the good of others,
has already secured his own.
—Confucius

It's time to think about building your high-performance enterprise architecture team. You have so much to do and you won't be able to do it alone. If your organization already has an enterprise architecture team in place, you may be all set. Most often, you'll have to assemble your team or go mining for architecture skills and learn how to excavate and cultivate to build your dream team for the architecture at your organization. One of the biggest problems you'll face when it comes to your architecture team is that there is almost always a shortage of resources. Specifically, it's hard to find good architects who are already skilled and willing to be a part of your team. In this chapter, you'll learn how to recognize the right skills and how to excavate the EAs you already have in your organization. You'll find out how to build the team that you need and get the tools a leader needs to foster and grow enterprise architects.

Scheme Your Dream

You'll need a strategy to build your dream team. The steps included here are from real case studies and my personal experience. The steps laid out here are for constructing your team from the ground up. To build your team, you will need to visualize what that team looks like. You'll need people who are talented and motivated. They will need to come with a cross-section of skill sets and believe in the vision you created. They will have the ability to see the big picture for both their own careers as well as the company. They are individuals who put the vision ahead of personal goals and work well with others. Choose people who have a history of being on time with deliverables, meet client expectations, and work independently.

One of the first steps you will need to take is to identify the sponsor of the enterprise architecture program. This might be a CIO, CTO, or CFO. You'll also need to identify a program lead or chief architect. If this person is you, you'll start by defining the program and identifying a few outcome goals or possibly even the first draft of the enterprise architecture plan. The next step will be to determine the structure or team composition.

Determine Your Team Structure

One of your first decisions will be the structure of your team. Will they be dedicated 100 percent, or is there room for a virtual team in your organization? Most of the time, virtual teaming is the common model of the enterprise architecture team within a company. Consider the time commitments and the activity management you need for the team. You'll want to clearly identify roles and responsibilities within the team up front. For most organizations, this task tends to be one of the biggest challenges when setting up their enterprise architecture teams. Clear responsibilities, defined activities, and established goals are imperative for a successful team. Keep in mind also that if members will contribute on a part-time basis, you will need to set up extra communication vehicles with those who manage them.

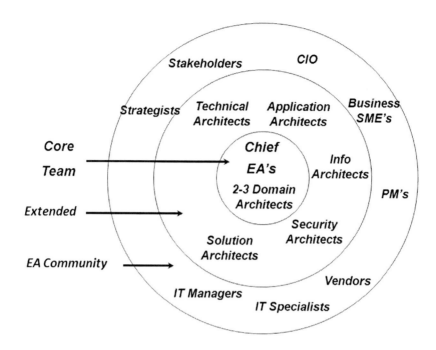

Figure 8. Enterprise Architecture Team

The typical team structure is composed of multiple groups with varying levels of influence and contribution. Create a small group at the core to own and operate the EA program and process. They will plan and design the enterprise architecture. Keep this core team very small, especially if you have a virtual team. Large virtual teams are relatively ineffective, as they easily lose momentum and can't gain value quickly enough to justify keeping this talent together for a long period. Instead, inside this core you may install the EAs you have and a select few domain architects. Where possible, aim for this group to be five to seven full-time employees at the maximum. They should have expertise in the areas of business, solutions, services, applications, information, data, process, and technology. Your selections will depend on your current focus and immediate goals for the enterprise architecture.

An extended group should consist of subject matter experts selected from the available architects from across your company. This will depend on the size of your team as well as the size of your program. It should include additional domain architects who may be engaged in projects or technical specialists within your company. Your EAs from your core group should explore this extended area for participants. Some key contributors will not be able to participate as core team members due to project commitments, lack of interest, or lack of availability. They'll contribute to the current state or some specific key strategic projects for the future state architecture. These resources are usually project or solution architects. Pull from the same domain category list as you did for the core. They might be business application or solutions experts or information and technology architects.

In the outermost group, you'll assemble contributors from an architecture community. This will include interested parties in the enterprise architecture program. Your cast will feature senior executives or corporate leadership as well as business strategy teams. You may line up some business management experts to strengthen your vantage point. There can be those who are involved in strategic planning at a corporate level. You might include some governance team members, depending on your governance structure. Add some IT leaders and IT business relationship or account managers, and consider your program portfolio managers. You may include some users who will participate from time to time as contributors or subject matter experts from various projects and the business. Get broad participation that affords a sense of ownership and credibility to the entire enterprise architecture process.

Search for Your Candidates

If you are not flush with EAs on your team, you can start with a search for potential candidates inside your organization. Can you find someone who is already an architect? Does that person work under a different title but still conduct architecture activities? If this doesn't describe your potential candidate, he or she might not fit your core team. Don't dismiss this person, as he or she might fill the role as an ally or a supporter of your architecture program. Keep this candidate in mind, especially if he or she is an architect. If you've found an architect, what type of architect? Is your candidate already skilled or playing the role of an EA? If not, consider the candidate's potential and whether he or she has the talent, the skill, or the desire to become an EA.

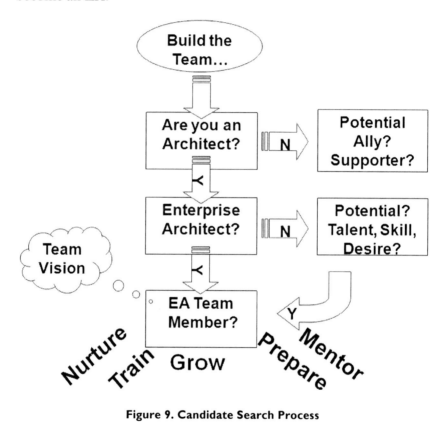

Figure 9. Candidate Search Process

If you answered an emphatic yes to that question, you've found a potential team member for your core EA group. You may need to nurture, train, grow, prepare, and mentor any potential architects for your team. The same may be true as you adjust and shape the team you assemble. Consider the main differences between an EA and a domain or project architect. The EA has very broad knowledge and diverse experience versus deep subject knowledge. EAs possess premium soft skills as well as a big-picture mindset versus attention to detail on a project-focused target. They have varied business knowledge and are driven toward long-term goals.

What are the signs and potential that you have found a candidate for your architecture pool? Who are the gems? Look at people that you would consider big conceptual thinkers or great relaters and how well they get along with the individuals in business and IT. Ask more questions, including the following:

> Are they astute politicians? Can they negotiate their way around the delicate and controversial issues?
> Are they boardroom friendly?
> Are you cautious to bring them to meetings, or are they the first people you think of as partners who are supportive and can contribute?
> Are they already strong leaders in the group they work in?
> Are they sharp strategists? Have they put together strategies for the work they already do or on the projects they have completed?
> Are they worldly communicators?
> Do they understand the big picture of the enterprise well?
> Are they culturally savvy? Do they understand the demographics within your company?
> Are they able to use their political and cultural skills to advance their purpose?

Practicing architects can recognize a good architect quickly, so consider asking those that you've already got on your team whether they can see potential around them. Look at your candidates' career background. Have they demonstrated a path of vision and commonality to the architecture field before? Who has a passion for transformational change and standardization for your organization? In your conversation with your team, let them know you are looking for people who focus on meeting objectives, keep their eye on the business, and are able to give good whiteboard. You are seeking out the self-confident modelers who are also politically astute and knowledgeable without being aggressive or obnoxious.

Your Mining Expedition

When searching for architect gold, the most critical component is talent. Identify the potential architect's talents that you note as a gap in your team. Seek latent or unrecognized skills that may be grown with some experience or mentoring. Do the candidate's current skills fit within the team you envision? If you are seeking to fill an enterprise architecture team, remember this is a separate set of skills than those your project architectures or your domain architectures demand.

Here are more questions you should ask/answer:

➢ Are your prospects capable of building the needed skills?

➢ Are they virtual team candidates?

➢ Could they possibly assist your team if they are not part of your core team?

➢ Do they have the desire to act on one of the architecture teams or have a career in IT architecture?

➢ Do they share the enthusiasm for the big-picture vision?

➢ Do they have the desire to build or grow their needed skills?

➢ Are they resilient enough to endure an enterprise architecture journey?

➢ Are they competent in dealing with change?

Build Your Dream Team

Your building adventure starts with recruiting. Start by identifying the EAs or the go-to individuals. Who appears when there is a large problem, challenge, or opportunity? Engage them by soliciting ideas on such a team and gauge their interest and promising contributions. Do their talents meet your organizational mold and vision? To build your dream team, ensure that they have team participation skills, that they would be able to get along with the rest of the team, and that they want to be there. For the perfect mix, you're going to need a visionary, a leader, a contributor, a communicator, an analyst, a strategist, and a facilitator. Some individuals are multidimensional and possess more than one of these skills. One of these individuals might be you (the leader?).

Consider potential conflicts with those with very strong personalities but opposing opinions in the same areas of strength. Do you have multiple suitors who love to be in control of the presentation? Is there more than one master of the whiteboard? Do you have multiple souls who insist on creative author control over documents or who love to intensely debate the wording of decision statements? If you have the luxury of such a multitude of choices, make them wisely. These can be momentum killers, but they often are "features" of your team that you must learn to manage.

Make sure you cover all your bases both from the enterprise and the domain perspectives. Establish clear leadership on your team. You need to confirm a unified vision and strategy and install and communicate team collaboration and decision models to the team. You'll also need to identify leaders and position leaders in training. If you are considering a potential leader, determine whether he or she has done this before.

Determine the growth areas and prospects for your team. Think about the work to be done and the opportunities. Consider who is available and match these adept souls with the work you have. Envision the work as matched to the team member as best you can. Planning ahead for placing team members together will prove invaluable in the long run if you have great bench strength from which to draw. The team needs to evolve over time; hence, people will migrate in and out over the long term. Your success depends on your ability to define core roles and skills as well as the core leadership in a crystallized fashion.

Grow Your Crop of EAs

So how do you go about cultivating EAs? First, review the work that needs to be done on your enterprise architecture plan. You might call this the development work. It is what you need to do to develop the architecture. Match the architectural talent and skills to the tasks and activities at hand as best you can. You ultimately won't want to waste any team member's skill or expertise, or he or she will quickly become bored and disengaged. Make sure that everybody who will be engaged is truly passionate about being engaged.

There will be growth projects for eager individuals to ramp up their skills. Consider resources that have done tasks similar to the ones you require. Assign the task as well as a suitable mentor to allow the protégé to gain experience.

As you examine the roles, responsibilities, and the work to be done, consider the fit within the team versus what the team needs to accomplish. Observe the potential gaps between the current roles and the responsibilities of your resources and discover which targets are realistically reachable. Consider the growth opportunities that exist for the team. When cultivating EAs, there is a skill area that you will need to grow the most, as previously highlighted throughout this book. These are areas of leadership, politics, culture, communication, and organizational behavior.

Plan Your Team's Workload

Review the work that needs to be done within the architecture team. It can be segmented and described as the planning, development, implementation, and then management of the enterprise architecture. The division of this work is crucial in both accomplishing your goals for the program as well as matching resources against the work in relation to their experience. At this point, a match between the skills you need on your team to complete the work against what you will need to get done is of value.

Recall the elliptical diagram of skills required as an EA. Now we'll apply the work to be done against the activities you may assign to give more junior architects the chance to grow. If you are reading this book and you are the junior architect or one who wants to experience all that you will need to do to become diverse in your career, do what you can to get working on these activities. All areas will need to eventually become actionable. It will take a broad team much time to get it completed, but if it is properly prioritized and the team is adequately assigned, it can become a reality.

The activity of planning the work to be done is taken on by those who already have enterprise architecture experience. This is an area you'll need to supplement if it does not exist in your organization. An external coach or mentor fits well in this area to get you started. What do you do if you really want to get more growth in the area of enterprise architecture at your organization but your team is somewhat junior? There are many ways these less experienced members can participate on the team to gain experience and expand your depth chart.

Grow Technical Skills

Consider the ellipse of skills ranging from technical to soft skills when searching for growth areas. Starting from the outer ring of technical expertise, there are several activities you can delegate to help someone become skilled as an architect practitioner. In the area of technical growth, assign work on current state deliverables such as the models or some of the inventories. Allow the apprentices to participate in the gap analysis exercises to stretch their analysis skills and learn how to judge between the current and target state. Assign repository updates for the artifacts and modeling exercises on some of the current components you need to see before planning the target state. It will be easier to learn both of these skills on something that is in existence and less abstract than teaching on something that is not present. Assign a task in metrics collection and analysis of the metrics to enable the student to gain technical skills from a different perspective.

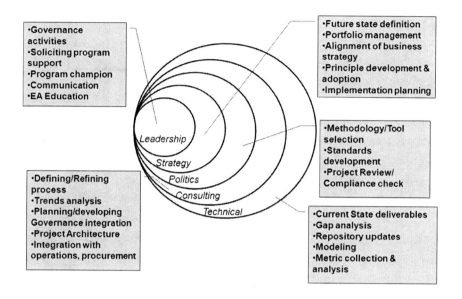

Figure 10. Growth Assignments

Foster Consulting Skills

Consider the skill area of consulting as an architect. There are many opportunities for you to behave as a consultant within your IT department, with the business users and executives, and potentially with customers or vendors.

Acting as a consultant, you'll find there are various growth areas. In the area of gaining domain knowledge, you'll need to expand some solicitation techniques. You'll also need to become skilled in the areas of negotiation and feedback, as you will be finding middle ground with various groups in the areas of standards and potential solutions. You are going to have to strive to build good relationships while participating in these various activities as well as determine the feasibility of any implementations or technology you plan to implement.

You are going to provide advice on a regular basis to various team mentees as well as business people. You'll need to learn to influence people rather than use authority to direct them. You'll need to figure out how to get commitment for decisions by stakeholders, whether they are IT team members or representatives from the business areas. If you have previous experience as a systems or a technical analyst, you may have to consider how to stretch this experience where we treat our subject matter expects as our clients.

Take on some activities in the areas of defining and refining business processes. You may help the business define a process in written terms or model it for them or with them. You may not be asked to go away and do the work for them, but to work with them. If you are doing the models for them, you'll learn a lot by exercising a feedback loop mechanism and employing your great listening skills. You may analyze information from a trend-analysis view of the business. This may include trends inside the business environment, the competitive landscape, and their internal business processes. You may also help with the planning and development of governance integration within your company. This may be done by asking you to review projects that have been submitted for governance reviews in advance of the review and passing on your feedback to more senior team members. You may also be allowed to attend these meetings as an observer or as a scribe.

You may work within the structure of a project architecture where you are able to consult with project team members and business team members. Projects typically ask for architecture involvement when they need modeling done, solutions crafted, decisions made, and prototypes built. You might assist with integration of procedures with the operations department and possibly even the procurement of components, if the solutions you are putting together are to be procured from a vendor. There is much research and preparation work to be done when a proof-of-concept activity is planned.

Foster Political Skills

It is somewhat of a stretch to easily isolate growth areas in the area of political skills. All architects need to have these skills if they are going to advance in their careers of architecture, and most learning opportunities will come through observation and identification during debriefing sessions with senior architects. Architecture is change, and change is political, no matter which company you work in or the department, executive, or external stimuli that initiate it. Consider the area of politics within the IT community alone. A contentious issue most architects will experience might be the selection of the methodology and tools to be used within the architecture team. The process, approach, and framework are common, but most times these are selected before most of the team and less experienced staff become involved.

As you gain more experience as a practitioner, you'll morph from being an observer in many meetings and discussions to an active participant. As you gain confidence and knowledge, you may take on a leadership role and that of a decision maker. This will most likely be the most important area on an architecture team, and you should observe those who have gone before you. Take their lead to learn which situations they avoid or back down from. You might also help various IT teams with standards development, which will be a great learning experience. This activity may include negotiating with and facilitating groups when exploring the standards you need to set for your solution and technical environments.

If you're involved in governance, you'll learn some of the most important political lessons for an EA. Project reviews and architecture compliance checks are often part of the enterprise architecture, and there is much to be learned from these reviews. You'll see how the most experienced architects recommend that the teams proceed, and you'll witness some rigor and process in and around decision making. The EA is involved in standardization of methodologies and tools as well as standards and project reviews: all require a very skilled politician to handle some of the very hot opinions that you'll encounter in the different teams that you'll work with and observe.

In addition, you will need to learn how to wordsmith responses. Your articulation skills among management and with those resistant to change will have to be very delicate. Also, you'll need to consider those in the operational areas. Many have become married to technology, as it has been their identity and badge of honor for years.

You have to know when to take things offline and to respond later to keep things moving when it comes to having conversations and decisions that are getting made.

You'll also need to put limits on the solution and make sure the context is set very carefully in meetings and on projects. You'll have to be aware of political situations that exist before stepping into them. You'll want to have a good understanding and knowledge of the key stakeholders and how they interrelate across your organization's other projects and divisions in your company. You'll also want a solid understanding of personal and business objectives of the various stakeholders. Understanding what each person truly wants and being able to see and sense what it is that they are driving for as decisions are getting made is just an invaluable skill.

Mature Strategy Skills

Moving farther from your comfort zone and toward the pinnacles of enterprise architecture, you'll need to become a very good strategist. As an architect, you'll have to become advanced to work in the capacity of these key strategy areas:

- ➢ Future state definition
- ➢ Portfolio management
- ➢ Alignment of the business strategy with the IT strategy
- ➢ Principle development and adoption
- ➢ Implementation and migration planning

In the area of future state definition, participating inside a team will give you a vast amount of experience. You might see an awful lot of opportunity as a junior architect or as a practitioner tasked with work in the portfolio management area. You'll be required to inventory your organization's IT assets. You'll get involved in planning and estimating for future IT projects and improvements at your company.

You'll do this by either reviewing the current asset list or building the current one from scratch if it does not exist. You'll list the assets in your infrastructure and then move toward the project and initiative areas. This will require interviews and communication with all IT areas on what is in flight and planned for the upcoming year. Upon this, you'll layer new or backlogged requests from the business areas.

The most experienced of technology architects will recommend the upgrades and replacements most in need, and it will be up to the EAs and senior management right up to the CIO to provide an IT position on what should be scheduled for the upcoming year. In a full-scale portfolio management exercise, ranking, estimation, and costing may be required. As a contributor and a student of strategy, take these tasks and do your best to understand and learn the process. Alignment of the business strategy is typically reserved for those in the area of enterprise architecture, but you will learn a vast amount if you are fortunate enough to become an observer or participant in the modeling. Principle development and adoption is something that's common, if not a mainstay in the enterprise architecture program. Working on selection or development of such broad goals will provide a great learning platform.

Another area for strategy growth is in implementation planning. As your team tries to make your architecture actionable, you can gain great experience while figuring out how to put solutions into place. Pay close attention to the order in which the most senior architects prescribe that the implementation should occur. Most often, they'll take the large stone, medium stone, small stone, sand, water approach. Large stones, such as major network upgrades or entire platform changes, are placed into the schedule first. In this pile, you'll find enterprise-sized application and project initiatives.

Most corporations don't plan for more than one or two large projects in a year. The next layer will be some medium-sized projects, such as technology upgrades, migrations, or second and subsequent releases of projects. Some custom projects fit into this space, and companies will try to minimize the number of these in a year to fewer than three, depending on company decentralization. Small enhancements, mini-projects, and regular system maintenance activities should follow.

Build Leadership Skills

*Leaders are made, they are not born. They are made by hard effort, which is
the price which all of us must pay to achieve any goal that is worthwhile.*
—Vince Lombardi

For you to become a great leader, you will need the opportunity to
practice. Look all around you—it is abundant. As your leadership
skills improve, you will see great career opportunities. In a way, any
person who wears the title of architect is in fact already a leader. You
may demonstrate leadership through your work, your statements,
your decisions, or your participation in various corporate activities. If
you get the opportunity to participate in some of the governance
activities, you may demonstrate great leadership abilities and skills as
an active participant. Otherwise, as an observer, show your keen
interest in the process and potential for the future.

As an architect, you must solicit support for the program; this
will be asked of you when joining the team. Learn by fully understanding the vision to carry it forward. Ask questions if you must.
You'll have to solicit support from business areas as well as other IT
members and managers. As an EA in training, you may do this in
very small ways, but you should be aware of your need to do it.
Become a program champion even when you might not feel like it.
Face it—making change and participating on large initiatives that may
take years to demonstrate value are not always uplifting activities. But
if you believe in the strategic vision for your team and for your
organization's architecture, you can affect the smaller portions of the
projects and domains you are working on.

As a leader, you will get great experience in communication, both
in written documents and with various artifacts you need to produce.
You'll grow in the area of presenting and communicating with other
groups with respect to visions, viewpoints, and decisions. You can
assist in the preparation of documents or you might be asked to
author chunks of some of the larger deliverables. As you gain
experience as a leader, you may be asked to educate or mentor co-
workers about the enterprise architecture program. A perfect exercise

in growth for the budding EA is to give "lunch and learn" seminars on the enterprise itself. By answering questions and replaying your take on the vision, you can develop confidence and gain respect as a leader.

You'll become a mentor and probably were always known to others in this way. You'll show a softer side by empathizing and understanding what the various groups' needs, feelings, and emotions are with respect to ownership of solutions and the standards in technology. You need to be a change agent, a skill tightly bound with leadership. You are participating in a series of activities that cause change, so you need to be skilled at making it happen and in moving it forward. You are going to have to know and demonstrate how the features, functions, and business priorities rank for a specific architecture solution.

You'll need to solicit input and get the information necessary to formulate a solution. As this information forms the basis of the solution, think in terms of agreements, tasks, and statements of work. If you are going to be working with business people, establish agreements on various decisions. You'll have to establish a collaborative relationship with team members and give your undivided attention to both the technology and business problem as well as the relationships with stakeholders.

It is critical for you to understand what the developers want and actually need from the architecture. By producing documentation that describes standards, you are shaping what they will develop. There are some things you can do to nurture your communication skills. Start with some of the knowledge areas you will impart to each group of stakeholders. They need to understand how the architecture meets their requirements. You'll need to create customized views of the architectures that are directed at different groups so they may understand and accept them.

Your presentation and facilitation skills will need to be sharp, and you'll want to explore the suggestion of adapting your view for each group. No matter your audience, any architect who wants to communicate effectively must know how to model. One of the main jobs of an architect is communicating the architecture, and you must become the solutions champion. If there is bad news to share, it will be your job to do so, so you'll need to gain skills in that area. You'll need to share this news as early as possible while being very aware of the needs of your target audience.

Speaking of your audience, you'll need to study those whom you will prepare for and deliver to. You'll need to find a way of being very objective with the news and focus on the process, not on the people themselves or lay any kind of blame. You are going to have to provide a solution and options to get stakeholders to make a choice. People like to have options, and they want to clearly know what their choices are as well as the benefits and the drawbacks of each. Provide or suggest the next steps and recommendations when circumstances warrant it.

You'll gain more communication skills when communicating the architecture, selling the vision, and keeping it alive in the face of challenges your team faces. Consider taking one perspective for each audience, adapting it, and developing others for presentation to small groups. You'll gain the ability to adapt your leadership and communications style to fit your audience. You'll also expand your modeling style and perspective depending on your audience. Choose whatever aids you need to be effective. This might be audio, visual, telephone messages, meetings, e-mail, or whatever it takes to be able to communicate—both the good and the bad.

There are many ways in which you can mentor as the leader. You'll need to articulate a strategic vision among your team. Architects are leaders who make things happen and who are focused on the big picture. You'll act as coaches of project teams and architecture groups and be champions of the program. You may mentor your team members or find suitable mentors for them. As the leader, you possess traits of inspiration and motivate others. You are committed, dedicated, and passionate toward the organization as well as the program. You'll create a shared purpose, vision, and direction within your team, and you will strive to position team members to contribute. Your vision and trust in your team will allow you to actively encourage the participation of all affected. You'll take good ideas from everyone and try to make them a part of a cohesive whole.

When leading groups and teams to understand the architecture, you'll share its values and its reasons. You'll also be responsible for architecture decision making. Leaders contribute to all governance initiatives in and around IT as well as the architecture. Show your great sense of community. Be open to learning and help others learn as well. Use your diversity in your perspectives to be creative in your solutions. As a leader, you'll need to learn how to influence others without authority because you are not management. You'll need to keep relevant people informed while building your network.

Achieve your vision by making compelling presentations about the architecture to a broad base of people. Listen to your audience while gathering their feedback. Consider multiple viewpoints to understand all parties. Show patience while being the focal point of change, as it is always a challenging endeavor. You'll need resilience and sensitivity to the powerful forces that resist change while trying to advocate it. Establishing good working relationships around your company is critical, as is trying to understand and tactfully get close to the leaders. Seek out those in the know in the operational and development areas, as they will be paramount to your success. Having some sort of organizational and cultural sensitivity is also a benefit in this area.

When You Are the Mentor

To prepare architects to join your team, they will need to be trained, oriented, and mentored. Develop a professional development plan (PDP) for all architects so that they may focus on short- and long-term goals that will benefit both themselves and the company. See www.zoomfactorbook.com/book-resources for more information. Training in communication and in the areas of your organization's business process and industry vertical will be necessary. You'll also need to prepare an orientation to the organization (if one does not already exist) and to your team. They'll need a primer on organizational politics and briefings about key stakeholders. You'll also need to mentor and hold some team-building exercises in the area of process strategy.

When mentoring your architects, let them come to you first. Mentoring sessions should be something you hold privately between yourself and the architects. Keep your conversations positive and professional: your job is to elevate architects to new levels. Help the architects leverage their strengths and acknowledge their weaknesses. Keep an even balance between the planned goals for the architects within their PDPs and what you need to achieve on your team. Be sure to promote a balanced life between the architects' long-term career goals and their lives. Be careful to uphold realistic goals for the architects in terms of their career path and their salary expectations. Above all, be knowledgeable about the subjects on which you mentor. If you need help, seek it either internally from a colleague who has the facts or externally from a coach.

Get your students assigned to business areas so they can gain deeper knowledge. Acquiring some broad-based skills in each of the business areas is paramount to their success. Discuss political and cultural concerns and recommendations with the architects. Allowing them to shadow other architects during governance activities is a great way for them to gain knowledge about the whole process. Give them the experience that they need, assign work to them that will challenge and stretch them, and assess them along the way. Focus areas should be in the current architecture when they are most junior. Give them communication tasks such as delivery of a presentation within your team as a start, branching out to the rest of IT, and finally to the business. This will make them comfortable. Give them some tasks in the area of portfolio management as well as some activities within the development of the enterprise architecture plan.

How Do We Engage Architects?

How does a project team or manager decide to engage an architect for a project, decision, or some other work? Articulating this will benefit all who wish to use your services in a harmonious manner. Engagements may come from a request from project managers to have an architect position filled within their team. This can be tricky in that most project managers want a full-time architect to reduce their risks.

It should be up to the resource managers for architects or the architects themselves to assess how much of their involvement the project will require. If your organization is following an RUP, architects will be heavily involved through the inception and elaboration phases and will be greatly reduced through construction and transition. Consider involvement in terms of a sliding scale from top to bottom or from high to low from inception through transition.

Other terms of engagement may stem from discovery as teams make suggestions or observations during their normal course of work. The team may discover that other IT resources may need an architect by consultation. The CIO may also have a special project where an architect is identified. Through portfolio management analysis, each project may determine a set amount of architecture resource time to be applied to the project.

An architecture review board (ARB) needs to be in place to review architecture change decisions on a regular basis. Typically, the ARB will meet monthly to discuss any major decisions that are put forward. The ARB may be comprised of IT leaders or include business leaders where an enterprise or organization is very mature. Other processes required to engage architects may be the change advisory board for large projects and infrastructure. Change advisory boards review major changes applied on a weekly basis as part of a regular change management process or release management process when the organization follows the ITIL method. It is crucial that the EA receives an itinerary in advance and have optional attendance. Express invitation works best in this application of the EA's time.

A final mention of engagement for architects may come through the transition plan or through the enterprise architecture planning process itself. Depending on the structure of an enterprise architecture team at an organization, the chief architect or EA may request that individual domain architects research, develop, and provide input to the enterprise architecture plan. The EA will be involved and committed to create the transition plan from the current state to the target state architecture. The domain architects will be responsible for documenting current architecture portfolio contributions. During target state planning, the same architects may be invited to provide valuable input.

Be on the Lookout for Talent

There are a few other critical points to remember—always be on the lookout for latent and emerging talent. Your architecture team will evolve, and so will the enterprise architecture at your organization. Choose your team members very carefully. Keep your core enterprise architecture team and your architecture team small. Lend your skills to create the best mix and leverage the strengths from each of your team members. Even if a resource can't be a permanent team member, he or she may join for specific reasons on a limited basis. Know that the best enterprise architecture teams are often virtual in nature.

Soft skills are much more essential to the enterprise architecture team's success than technical skills. The team should evolve over time. Build teams suited to the tasks at hand and set goals for skill development at each phase. Set deadlines when you assign the task as well as some concrete deliverables, and then monitor carefully.

Last but not least, remember that relationships matter more than just about anything else. Know the political connections within and in between people. Study them, learn from them, and then benefit from them. It will take a steady-handed leader to succeed in this area.

Zoom In—Action Steps You Need to Succeed

Hiring or assembling your team will be one of the most critical activities that you undertake. Here are a few suggestions to find the key skills and background that you will need:

- ☐ Ensure that you have a clear budget and a purpose for the role.
- ☐ Have firm descriptions of the role as well as planned projects and initial assignments when you interview candidates. Know available career paths within your firm if they

exist. Use the sample one from the website resources, www.zoomfactorbook.com/book-resources, or search one of the popular job sites for an example that suits your purpose.

☐ To start a program from scratch, at minimum search for a solution architect, a data architect, and a technology architect who will work at the enterprise level.

☐ Formulate a first set of questions before initiating your interviews and invite a second person to get plenty of perspective. Ask for the invites' definition of architecture and an account of some of the architecture projects they've completed in the past.

☐ Find out what it is they want out of their career. Determine whether they are looking for position advancement, a structured path leading upward, or just looking for new and more exciting work.

☐ Ascertain their background to determine their capabilities for doing your architecture work.

☐ Establish their background in the area of process and methodologies. It is critical that architects know how one wraps process around technology and solutions, as well as how to document them.

☐ Discover their experience in building models and prototypes. They should recount situations in which they tested and found proof of technology solutions before they made recommendations.

☐ Ask them about their background in mentoring technical resources such as operations or application services staff and database analysts.

☐ Find out what kind of experience they have in creating and delivering presentations or programs for educating others.

☐ Inquire about the mentoring they have received. Find out whether it was from a third party such as a coach or trainer or from a more senior resource in their own firm.

- ☐ Use scenario-based inquiries. Ask for examples of some of the more difficult or creative architectures they've created, and ask them to describe the challenges they faced.
- ☐ If it is important to you, determine what certifications they hold and how they went about getting them. Did they challenge an exam or take the training prior to it?
- ☐ Ask them about prior architecture training.
- ☐ Ask about architecture projects they suggested and projects that never made it off the ground.
- ☐ How well-versed are the candidates in general business knowledge, consulting skills, and soft skills? If the architect is to take a role as a domain or project architect, do the candidates appear to have the ability to lead and provide assistance and support to a project manager?
- ☐ Establish the extent of experience they have in interactions with business executives and gathering requirements from them.
- ☐ Determine their history in formulating or contributing to an enterprise architecture plan.
- ☐ Learn about their strategic planning background, and ask about their relationship to their past CIO.
- ☐ Determine the roles they played and the amount of direct contact they have had with C-level executives.
- ☐ Be sure to ask about their architecture governance experiences. Determine whether they helped to evolve the process in their current role or just know the definition.
- ☐ Get a description of the roles they played in the past. Ask about their portfolio management experience and their role in denying or accepting the use of non-standard technologies.
- ☐ What kind of changes did they make to alter the current standard set at their organization?

Interesting facts about their background might include the various methodologies and procedures they used. Be sure to determine whether they are able to distinguish between a framework and methodology or approach used to fill it.

Delicately scrutinize their experience in leadership, politics, and culture while obtaining other answers. They should identify areas such as the ease of transition or migration, the availability of standards, as well as resources with those types of skills. An architect who understands all of these things is looking at the big picture and is somebody who will be valuable to your team.

Zoom Out—Big-Picture Concepts

Group dynamics apply when growing and establishing your team. You should consider traditional team-building exercises, but your enterprise architecture team will come from a unique breed of talented individuals. Here are some things you may want to keep in mind to grow your team:

☐ Keep in mind that you have people with an extreme amount of talent, and your adventure may be different than that of other IT managers in your organization. They may struggle with getting team members motivated, while you may need to work on tempering enthusiasm for change the organization may not be ready for.

☐ Your team may struggle with letting go of old tasks and responsibilities from their previous roles. Be patient and firm and provide the guidance and support they need to sever unnecessary drags on their time.

☐ If you faced a healthy selection pool from which to choose and chose your team well, you will have fewer challenges than if you had to settle with those who existed in these roles before you became the leader.

☐ Group dynamics will require that you engage in some of the most basic of activities when getting to know your team. Activities such as exercises geared toward getting to know each other and reducing friction that may exist are always time well spent.

☐ Establish the rules of the road between the group members and be patient while order and relationships are established.

☐ As the group adjusts, it will become able to operate as a well-oiled machine and achieve the vision you have created.

☐ Take the time to study models of group development other than the example of forming, norming, storming, and performing established by Bruce Tuckman in 1965.

☐ Find out which activities your team members like and dislike. Find out which soft skills you want them to develop and the ones they want to work on.

☐ Ensure you are in a position to back your team members. They will go through the grueling task of presenting contentious positions, and your support is critical to their development and confidence.

☐ Your team is just like any other—you must plan for growth and study the ways and methods for doing so in a positive and facilitated manner.

Part V:
Achieving Architecture Altitude

In this part

- Chapter 18: Become a Master Strategist
- Chapter 19: Ignite Your Entrepreneurial Spirit
- Chapter 20: Be the Change Master
- Chapter 21: Get Your IT Career in Gear

Part V includes topics and specific activities, such as strategic planning and fostering alignment between business and IT, and it discusses the various components in the alignment process. This part also shares techniques that will help you prove quality in the architecture through metrics and portfolio planning. It also focuses on the key business knowledge areas you must strive to learn to gain the respect of and to work alongside business experts. The topics of the EA as a master of change and the next steps an architect may take to gain even more expertise close out the book.

CHAPTER 18:
BECOME A MASTER STRATEGIST

A strategy delineates a territory in which a company seeks to be unique
– Michael Porter

The goal of this book is to outline the skills and knowledge you need to achieve architect "altitude." You may achieve altitude by taking multiple perspectives on the task at hand. Architecture altitude is the culmination of the skills, knowledge, processes, and techniques you need to position yourself in your career, creating great successes for both you and your business. The more perspectives you acquire, the faster and more efficiently you move. I believe that architecture altitude applies to zooming out to get broader perspectives so that you can zoom back in, zeroing in on the details more efficiently and more effectively. This book was written from the five perspectives you need to reach the ultimate reach the destination of excellence as an EA!

This step addresses the highest levels of knowledge you'll need to get to the top of your career. You may notice that this step is more about the business than technology, which is where your career will head as an EA. One of the final skills you'll need to master as an EA is in the area of strategy. You need to orchestrate change and apply and transition these strategies to your target state. Turning your vision into reality will allow you to see the business community prosper from your efforts. The outstanding EA is a scholar in the area of strategic growth and thrives on executing the business strategy through technology. You'll understand, evaluate, and select the best technology opportunities within a strategic plan for IT while striving for the utmost quality in the enterprise architecture that is built for agility.

Earlier chapters addressed many keys, skills, and traits you'll need to accelerate your career. Revisit the order in which these were introduced—a baseline foundation in technical skills and experience, core and critical architecture processes, human factors and soft skills, and most recently, the perspectives you'll need to have an all-encompassing view of the enterprise. If the first four steps resonated with you and you possess these traits and skills, you are at an important juncture in your career. You are likely ready and able to serve as the chief architect or lead EA of your company. Or you might assume an EA role responsible for a subsidiary company, a business vertical division, or some other similar organizational area. Regardless of the status of your career, the chief architect is allocated more decision-making responsibility, more strategic-planning opportunities, and greater involvement in governance activities.

You may or may not yet act in an official leadership role as the director of your team, and you may or may not have staff responsibilities: this will depend solely on the culture, style, and management structure of your organization. In any case, you have likely arrived at the highest IT position in your company next to the CIO and will need to show leadership qualities. You may have joined a purely strategic team that did not evolve from the ranks of IT. If you've landed in the role of the CTO, this is characteristically an executive position with visionary responsibilities and weekly touches with the executives.

Why Is Strategy Important to the EA?

Systemic issues between IT departments and their business organizations stem from the absence of shared articulated business strategies and goals. This may be due to the perception of IT's role or treating the department purely as a cost center. It is difficult to grasp how a business believes that IT can deliver systems of value and financial assets for the organization without sharing strategy and goals. Nevertheless, this behavior is all too common in many traditional companies, and the same problems ensue if the leaders in an IT organization won't share strategy with executives or their staff. The situation improves when IT shows the business acumen and leadership needed to adequately plan the IT strategies in line with business strategies.

Unfortunately, clearly defined enterprise architecture strategies, frameworks, and/or strategy development methodologies may still be absent in your organization. The steps in any strategic-planning activity are intertwined with enterprise architecture, especially those that represent growth activities at your company. This makes it critical that the EA knows about strategic planning and exerts effort to fully understand the goals and intentions of the executives and business areas.

A clearly articulated business strategy is the catalyst for the IT strategy and drives the development of the enterprise architecture. How will you know what your framework should include if you don't know the business drivers or goals? In my experience as a coach, one of the most common things experienced is that it is difficult to get information about the business strategy. Many will claim they know what it is, but that it just hasn't been documented. The problem with many who believe they "know" the strategy is that confusion and conflicts arise from misconceptions in the various business areas. Challenges then trickle down to the IT groups trying to analyze requirements.

As the EA, you'll need to get something about the strategy in writing. Even better, you might get involved in the strategic planning activities, or gather what many "know" about the strategy and validate it. Resolve any conflicts or ambiguities. Get priorities on paper. If you use the backward chaining approach in starting from where you want to end up and document what you know for sure, it will be easier to gather information from others. Groups work well in brainstorming situations, especially when asking for opinions on what they believe current strategies include. Facilitate the activity, keep them focused on the core business strategy alone, and then put your effort toward validation. These actions will take a lot of effort and intensify the political element, but this is an improvement over moving forward with what everyone thinks are foregone conclusions about the strategies in play.

You can't realistically take a reactive approach to strategic planning. It is too solution-based and offers little aid to true alignment with the business strategies. You cannot adequately employ architecture to solve current problems in the short term. If we use it only to cover our weaknesses or meet management's initiative of the moment, we lose the benefits of the planning effect. We can't effectively direct and guide the development of strategic solutions as we react to deficiencies and view everything from a current state perspective.

A more proactive approach allows us to plan for the future and escape the problem-solving cycle. Our thinking about solutions and alignment for the business becomes simplified when we are able to zoom out and see the big picture. We can clarify the vision and direction we wish to take when we come from a position of future state and see the path backward through our migration. Consensus is much easier to obtain when we have the time and space to consider many options and various strategies to get to where we believe we want to go.

Strategic planning is important and allows you to focus on the company's future by aligning your plans within IT to achieve a position of balance and control. By using this approach, you may build better relationships with the business and achieve commitment to your strategic road maps. If you strive to enable desired business capabilities and prevent problems, risks, and crises as the EA, you will give your business clients what they strive for, desire, and need.

Your Role as the EA Strategist

As an EA focused on excellence, you'll exhibit value-centered thinking. You'll lead your teams to alignment between the strategy and the architecture. You'll also have a high desire to make your company better. Your personal traits will include humility, and you'll be self-actualized and not seek ego-building projects. By the time you arrive at this stage in your career, realization of the architecture is what you strive for most. You'll enjoy the strategic nature of your job more than most other activities, and team activity will be your daily boost.

So how will you know when you've arrived? How will you know you've succeeded as an EA and with your architecture program? You'll start to see a move toward business requests for the architecture assets. They'll start with your supportive CIO. People will request to see models and documents and use them for their presentations. Requests will emerge to update your frameworks, models, and artifacts based on changes the business has made. Business leaders will appear and say, "Hey, are you thinking about this and how it might affect the plan?" If you are balking at this possibility, I've seen it happen in less than one year's time with some of most challenging industries in which I have worked.

The CIO might actually refer to some of the key enterprise architecture frameworks when he's running a town hall meeting or maybe even executive meetings. You may have heard that using some architecture terminology around exec types is suicide, but I'm supposing that the day will arrive when it's accepted. Gently forge your way ahead. The executives in mature organizations may favorably reference these frameworks and analysis tools in their internal communication. The trick is not to sell them as frameworks, or you will see eyes glaze over. Executives understand grids and matrices, but just be careful with labels! The secret lies in zooming in on strategy.

Your initial role as a strategist is to become involved in the planning process. Once you have a place at the table, hesitate before offering technical language and solutions. It is crucial that you understand the method and approach the team will take and the steps in which you should contribute. Your role is to prepare and bring innovation to meet their desired growth capabilities. You'll need to articulate and demonstrate how the right mix of technology and IT performance will maximize value for the business. Most often, you'll do this in conjunction with your CIO and IT management teams, portfolio management group, and project management offices. Strategic alignment is the largest EA contribution to the enterprise and organizational relationships as they meet technology.

Strategic Planning 101

To set a baseline for this chapter on strategic planning for the EA, let's visit the most elemental steps of strategic planning:

1. Business strategic planning
2. IT strategic planning
3. Enterprise architecture strategic planning

This is somewhat oversimplified. There are many inputs and outputs and some overlaps in process, so it is necessary to drill down a level. At each step, you must evaluate current performance, consider the growth options as well as the required imperatives, and then analyze and weigh each option's costs and values. The main components for the business strategy are the business drivers, goals, policies, and trends in the business arena. The approach includes several steps, which include an evaluation of the internal dynamics within the company, a review of external factors, and then blending both with the approach taken by management and the culture. The combination of these components makes up the critical elements for formulation of the business strategy.

IT strategic planning takes a slightly different approach. The business capabilities are required as input to the IT strategy. IT's imperative is to maintain the operational structure for the organization in addition to providing development and innovation allowing your company to compete and thrive in the market. To add this competitive edge, you must evaluate and keep pace with technology trends and apply them to your IT environment as best they fit strategic drivers and your enterprise architecture plan. The enterprise architecture strategy will take inputs from the IT strategy while also taking a high-level perspective on technology trends and the IT landscape, aligning all back to the business. This should provide prioritized value through a strategic road map or an enterprise architecture plan demonstrating a transition path. Road maps are all about executing strategy.

Confused? Let's break down each of the components to lay out the method for obtaining the information and doing the analysis.

Figure 11. Strategy Relationships

➤ The business strategy should address the business drivers, and illustrations might be to acquire lower cost materials, to remove a distribution link in the supply chain, or to acquire an international partner.

➤ The business drivers could include price competition, improving customer service, simplifying supply chain, or expanding into international markets, for example.

➤ The business capabilities needed in the future might be profitability measurement, electronic commerce, and an upcoming merger and acquisition.

➤ Technology strategy might focus on architected environments, increased speed of delivery of new capabilities and products, common shared services for infrastructure, and distribution services.

➤ Technology innovation trends might include Radio Frequency Identification (RFID) technologies, cloud computing, SOA, analytic software, and middleware consolidation.

> ➤ IT tactical groupings might include increased investment in storage, access, and accuracy of supplier information; focus on efficiency analytics; or support of electronic commerce in distribution technology.

> ➤ Enterprise architecture strategy might include improved governance of IT solutions, establishing portfolio management integration with architecture annual planning, and reducing the number of tools and methodologies for development and infrastructure.

Volumes have been written on the subject of strategic planning. I suggest you choose a few from the bookshelf, www.zoomfactorbook.com/bookshelf, and get reading if this topic is new to you. I need to call out a book entitled *Enterprise Architecture as a Strategy* by Jeannie Ross as one of the first places you should start.

The Business Strategy

If you need to search for a documented business strategy, it adds a layer of challenge to the IT strategic-planning stage. If this matches your situation, go on some exploration activities to see what already exists. Search for business plans or annual reports. Start your archeological expedition by trying to gain access to some of the executive reports or briefings. A great place to start is to ask the CIO for the strategy from his or her perspective. It should be traceable back to business drivers. If you are fortunate and already have a place at the strategy table, interact with the strategic players in your organization to get this information.

It would be helpful for you to understand the steps that the business goes through in developing its strategic plan. Strategic planning can take many shapes, forms, and approaches, and it is perhaps the simplest approach to give you some of the most common tools a business uses to set the context for assessing its current situation. Your business might start with some key known facts and assessment before starting its detailed analysis:

> What is the form of your business?
> Who are your main competitors, and what is their size relative to your company?
> What is your performance relative to a competitor of similar size?
> Are you satisfying your customers' needs? What could or should you be doing differently? What are they asking for?
> What is the pace of your business?

Some organizations have an in-house strategy team or may engage them to do perform the following activities as the basis for the strategic planning exercise:

> Benchmark your business by setting a baseline or finding a generally acceptable industry average for a business of your size.
> Measure costs, prices, production, overhead levels, marketing budgets, sales, and turnover.
> Rate products on a variety of factors with key performance indicators as your market dictates.
> Measure customer information by number, turnover, and satisfaction.
> Measure information about your workforce, including employees, their skills, and their knowledge, as well as outsourcing.
> Measure various aspects of management practices and expertise levels in sales, marketing, productivity, administration, finance, and distribution.
> Finally, financials will bear some of the heaviest scrutiny.

For various facets of the business, market, and external forces, you may apply some industry-accepted tools and practices to perform your analysis and assessment:

1. SWOT Analysis—Strengths, Weaknesses, Opportunities, and Threats:

This tool is one of the most common and assists the business to provide an honest and critical review of itself. Results are recorded in grid fashion. Strengths and weaknesses are normally internal functions of the business, while opportunities and threats are usually external factors. The intention is to figure out strategies to capitalize on your business's strengths while minimizing the effects of its weaknesses.

2. PESTEL Analysis—Politics, Economics, Social, Technology, Environmental, and Legal factors affecting your business.

This categorization of the external effects allows you to evaluate the most common issues your business faces. The political landscape may be such that various opportunities exist that you may wish to take advantage of. For example, the economic downtown of late has offered several stimuli that businesses should not ignore. The economics review should include banking and market issues, such as rates and various incentives for your supply of materials. As a society, it is an age of community and collaboration. Demographics of an aging workforce and pandemics have affected the markets in which we work, and your strategies must consider them.

Technology advances are always an area that both the business and IT must review, especially those that allow the company to compete, jump ahead of the competition, or even just keep on even par. The environment has never been a bigger concern than it is now, and in combination with the economic times, government, and political landscape, it creates both concerns as well as opportunities for businesses to improve their footprint. You may be in an industry forced to keep pace or drop out. As a final factor in PESTEL, assess the legal perspective. Whether regulatory changes to the environment or customer protection factors are in play, you may be sure that legal restrictions will be one of the leading considerations in business strategy each year.

Regulatory factors are a large group of related strategies and one of the biggest areas in which our architecture can speed agility in change.

3. A third tool worth mentioning is Porter's Five Forces Model.

    You can ask yourself the five questions of Porter's model before entering a strategy or about your existing business. The factors include the threat of entry by competitors and what you need to do to keep the cost of entry high for your competitors, the power of buyers in your market, the power of your suppliers, the threat of substitutes, and the competitive landscape for your products and market.

You can read more about SWOT, PEST (a shortened version or PESTEL), and Porter's at my decision-making information site at www.decide-guide.com/models/.

Your business resources will often start with an external view, later applying the key focal areas they find relevant to their internal analysis. They might address external and internal forces in tandem as they review each external point with a comparison of in-house practices. Know that there is no right or wrong method for doing strategic analysis, and the method will depend on the background and experience of the strategic players in your organization. External forces are what drive the business strategy the hardest and typically consume the most analysis. These are items like the financial and economic landscape as well as your customers, partners, and suppliers.

External perspectives will include a review of the industry environment and a breakdown for each market. The review might expand to consider the various markets your company touches and a review of your distribution partners or suppliers. For each area addressed, concentrate on growth areas, declines, and flat areas. Where possible, try to join the business to evaluate the customer, and evaluate and determine their changes and needs. Look at various business areas or departments within your organization, being aware of how your business is changing. Consider all of these context reviews from both a macro and micro perspective. If you have some knowledge in the area of business or economics, apply it. Look at what the trends and waves are within your business sector, and then within each of your departments, cost centers, and profit centers, and get into the details.

The business should strive to remain at the minimum competitive level in almost all capacities and capabilities. You will also want to be a differentiator in areas in which you are able to dominate in the marketplace and advance with your unique selling position as a company. Your tagline might include a position as an innovative company, a premier service company, or a price-savvy competitor. You should know the biggest risks your company faces. I once sat down with the president of a multibillion dollar company and asked what kept him up at night. He was quick to respond that he was always aware of the five biggest risks he faced every day and what he was doing to manage them. You should know this too, both from a business standpoint and from an IT and EA perspective.

So what do you do if all of this analysis isn't available to you? If possible, find an EA-friendly ally in the business, and use your ally to help you validate what you are able to uncover. At a bare minimum, you will want to get at least three key business drivers: for the customer, for the corporation, and for IT. You should model a set of business capabilities that you want to maintain and build within your company. There will likely be a need for some kind of corporate vision or strategy statements and the approach that your management wants to take. Stemming from this will be a list of your key business goals and drivers.

Business strategies are born out of improvements to existing operations as mechanisms of internal growth or through external methods. These are often achieved through mergers and acquisition of other companies, diversification into new products or markets, and collaboration or partnership with other firms. Joint ventures and partnerships in both the product and supply sides of your business are also common. All strategies will translate directly to key business imperatives. Examples of such drivers might be the desire to reduce costs or extend customer service or any other variety of organizational goals.

Ultimately, you discovered a nicely organized existing document that encompasses all of the business strategy. More realistically, you will need to gather pieces from various sources, and you may not be able to get anything at all. You will then have to note it yourself or with your team. Throughout this process, keep your ears open. What things are being discussed by the business? What do you hear often? What does your business seem to be studying? A great source of information is simply a list of the various projects the business is involved in. Something just as simple as an executive meeting agenda may provide hints to you that can prove valuable.

The IT Strategy

The business strategy will drive the IT strategy, and of course, the IT strategy needs to drive the architecture strategy. IT maintains various support functions and operations to keep the lights on and keep your infrastructure healthy. These functions and initiatives to sustain them will form the basis for the list of your IT imperatives. If you are using the strategy of EPfM as a means of managing your IT investments, you'll now see a convergence between strategy and all that was addressed earlier related to road maps and perspectives. The IT strategic plan should be a collaboration between EAs and IT leaders, and should overlap some facets of the enterprise architecture plan. The review of current and upcoming technology industry trends is just one example. Realistically,

To create this plan, you'll use as input the business strategy and drivers. You'll filter the various strategies and match them with your IT organizational capabilities, budgets, and the longer-term enterprise architecture road map to plot out your short-term and long-term strategies. The IT strategy will break down into individual strategies for each business department. You should lay out these individual strategies based on the various tactics that you'll deploy, and you'll want to create a visual to demonstrate the mapping from your tactics to the strategies so that it is abundantly clear.

You will survey key business individuals who have a deep understanding of the solutions which serve their business areas. Consider some of the approaches the EA can use to respond best to maximize business clients' value. Your end goal is to improve the team's value to the business and gain the most leverage from your IT assets. Each business strategy will break down into multiple potential solution strategies. The solution may be enhancement, replacement, or augmentation of existing solutions, or something that has been conceptualized to fill a void in the business landscape. As an EA, it will be necessary to evaluate critical issues and trade-offs while meshing innovation and infusing new ideas into the existing technology landscape.

The IT strategic plan often takes shape within a document called an IT Strategic Road Map. To give you an example, I once worked with a company that started out with a goal to create an e-business strategy. It decided to use portal technology to try to solve its application challenges with one large technical solution. To put it bluntly, this exercise was derailed in the budget process, and the road map planned for the e-biz strategy turned into an IT strategic-planning exercise. It was probably the best thing that could have happened to that particular company.

We mapped out everything in the organization, including all of the applications, and assessed the inventory of systems and solutions by interviewing the business leaders responsible for the solutions. We reviewed the biggest questions that the CIO and management faced. We further investigated the answers that they were trying to get and focused on the biggest initiatives on the horizon. We wanted to look at what the market was dictating and found a context and a frame to put it into. We tried to narrow the scope as much as possible so that we were able to focus on the types of answers and the strategies to come up with an achievable plan.

The Enterprise Architecture Strategy

The EA must map, define, and standardize technology, applications, data, and business processes that make the business strategy possible. Taking both the macro and micro views, you'll translate the business strategy into your architecture approach and in the end work out the detailed initiatives and projects from a micro view. The enterprise architecture strategy first starts with a plan for the EA program itself. You'll need to decide which approach works best for the program to reach the goal of business alignment.

As you review the IT strategic plan, you'll need to select or develop overall guiding principles you'll use to guide the enterprise architecture strategy. Your enterprise architecture strategy will consist of some overarching goals that dictate what you hope to achieve with your program. You'll choose the framework, standards, and products that you'll employ and lay out the scope and boundaries of the domain architectures to come up with your conceptual architecture.

You'll analyze the business capabilities required in the context of the conceptual architecture that you have set out. Review the strategies you selected for each for the major business drivers you've highlighted in the IT strategic plan. You'll need to decide just how much work you'll put into to your current state architecture, and you won't know the full extent of this effort until you have a good draft of what your future state will look like.

Researching and studying the latest technology trends will allow you to select and test the few trends you may leverage to advantage your chosen IT strategies. Combined, this will describe what composes the target architecture and the approach your organization will take to build it. It will be up to your team to match the strategy, approaches, and solutions needed to map these technology trends and capabilities to the ones your organization needs.

To ensure alignment, measure each solution by plotting and ranking its business value against its alignment value in terms of IT readiness and capability to deliver. Create a clear picture of the solutions you want to keep on your radar. Study each business area for business capabilities needed and the potential solutions. To achieve the highest level of value, you can now apply your enterprise architecture mapping strategy.

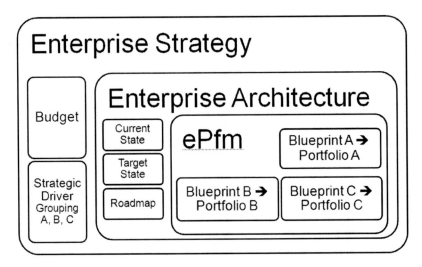

Figure 12. Enterprise Architecture Strategy

You can extend your road map, which is wound around a tight strategy, to become a detailed long-range plan for the architecture. You'll describe the organization and management of the enterprise, the business processes that you'll enable, and the IT functions and standards that you'll use to leverage the technology. The list of applications and the data and technology components to be included or built will evolve from the identification and analysis of gaps between the current state architecture and the future state vision. The road map will be filled with activities and processes in a sequenced fashion that fill the gaps within a high-level timeline.

Within the road map, you'll include the business drivers affecting IT and IT architectural principles from both an enterprise architecture level and those that are domain-driven. Along with the current state IT architecture and a high-level future state architecture, you'll generate a transition plan. This plan will include a very high-level plan of all projects it will take to realize the target state architecture. Included will be a pure technology road map. You should review the potential return on investment of IT investments at a high level. Based on current processes, data, and applications, assess inefficiencies against optimal levels and strive to create a balanced blend to support the business goals.

Drilling down into the individual domain architectures, there are some additional areas of focus. Within each of the application and solution architectures, information and data architectures, and technology architectures, you'll see synergies with respect to timing of the transition toward your current state. Grouping the solutions based on the timing in which you wish to deploy the infrastructure and resources will achieve even higher value. For example, you might find solutions in three different business areas that require some service-oriented infrastructure and middleware. Your strategic vision might include deploying the SOA infrastructure as a tool for one of the departmental business projects, matching the sense of urgency by the business with the project that makes most sense with respect to risk and timing for the architecture. These will form the strategic projects and allow you to lay down the migration plan for your enterprise architecture strategy.

The tactical groupings you expose by evaluating cross-cutting concerns for the organization form the majority of the strategies you employ. In performing your gap analysis, you'll see points in the framework for which there is value to answering the questions, creating models, and moving toward the target state. Most of your plan will be enveloped in an artifact called the enterprise architecture plan.Some will go into decision documents regarding the changes you foresee as necessary to your governance, methodology, and standard procedures to enable your IT organization to handle the required business changes. The output will be an implementation plan and design that the portfolio management and project office teams will create with your input and guidance.

Your work will encompass decisions about which business goals to tackle, which architecture decisions you'll need to make, and which resources you'll use to make it all happen. All will translate to desired results and will be used to evaluate IT against the value the business receives.

Zoom In—Action Steps You Need to Succeed

☐ Consider following these steps as they relate to EA when considering your strategic-planning activities:

☐ Join or set up the strategic-planning project and set the foundation and oversight processes.

☐ Institute or join the strategic management team with roles and responsibilities for strategic-planning activities. Align with the enterprise architecture team where possible.

☐ Analyze the situation: Research, analyze, and understand the environments in which the IT organization exists. **At this point, a linkage and coordination with current state architecture findings occurs.

☐ Weigh up the external environment: Analyze the conditions outside of the company that might require it to adapt or change its course in some way.

☐ Assess the internal environment: Analyze the conditions within the company that might require it to adapt or change its course in some way.

☐ Evaluate the technical environment: Analyze the current services, solutions, infrastructure and relationships to the organizations within the company.

☐ Assist the CIO to formulate the IT strategic direction: Establish goals and initiatives. Include guiding principles and ways in which the value will be measured, aligned with business and communicated. **At this point, a linkage and coordination with potential future state architecture is evaluated.

☐ Identify tactical groupings of business drivers and capabilities needed, as they relate to goals and projects that match the IT portfolio: Determine the most important initiatives and the measurable steps to achieving them.

☐ Classify critical success factors: Identify factors that are critical for achieving the vision.

☐ Discover desired metrics: Create the measurement and analysis system for assessing progress on the overarching goals.

- ☐ Identify solutions, projects, and initiatives: Establish the highest-level organizational initiatives needed to achieve the goals of the IT strategic plan.
- ☐ Assess ongoing initiatives: Review existing initiatives and adjust them to meet the new strategic goals.
- ☐ Define new initiatives and solutions that match the new strategies.
- ☐ Layout the transition architecture roadmap (if not done already) by considering the map from current to target states, taking into account the above factors and considerations. Prioritize the architecture initiatives most critical to IT's strategy goals, and integrate them with the strategic plan. Iterate and validate as necessary.
- ☐ Prioritize initiatives: Ascertain which initiatives are most critical to IT Strategic goals and match the organization's investment portfolio and goals.
- ☐ Refine and begin to share the plan: Communicate for feedback from all involved. Ensure alignment between IT Strategy Plan and EA Plan.
- ☐ Coordinate and publish: Formally document the strategic plan and publish the IT Strategic plan.
- ☐ Strategic plan implementation: Further define projects, allocate resources and delegate authority and responsibility to achieve the plan.
- ☐ Govern operations: Governs and monitor strategic indicators for performance against the IT strategic plan.
- ☐ Adjust plan: Make intermediate adjustments to the IT strategic plan and its implementation as discussed and required by the business.

Zoom Out—Big-Picture Concepts

If you operate within a large operation, you may need to coordinate many teams to gather the information you will need to come up with your strategy. If you have a strategic-planning department within your company, this process should have been established. If you are trying to figure out how you may approach this complicated scenario, consider these tips:

- ☐ Take a general overview of the business in each location or company.
- ☐ Review the trends at that location or company as well as the critical business issues.
- ☐ Ascertain the problems and opportunities. You essentially want a snapshot of the current situation and a measurement of the pulse of the business.
- ☐ Create an interview guide and a checklist for each location, business division, and group you wish to collect information from. Your organization and preparation in advance will pay off in spades.
- ☐ Collate your notes after each visit and before the next. You'll need them not only for analysis once you've collected everything but also for future reference.
- ☐ Ensure you did the previous step. If you have many people and groups to interview or gather information from, then the pieces of information you gather will quickly blend into each other and confuse and mute some distinct decision points that you should preserve.

CHAPTER 19:
IGNITE YOUR ENTREPRENEURIAL SPIRIT

I am careful not to confuse excellence with perfection.
Excellence, I can reach for; perfection is God's business.
—Michael J. Fox

It would have been quite easy to title this chapter "Building Extraordinary Value" or something to that effect. By being a business-savvy architect, you are genuinely interested in creating more value for your business. Understanding many of the methods and factors that contribute to value consumes a great portion of your efforts. Igniting your spirit by learning some of the dramatic improvements you can add by gleaning the potential value of IT strategies, return on investment, and various other business activities, you more than double your effectiveness as a leader in enterprise architecture.

Your efforts in and around governance, technology-based innovation, and strategic planning will enable your company to leverage IT value. Being aware of how the business is changing allows you to inject that knowledge into the plans for IT's support of change. As opportunities emerge, you'll investigate and decide how technology will play an appropriate role for your company. Consistency in both day-to-day and strategic decision-making processes will allow your enterprise architecture group and IT to provide value on continuously increasing levels.

A keen entrepreneurial spirit will serve you well as you study and use a few key business activities and measures to keep on top of the value and effectiveness of your enterprise architecture program. At this point in your career, you may even be more interested in spending the better part of your workday with business resources rather than those on the IT side. Being aware of current business issues such as e-business, the global business marketplace, and diverse supply and marketing channels that change the ways business is conducted and technology is leveraged are invaluable to the EA.

Your work with the enterprise architecture road map has exposed possibilities for your business to become agile enough to gain distinct advantages over the competition. You see your business's core competencies as the price of admission to being in your sector. You recognize the specific elements that differentiate your company from the pack and realize measurable competitive advantage, especially as you use technology as a leverage point. Finding courage in leading technical change, as well as your lack of fear in failing, makes you nimble, resilient, and a star in your career.

Make Quality Count

Quality is everyone's responsibility.
—W. Edwards Deming

As a business-savvy EA, it is your responsibility to understand all there is to know about making quality a priority in your architecture. Consider the choice between any two of the three constraints that include scope, time, and cost. Otherwise known as the good, fast, or cheap triangle, you may choose just two at a time, or any one, but it is impossible to have all three. This triangle seems to parallel the business cycles or seasons. The new millennium brought the Internet boom as the "fast" cycle. The "cheap" cycle has emerged as the world tightens its belt and the economy rebounds. "Quality" cycles almost always follow, when we as a society are broke and tired of failures and broken promises.

As an EA, there are many ways you can instill quality. Keep your ego in check and seek peer reviews and feedback on your design work. Ensure peers believe in the architecture and that each part is cohesive with the whole. It is important to understand that all capabilities and components are in rhythm with each other and align with the business drivers. New efforts must be in complete concert with business goals and satisfy any efforts you apply in business transformation.

Seek to get business support for functionality that aligns with business goals, as well as financial support for solutions and the architecture program as a whole. Business leaders, teams, and subject experts should understand, agree, and support the transition road maps that will bring them closer to their goals. The architecture team, the IT implementation groups, and the business support resources should find excitement in the journey you are planning. You can't expect to get full support, as it is likely that there will be initial reluctance to embrace the vision. This is a matter of change management, and you will realize that many resist change to the processes and technology on which they have built their careers. Use your business knowledge to enable you to build a boardroom presence and effectively lead change.

By the time the target state is being constructed, appropriate communication should have been delivered to all involved. In general, most should support the target state architecture. The application and solution teams should be excited about your plans. You should believe that the solution or combinations of solutions would help the organization meet the business requirements. You must feel the data that is going to be produced, managed, and created will be of the highest quality without concessions. The business should benefit from using the new information being made available, and you should find it convenient and qualitative.

Inject Your Integrity

Your integrity is demanded when you take on the role of EA. You'll inject that integrity into the architecture in various manners. Ensure that the solution is only as difficult as it needs to be and understand that achieving simplicity will come only through experience. One sure approach to ensure that quality exists in the architecture is through prototyping.

At various levels, starting with conceptual and extending to horizontal and vertical where warranted, prototyping is the best test to ensure that quality will be everlasting. Prototypes may be constructed at various stages in the architecture. Test various scenarios, asking how might you bend or extend the architecture. How might you break it? Consider the removal of any major element or the application of any of your most common business changes, such as legislative or regulatory ones. Always test the architecture against common quarterly, semiannual, and annual business requests for change.

You should feel confident that a proof of concept has either been planned or vetted in various stages of the architecture project when including new products and technology. While you may strive to make your solution waterproof, understand that there is an even balance between scoping time and testing. As mentioned earlier, you'll want to walk through each component and each piece of the architecture at the earliest possible stages and at the highest possible levels. Paper-based walk-throughs are cheaper than prototypes and can help you work out big kinks early on.

There should be no known faults or pieces that may break from day one. This does not mean you didn't make trade-offs during design. It just means that you should not recommend solutions that you already know may fail or that have known deficiencies. Ensure the architecture you have come up with has no known flaws. Measure and size every component that you can to determine whether it is robust enough to handle current and future state demands out to some reasonable time in the future. Consider too what kind of changes you would have to make when that capacity is sated. If there are known flaws, they should be minimal or almost nonexistent and documented. In short, you will have overturned every rock.

The Enterprise Architecture Value Proposition

As you advance the enterprise architecture program, strive to get business executives to view enterprise architecture as a necessary tool for business, technical, and operational decisions made at their level. Value usually begins by standardizing infrastructure, creating technical standards, organizing and managing information, and designing and integrating systems. It becomes harder with an increase in the reward level for streamlined development processes, EPfM, business process modeling, and strategy.

When enterprise architecture is used strategically in concert with EPfM, the need for proof of value is reduced. It is important to understand the value chain in your organization as it relates to your enterprise architecture efforts, although opinions on value may be prejudiced by the impact of change. Linking any of the activities within an enterprise architecture program to a specific business driver is hard enough, and your passion in creating these links may be questioned. Instead, consider a more simplistic chain such as this where you are able to demonstrate the linkage:

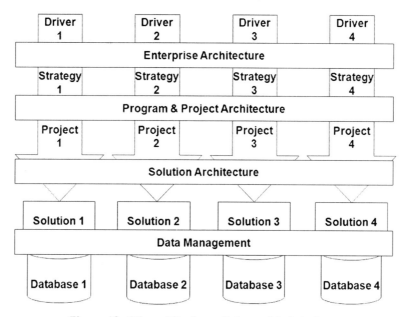

Figure 13. Aligned Business Driver with Solution

Architecture can easily trace to IT and further relate to business support. Departments track their performance, which should translate measurement to the bottom line. As enterprise architecture is abstract in nature, it is usually impossible to show the direct financial benefit. Easier to prove are opportunities in which you may provide input to existing business processes, such as process modeling, risk assessment in the area of technology components, or in innovation. A few examples that express value directly within the enterprise architecture program include:

1. Technical standards
2. Solution selection/application design guides and guidelines
3. Technology strategy development
4. Current and future state models
5. Reuse of models and methods
6. Enterprise data models
7. Proof of concepts for new solutions/technology
8. Enterprise architecture governance
9. Metrics collection
10. Templates for models, artifacts, decisions, documents, etc.

It will benefit you to know where you provide value on both the revenue and the expense sides of the business. It is valuable for you to know which architecture components, processes, and services are being used to leverage technology to gain competitive advantage, increase quality and efficiencies, and improve the company bottom line. Information you can provide will aid planning decisions regarding the resources and capital needed and once again prove value in the EA function.

Demonstrating value is difficult, but knowing where and when it is created will help you determine how and when you should measure it. Enterprise architecture should result in less:

➤ Overlap of products and product functionality and their licenses
➤ Production problems
➤ Support costs
➤ Reactive planning

Reductions are often easier to make and quicker examples of proof. Baseline numbers are required before change is made to numerically prove reductions or to communicate them later.

Enterprise architecture should result in increases both in the quality and in the breadth of functionality in the following areas:

➤ Business alignment
➤ Business capabilities

- ➢ Business intelligence
- ➢ Business value
- ➢ Cost savings through consolidation and standardization
- ➢ Operational efficiencies
- ➢ Project success through improved process and design templates
- ➢ Resource capacity
- ➢ System availability
- ➢ Strategic planning

Enterprise architecture can speed up:

- ➢ Development using components, frameworks, and templates
- ➢ Decision support
- ➢ Return on investment (ROI) for IT
- ➢ Planning
- ➢ IT budget process

The business expects to use some critical services from IT. Consider the enterprise architecture process as an enabler as well as a focused view of requirements. Two examples of services that are the most visible are secure data access and distribution throughout the organization and orchestrating the delivery, timing, and sequencing of automated business functions. Most recently, the business is seeing more enhanced strategic value through EAs' knowledge and delivery of technology innovation, such as collaboration, knowledge management tools, and additional online customer and vendor channels.

A few illustrations of value due to enterprise architecture are warranted, and they often come in categories such as price, speed, and adaptability. Reusable components enhance development capacity, thus leading to increased business capacity, enabling your company to sell or create more products. Consolidation of infrastructure, products, and licenses is just one example of gaining efficiency quickly without adding cost in effort and savings. A great infrastructure example is in virtualization, which you can use to enhance your development environments and reduce the cost of expensive equipment. Tools such as decision guides, development guides, and common components that development groups will further streamline IT efforts.

Development methodologies and patterns should be highlighted, as they increase efficiencies and productivity and speed applications to market for your business customers. Use of SOA and solutions will most likely help to gain in this area. Support the business by documenting its processes using your modeling skill sets and solutions.

Examples more visible to the business are in enterprise applications such as call centers and customer relationship solutions, which allow you to enhance the customer experience and obtain information about them. Data models grant better decision reports, business intelligence, and market research, leading to more customers. If you comprehend how this will help the business determine to how to find better and more profitable customers, you are much further ahead in the game.

While knowing how the enterprise architecture increases or proves value, you need to measure gains to keep your enterprise architecture program afloat. The enterprise architecture value chain is subjective and thus difficult to measure. Your business customers will seek help in achieving savings by bringing in new systems and products, and their success will be measured by their speed to market and their bottom line.

Earlier, a need to take baseline measurements where possible was mentioned. If there are regular, repeated processes, measure their duration. The number of products and license costs and combinations of costs that single solutions replace are easy to quantify and measure. A set of dimensions that visually depicts value is most easily shown in something called a spider diagram or a web diagram. Each of the given dimensions or "points on the web" is given a rating or numerical score depending on your rating system. These, as well as scorecards, are your tools for measuring more intangible contributions.

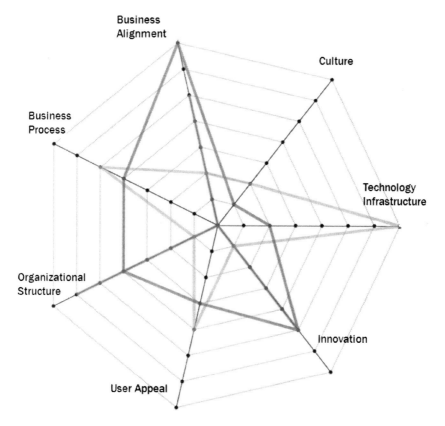

Figure 14. Spider Diagram

ROI

The mathematic definition of ROI is cost savings (benefits) divided by the investment made. Commonly known as the rate of return, the break-even point is a measure of the number of months, period, or the percentage at which the benefits pay for the costs incurred. Often, ROI demands that the costs of the investment are returned within the scope of the project at hand, making it too tactical and off-point for an enterprise architecture measure. Instead, you may need to introduce another strategic measure: return on assets (ROA). This forces businesses to build value based on increases in productivity of capital assets, which is better aligned with the practice of EPfM.

When using ROI with your enterprise architecture program, one of the biggest mistakes is to measure the cost of the entire program, including full team resource cost, against specific initiative gains. Instead, use small investments to grow the architecture incrementally. Small processes can become mature while realizing small, visible gains. ROI in enterprise architecture is typically a recursive baseline of costs. It is cost savings through integration and consolidation as well as standardization.

You must measure opportunity costs today versus tomorrow by analyzing the cost of the opportunity today, such as an improvement to the systems, against the savings tomorrow. As a reverse tactic, you may measure the lost opportunity cost today of using investment money today on IT systems instead of a business-related investment. Calculating opportunity costs today or the current cost for the opportunity and the increased systems needed to weigh against differences would be massive effort with little degree of confidence. Examples of costs more easily measured are a move of hardware, consolidation of hardware, rationalizing vendor licenses, IT asset management, or consolidation of architecture.

Business investment usually wins over pure infrastructure projects, but the costs of forgoing such IT investments are usually much more visible when the effort to improve the systems isn't made before disaster strikes. Usage costs are harder to measure unless they were set up to be tracked by activity-based costing. Maintenance costs are measured in break/fix time collected as metrics per environment and on change events.

Make the immediate value of enterprise architecture evident by demonstrating the transformations that your road map can facilitate. Current state models show where the organizational focus has been while visually exposing inefficiencies and costs. Transition management is created through planned key projects in alignment with business goals. The future state focuses on things like enterprise architecture governance and managing change.

Manage Your Executive Dashboard

Many executives manage by dashboard, meaning they rely on the visual representation of the key performance metrics that drive their business. Your keen understanding of the business indicators that drive your executives will catapult your career as an EA. Other numerical monitoring is often done through benchmarking processes, and knowing which numbers your business relies upon will allow you focus on where the architecture can provide value. Business executives also use scorecards to follow information that is more subjective. This is a massive topic, and a short description follows that should point you in the direction of the topics you may wish to explore further.

Dashboards

Another way that the architect can demonstrate value is through executive dashboards. Dashboards enable agile and quick data visualization of the KPIs your business cares about most. Statistics allow leaders to drive better business results and use the data you provide as actionable information. A strong suggestion would have you to improve your understanding of critical business data, and what better way than to have a conversation with your business executives while designing something for them to use.

The business can improve and make operations more effective using something as simple as a spreadsheet and a half-dozen statistics updated daily. They'll keep tabs daily on the statistics that matter most to them. Numbers depicted visually will speed their decision making and allow you to generate choices for your architecture. Gartner wisely coined its dashboards version as "Magic Quadrants," branding its assessment of the state, quality, and popularity of technical solutions. Most of what is displayed on such quadrants is information from its own analysts, but the quadrants also include information from customer surveys, adding a subjective element. Executives love to see this type of data visually, as it would normally consume far too much time to read textual descriptions of the information behind data points.

Architecture has been deemed difficult to measure, but through dashboards and scorecards, you can see both quantitative and qualitative measurements. You may get the best perspective of the status of various components in your architecture using this method. Attempt to start a matrix depicting information about the enterprise architecture program immediately. Using these statistics from the beginning of your program, as well as common IT statistics and business KPIs, your employee net worth will skyrocket.

Scorecards

Scorecards are a popular strategic management tool made popular in the early nineties by Robert Kaplan and David Norton. A specific example is the balanced scorecard (BSC), which was created to maintain alignment with business goals. BSCs are typically delivered in a four-quadrant style, usually including measures in financial, customer, process (operations), and employees (learning). They are widely used as a tool for businesses to communicate their strategic drivers and goals. Additionally, a SWOT analysis can be displayed in quadrant style and may be used to list the evaluation of the enterprise architecture program or any other business focus area.

Scorecards can be used for data that is more subjective in nature as a means of doing dynamic gap analysis. By taking a baseline measure and then collecting statistics on a periodic basis, the executive can view and see continuous improvement (or declines). Another form of scorecard is in a spiderweb format, where each spoke is given a numerical value or measure and then repeated over time to show progress. In enterprise architecture, the business can evaluate the business value proposition by using enterprise architecture metrics or specific business metrics.

Enterprise architecture scorecards are often used in a report card format with the business. They might rank something as to how they perceive the value in returns on their investment against the cost of the architecture. Also included may be judgments on the governance process, enterprise architecture advisory services, and enterprise architecture team involvement. Another fashion of scorecards used internally within the enterprise architecture program is a means of judging both enterprise architecture maturity attributes and progress. You might measure the progress in which you have documented and analyzed the target components within your enterprise architecture using a heat map or chart.

Make Metrics Matter

Metrics can be an overwhelming topic to tackle, especially when you have little or no experience with them. Starting to collect them can be less daunting if you avoid trying to boil the ocean. By attempting to understand what the business currently tracks as KPIs and getting a sense of the highest priority numbers, you can appreciate the value in the data. Look at these numbers and determine which can map to some of the business drivers that are core to the enterprise architecture plan, and then figure out which ones you can begin to collect or baseline today.

Another place to start is in the area of your enterprise architecture program. You can measure enterprise architecture maturity in a manner similar to the documentation status heat map or by using the various parameters and their scores in a spiderweb diagram. Some examples of measures that the executives like to see are in the financial areas such as the ROI on IT investments.

Businesses all track metrics appropriate for their focus. Common examples are:

> Earnings per share (EPS)
> Net present value (NPV)
> Net cash flow, discounted value
> Return on Investment (ROI)
> Return on Assets (ROA)
> Internal rate of return (IRR)
> Revenue growth
> Total cost of ownership (TCOO)
> Price/performance ratio
> Number of website visits

Know which numbers your business or focus areas track and know how they are calculated. Even better, know how you can use these numbers to suggest improvements or changes to your target state. Study and education in the specific KPIs for your business will show dividends in investment in your career.

Metrics for IT and especially enterprise architecture have been known to be difficult to collect. It is important that you know a few that will allow you to prove valuable to the business. Some IT metric examples include:

- Financial: ROI on IT investments, IT cost per employee, budget time cycle
- Customer: percent of satisfied customers, number of help desk calls, number of touch points
- Business process: time to market, solution fault count, number of products supported per category, reliability/uptime/availability
- Employee: percent satisfaction, speed of learning, market capital per employee. area in which user is dissatisfied
- Solution cost per user, cost per transaction, cost per customer
- Project performance
- Application performance
- Development characteristics (number of change requests)
- Management: costs/budget, schedule/effort/delay, utilization and loading, resource availability
- Operational view: process/activities, products/specs, policy/procedures, constraints/guides

These can be shown using scorecards or gauges on the dashboard (particularly for quality attributes), depending on their qualitative or quantitative nature. Some more architecture-specific examples could include:

- Audit/risk
- Application portfolio quality
- Architecture staffing/skills
- Architecture requirements vs. business drivers: a chart with critical/medium and low-priority business drivers down the

left vertically, and then architecture requirements across the top horizontally are given a rating

> Change velocity
> Decisions: ROI, business impact, price/performance, risk/opportunity
> Customer satisfaction (alignment)
> Quantity of capabilities added
> Governance statistics: work volume/requests, number of standards defined, percent of assets in compliance, number of redundant assets identified, percent redundant/reused, number of projects reviewed, percent of projects in compliance, percent of projects aligned with business goals
> Overall cost reduction via standard process
> Time to market: improved delivery of business deliverables
> IT expenditures: percent aligned with goals
> Business value of achieving goals

Get creative, but remember the keys to creating great enterprise architecture metrics. Your number-one goal is aligning IT to business drivers and goals, and your numbers should support this effort. Start small, focus on a few, commit, and improve. Scorecards are a great place to start—even internally for the architecture group and with IT—for the CIO, application groups, operations, technical, project managers, and middle management. You want to prove your enterprise architecture program is working.

For more information, see an introductory presentation on enterprise architecture metrics at www.zoomfactorbook.com/book-resources.

Govern Accordingly

Governance is a popular topic with all business executives and most likely exists within a hierarchy at your company today. It may be present at the corporate, IT, enterprise architecture, and domain architecture levels. It is a process and structure put in place to ensure order and control of various programs at the enterprise level. More specifically, architecture governance may be put in place to ensure that the processes you've chosen to employ are conducted correctly. It means many things to many people depending on their organization, but most definitions include the words decision, accountability, desirable behavior, foundation, sustain and extend corporate strategy and objectives, direction, control, and monitoring. Some include strategies, policies, and standards of IT. This book will give you a brief, high-level overview of architecture governance, but this stand-alone topic may require in-depth study.

In a research study at MIT, Jeanne Ross, acclaimed author of *Enterprise Architecture as a Strategy: Creating a Foundation for Business Execution*, found that ARBs and governance committees that include senior business leaders and oversee architecture initiatives are a major trait of more than half of all highly strategic effective firms. These same firms will subject as much as 80 percent of their projects to an architecture compliance review. An architecture governance program is comprised of a set of prescribed processes for review, documentation, and compliance with and exception to standards. The structure will include an ARB, which is a meeting of people to discuss architecture decisions put forward for approval within the architecture landscape. The principles behind governance drive alignment of IT investments with business direction.

If a business has provided a strategic plan for the organization, it should align with the planned IT investments appropriately. Governance and processes must be put in place to guide such investments. The architecture governance program typically falls within the IT and corporate government programs and depends upon the structures the organization's management prescribes. The EA must understand the importance of this process to the enterprise architecture program.

Architecture governance is needed to guide the planning and control of your program. EAs create standards as well as checks and balances to ensure the quality of the infrastructure solutions that they built in compliance with the architecture. You can use governance as a guidepost during the planning, design, and implementation stages of your projects. One of the critical value measurements for enterprise architecture is alignment to the business. If key business stakeholders participate in your architecture governance, this is the best chance for buy-in to what you have designed. The business process and application management through all phases of the system development and governance life cycle must be in place.

Governance is most often used to guide and document decisions made around IT investments. Involvement of stakeholders on governance committees or boards control the vision, priority, and centralized funding of major application and technology solutions. Leadership in solution decisions should be made available through this program on a scheduled basis rather than piecemeal. An enterprise architecture governance program offers many benefits, including cost savings in operation of standardized technology and in other non-discretionary expenses. The program allows your company to expand the budget for discretionary spend (change, improvements, business capacity, and innovation).

With architecture governance, decisions are optimized and predictable. Exception and compliance processes are known and practiced, reducing the exposure to risk. Standards are known and managed by an enterprise body. Architecture artifacts, including standards, decisions, patterns, and models, are managed, stored, and archived. Business partners become more satisfied as they are in control of better alignment to their strategies and investments. You may perform assessments of projects post-implementation and annually to continuously prioritize architecture and project efforts. Within the business, you can measure and communicate value. But the governance program allows you to spread the use of standardized technology across the various organizations that build and provide solutions. You will be able to standardize processes that allow you to align project priorities to architecture objectives. Finally, you can design the capabilities and services that your organization needs in an organized, prioritized manner.

The Roles and Responsibilities of the Enterprise Architecture Program within Governance

A simple, three-tier portfolio management model covers three stages in an IT life cycle. These tiers match the planning and design of solutions and infrastructure, the construction of those solutions, and finally the operation and maintenance of all of IT assets. In the planning stages, you'll build decision models and templates to ensure consistency across your programs. You'll align these programs with the prioritized business strategies to ensure the collaboration of architecture across the enterprise plan, your services, solutions, and functional teams. Your program will allow you to optimize and group architecture initiatives and achieve higher efficiency, awareness, and results.

Consider current investment planning to eliminate the bad and optimize the good components built to date. You'll review your upgrade list and potential for merger with projects in which you will increase business capabilities. Review the current project status and the state of the architecture road map. Are you still on track? You may need to deviate due to innovation or business change including strategy shift. Be sure to know the drivers of all of your costs, including operational costs as well as the shared or amortized costs of planned projects. Consider cyclical events, such as legislative changes, security issues, and operational events. You'll plan the frameworks and the repositories on which you base all of your architecture endeavors.

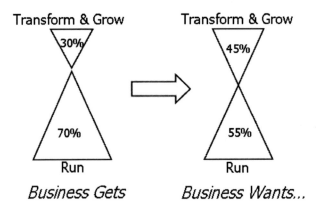

Figure 15. Portfolio Investment Optimized Shift

During the building or construction process, you will use reviews as a mechanism to authorize and direct the project teams on their architecture. Develop a lightweight checklist if you do not have a mature governance program or enterprise architecture program in place. You'll want to be aware of the current spend on support, operations, and development as well as the operational status. Notice any trends in statistics such as increased problems that may signal a need for upgrades or high support costs that signal an inefficient solution. Review incident and problem metrics relative to implementation dates of projects. Are any process changes or standards revisions required? How has the business reacted to your current operational levels?

Another part of architecture governance is the development of architecture competency throughout your organization. While enterprise architecture governance is not a training program, it does span from your team across the teams that develop and deliver the solutions. The governance program should ensure that as much as possible is designed to meet standards, increasing quality through review for compliance or exceptions. You'll use standards that you create in house and industry standards such as the ITIL, COBIT, Capability Maturity Model (CMM), Zachman, and TOGAF, as well as standards from the Institute of Electrical and Electronics Engineers (IEEE).

After all has been built, an enterprise architecture governance component is needed while you run and manage your infrastructure and solutions. You will have to manage the governance process itself, and the EA may participate in the IT governance process as well as the corporate governance process. Your program will need to manage your compliance approval and exception processes. Depending on your role in enterprise architecture governance, you will likely play the role of decision maker and must represent the viewpoints of both the business and the stakeholder. You'll maintain enterprise architecture deliverables, systems, patterns, and the technology standards repository in the architecture change process.

Technology tool selection processes and tool references libraries are held within the architecture governance program as well as the set of standards. You will want to track decision documents and provide an index for their speedy retrieval. Configuration management of both infrastructure and applications may fall within your governance program, although in my experience I have seen it run at arm's length while owned by the IT operations group. You should care about the metrics that operation of technology and solutions generate, and you should measure and report any savings. You should also track the progress and feedback on the quality of the architecture as well as the IT assets. The architecture governance program should be responsible for the creation of an annual site infrastructure health assessment program. Health is established within both applications and technology solutions to determine the longevity and the approximate life cycle of a specific technology.

There are many ways to set up an architecture governance program at your organization. You will need to create processes and documents as well as the organization of people and schedules who will manage it. Your program inputs will include cyclical requirements, such as legislative and security changes that arise through everyday business and on an annual, ongoing basis. The initial setup of your program should be quick and lightweight, borrowing what you can from organizations in your industry verticals or through standard processes. Implement a collaborative enterprise architecture governance model and process that complement those needed at the corporate and IT levels. Link the enterprise architecture framework to both technical and business architectures. Pilot your program, tweak it, and then select a repository.

There are multitudes of ways in which you can structure organizational resources within your ARB. In a perfect world, stakeholder representatives are on your governance board. As few as three years ago, attracting their attention was still a feat. Today, it should be simpler to get their involvement, as governance is one of the target strategies in most companies. You might include specific customers and internal subject matter experts from areas of your enterprise. You should also consider individual involvement from audit, compliance, and legal, depending on the structure of your organization and enterprise architecture program.

Formalized change management committees and corporate and line area departments may have a place at the table at enterprise architecture governance through one of the managers or directors. As mentioned in the design of virtual enterprise architecture teams, your team's size may become unwieldy if you add resources without a deliberate, specific purpose. Areas to watch out for are informal organizations that seem to form themselves in informal control mechanisms, such as bottlenecks through change approval and micro-approval organizations.

Running Your Governance Program

Process standardization will occur within a healthy enterprise architecture program. Review processes may occur to analyze requirements and move through the system's development life cycle with a project architect, with major reviews of artifacts and architecture at the ARB level. You must consider all stakeholder perspectives for choosing the solutions and determining the alignment of the solution with your stated standards and enterprise architecture direction. The ties between the technical solution and business needs are considered during this process. The governance committee will review and approve proposed modifications to the enterprise architecture.

The group must respond quickly and efficiently to architecture changes. The responses will provide impact analysis on other architectures. Some of the approaches are to consider the committee as the focal point of technology consequence, standardization, and integration within the organization. If IT initiates infrastructure and technology improvements without coordinating direction within the program and business concerns, they are headed for disaster. These improvements could include major application requirements without proper consideration for associated impacts on supporting IT applications or technology support structures.

A lack of communication or formalized publication of change is also something that may cause problems for an organization if not controlled within the governance board. IT-initiated infrastructure or technology improvements can create grief if not aligned with value to the organization and matched within a project budget. Communication of changes to standards as well as major decisions being made must flow quickly and consistently to the application and technology teams. Creation of an IT service delivery model and metrics must be in place to measure governance program tactics and strategies.

Create templates for solution reviews and an accessible place for your repositories. Choose a preliminary review board and have them set guidelines for meetings, reviews, exceptions, and compliance. They can start by setting up a lightweight checklist for reviews and compliance and should communicate and publish the results. The governance process allows you to feel that you are in control of your program and to continually ensure buy-in from your executive sponsors of both your enterprise architecture program and your IT asset portfolio.

Flash Those Entrepreneurial Skills

To gain advantage or be at level ground, you need to learn the common knowledge of the business people that you tend to spend more time around in your career. As an EA, you may or may not have that entrepreneurial spirit within you. As internal scholars in enterprise architecture, you will be intrigued and willing to read books in the subject of business that do not relate to IT or enterprise architecture. You might enjoy books on personal improvement and human skills to shore up your soft-skill set. As an EA, you are likely intrigued with the new e-commerce economy, innovation, and changes to the business landscape. You'll find information on some great reads at www.zoomfactorbook.com/bookshelf.

Be sure to flash those entrepreneurial skills. You have an understanding of how decision-making models work and how in business they are generally made based on outcomes, costs, and strategy. You are skilled in the area of risk management and have a good understanding of the concepts of probability of risk in the technology and solutions you employ. You work through the opportunity and the identification of risk and plan to manage it along with project managers throughout the solution development process, the architectural process, and the portfolio management process. You have a good handle on investment opportunities and justification and investment decision leverage points. You are typically involved with both the IT and strategic-planning cycles as well as in IT budgeting at the highest level by identifying items that require consideration. Take all of this knowledge and skill, blend it with your architecture acumen, and display value to your organization.

Zoom In—Action Steps You Need to Succeed

Here is a no-nonsense quick wins list that you can use to impress your business stakeholders and jump-start your enterprise architecture program:

1. Get the information you need for your program quickly to gain credibility. Examples are business drivers, process owners, and the current state inventory list.

2. Plan for strategic enterprise architecture outcomes. Choose three key metrics that you know will demonstrate that you have improved the value proposition from IT. Minimize your infrastructure where possible and choose consolidation projects that are quick and easy to do to show traction. Put up a straw man enterprise architecture road map as fast as possible.

3. Set out to build the relationships you will need to fuel your success. Become your CIO's trusted advisor and find out what wins your executive is looking for. Your team will be your pillar and executor of your vision. Learn everything you can about the CIO and what makes him or her tick.

4. Choose key projects to reduce pain in your organization. Solve some "big hairy issues" (BHIs) that seem simple to you. Carefully choose manageable, packaged solutions that will solve a multitude of business problems. Crisis gives you an

opportunity and visibility to assist, but you should allow others to do the implementation.

5. Exhibit the behaviors you need to lay your program's foundation. Construct a lightweight governance program immediately. Start collecting existing standards and make a quick list of those that are needed and target them. Model processes and behaviors that you wish all would follow, such as consistent decision making and documentation for actions.

Remember that in the end, it's about being visible and providing value. If you'd like to see the video of this presentation, visit www.zoomfactorbook.com/book-resources .

Zoom Out—Big-Picture Concepts

Your enterprise architecture program value list should include:

- ☐ Better agility
- ☐ Better alignment to the business
- ☐ Better information
- ☐ Better reputation for IT
- ☐ Higher availability
- ☐ Increased efficiency
- ☐ Increased financial impact and accountability
- ☐ New capabilities
- ☐ Quicker ROI for IT
- ☐ Reduced production and integration problems
- ☐ Reduced redundancy
- ☐ Reduced support costs
- ☐ Speed in development and maintenance

Find a way to weave a select few of these into your elevator speech when asked how the program is going or what you do for your organization.

CHAPTER 20:
BE THE CHANGE MASTER

Change has a considerable psychological impact on the human mind.
To the fearful it is threatening because it means that things may get worse.
To the hopeful it is encouraging because things may get better.
To the confident it is inspiring because the challenge exists to make things better.
–King Whitney, Jr.

Corporations are often limited in the ways in which they can find new revenue streams. That's where innovation plays a large role: it drives business growth through increased revenue and efficiencies, resulting in reduced costs. Most often, companies innovate by using new technological means to connect with new partners and supply chains, thereby gaining efficiencies. Current trends reveal companies searching for new markets, customers, and products using technology breakthroughs. These examples of business growth can be directly linked to IT, so be sure to leave no rock unturned when compiling your enterprise architecture plan.

Your first and primary goals as an EA are to provide leadership and a vehicle in which you can quickly accomplish change through business capability and designs in solutions and technical infrastructure. Your plans and designs will provide agility to your business strategies, and your leadership and communication will script the success that you may achieve as a change agent. The architecture program that gains traction is one that allows the business to take action and change rapidly. Companies gain value most often because the change orchestrated through architecture provides interoperability and better information to business users and customers.

Innovation invariably means change, and your mastery will depend on thorough understanding and the ability to forge paths through the inevitable jungle that awaits you. Methods and processes are one of the common ways that the EA can harness innovation to effect change. You can find ways to add additional capabilities and features to products, or you might apply new technology and infrastructure to extend your budgets, to increase your proficiency in existing functions, or to enable additions previously impossible.

Put the Business First

You'll strive to ensure that the business's perspectives are always put ahead of the IT perspectives. Be aware of the agendas and priorities of shareholders, stakeholders, investors, and customers. Your focus should be on realizing value for the business, while watching for opportunities for innovation. A variety of factors will drive out further opportunities for change at your company. These include a variety of management styles and agendas, the differences in stakeholder focus, the priorities of your peers, the chief investment officer's plans, and finally your team.

What You Need to Know about Change

Change comes in many forms. Rolf Smith, author of *The 7 Levels of Change: Different Thinking for Different Results*, has described change in an easy-to-understand framework. Consider his work as it pertains to enterprise architecture and ways you may apply his strategies in your organization:

1. Do what's right: Often this comes from spotting quick wins and seeing low-hanging fruit in your technical architecture. Apply the 80/20 rule to your architecture by setting priorities for change to become more effective.

2. Do things the right way by setting standards for what's right: You'll select and develop processes and standards so that you can achieve consistency in your architecture, which will yield cost savings, time savings, and increased quality. Take the time to right things that were wrong and that cost you on an ongoing basis.

3. Do things better with improvements: Focus on what is going right and do more of it, and use these things as models and patterns for future development and replacements of expiring technology. Make one of your principles to improve things as changes are requested to applications that have expected life remaining.

4. Do away with things: Cut the wheat from the chaff by eliminating redundant applications and technologies and allowing operations and development to focus on fewer selected technologies. Stop putting effort into things that don't have much expected life and be more productive.

5. Do things where others have succeeded: Observe and study how others have been successful in your industry with technology that may solve your problems. Find the best practices and copy them.

6. Do things no one else is doing: Consider the outlandish and try things you think may not work. Ask "why not?" when considering new technologies instead of listing reasons to stick with the status quo.

7. Do the impossible: What was impossible yesterday that is doable today? What would make things better or perfect that some think is inconceivable? Consider many ways of thinking about a problem and add creativity, strategy, reflection, and systematic thinking instead of using rigid paradigms, linear thinking, and risk-avoidance techniques.

Know How Change Works

Change disrupts the status quo and is the primary reason that most resist it at its first introduction. The EA's job is the hardest one around because you are always introducing change through new plans, strategies, processes, and technologies. Many IT professionals are content with their current slate of technology skills, and new ones really scare them. Most work with what is predictable and create a comfort zone for themselves. Their first reaction will be to resist the change, as it causes them discomfort and uncertainty. Some people may form groups to help them oppose the change as they feel their position, knowledge, and careers are being threatened. A similar reaction will be present among the business community.

Only when all groups feel that their new reality includes change will they embrace it. This is most often when they see it happening, with or without them. They may jump on board early if they love change or if they see how aligning themselves early will benefit them. Their careers will grow by embracing the change and being its champion, but they will experience much frustration and anxiety until they understand their role. Your responsibility will be to lay out as much as possible in your enterprise architecture road map to demonstrate how the transition will be made and to minimize or eliminate as much of the chaos and confusion that change entails. Keep in mind that fear is their primary emotion, and whatever you can do to minimize it will help you enable change through your architecture.

Know the forces for and against change. Your business strategies and stakeholders beg for new products and improvements in speed, quality, and quantity while gaining financial efficiency. Business and IT resources will resist putting extra time in to give requirements or to test the change in technology. They may be quite afraid of looking foolish while trying to learn something new or fear being left behind. They will ask that you minimize disruption in the implementation of new technology, and they will keep all change under the microscope from a cost-containment perspective.

You will use your soft skills heavily during the change process. If you consider the "ME factor" with those you communicate with, diligently prepare for each audience, and know what concerns them most, you will find yourself much further ahead with your plans. Consider how people feel when they lose an investment or when a new organizational change is announced. The reality is that enterprise architecture is affected more by people, the organization, the context in which change is made, and the company's culture than by the technology, framework, and models. Help others accept change by treading and leading carefully, and you will be much more successful.

Lead Change from the EA Cockpit

EAs are commonly perceived as change masters. This has been a recurring theme several times throughout your career journey. You will also need to drive change as a leader through process and planning. Decision making or choice selection is built around governance processes. You'll want to be flexible with approval on compliance processes, as it takes time to make change. As a leader, understand that introducing change will require time to grow familiarity. All those affected will need to understand the implications of change.

At this stage, your modeling and communication skills will become paramount. Your transition road map should lay out the big picture so those affected can understand that they are included in the future. Visible symbols of change, such as senior executive involvement in initiatives and the governance team, will show others that change is part of the future. Your role is sharing the vision and strategy while aligning IT to business goals. Motivate and inspire those around you to help the company move in new directions. Coach and mentor those who have difficulty with the change; you can do much by building relationships before the change has been determined.

As a leader, you will recognize that people are the major component in successful change. Your role is that of an influencer, and people are less afraid of what they see and understand than what is unwritten and verbally described inconsistently. Your passion and confidence in the change and the consistency of your message will help others accept it. Proving value and demonstrating that the vision is achievable and that it matches the corporate strategy will allow most people to see how being involved will benefit them.

Understand the need to accommodate speed bumps along the way. Creating a flexible road map for the transition and getting early volunteers to help solidify the plans will bring your first champions for change. Generally speaking, some people will always propose change and others will always be affected by it. People who will propose change will have either a weak or a strong commitment to the change, depending on its origin. The closer the proposal is to the person, the stronger his or her passion and appetite for change. On the other hand, those whom the change affects may have a weak or a strong commitment, depending on what's in it for them. When those who gave their strong commitment for a proposal converge with those who are affected by it, you'll have a higher probability of success.

When the strong who propose change meet those who are weak in commitment, things will get expensive and progress will cause great pain. If change is proposed with a weak approach that meets weak acceptance, rest assured that you will fail. When those who are affected by the change have a strong commitment to it but are weak in accepting it, you will witness lip service.

So what is the best answer? Nurture the support for change as part of your approach each time you propose a solution. Find the effective change agents around you and use them as marshals to help you move new technology into the future. Recognize where you need others to help you solidify and sell the change. Ensure that you have adequate resources to help you make the change both in dollars and people arranged in teams. Confidence in your proposal helps you build trust. Focused communication of the change coupled with honesty will bring acceptance from the masses. Use highly visible executive support to help shore up universal confidence in you and the change.

Communicate what will happen, the transition path, and, most importantly, the "on ramp" to those affected so they understand and accept the change. Discomfort about the timing of their involvement can disrupt and damage your potential for success. As you make the change, measure progress along the way, make sure you know which way you are going, and adjust as needed. Celebrate your victories publicly and lament your troubles privately. Your celebrations should enforce that change is coming and encourage those still standing on the sidelines to jump onto the moving train.

Make Change Easier to Embrace

To ease the challenges in making change, try to assemble a change infrastructure that complements the type of change you are making, including a very strong communications team. So how do you make change easier to accept? Draw out all of the steps in terms of what is required for your organization alongside of the value of and reasons for the change. By doing this, people will have a greater capacity to understand the catalysts behind the change. If you can carefully identify the problems that need to be addressed in your current state without insulting their owners, you will help those affected see the need for change.

As you try to embark on change, you'll need a mechanism to manage it and at the same time measure the strength of the resistance to the change. Determining the exact cause and nature of the resistance will help you build strategies for its containment. Secure management commitment to help your team ensure that there is sufficient support for the change. Assess the impact of change on both the workforce and the organization to allow you to better adjust your journey. At all costs, minimize implementation time to reduce pain and avoid those who are change-resistant.

You'll need the following resources to successfully make a change in your IT assets:

➢ Technology infrastructure
➢ Architecture, strategies, and programs
➢ Decision-making and problem-solving mechanisms
➢ Governance programs

Your performance in decision making, choices, and communication methods will be a large factor in your success. Involve your team in every step, getting help from your stakeholders where necessary. Make every effort to record your decisions and your issues as you go through the cycle of change to learn and adjust as you go. Identify the risks before the change, as it will be necessary to manage them throughout the process.

Either through hypothesis, prototyping, or human nature, architects are not afraid to fail. Trial and error seems to be part of your nature, so allow your team the time, flexibility, and support to make this change happen. If your culture puts architects on a pedestal and those around you are waiting for you to tumble, your team will still need flexibility to take chances and do the innovative things that architects do very well. Muster up all of your courage, as you cannot show that you fear failure.

Use Your Enterprise Architecture Plan to Leverage Change

The enterprise architecture plan provides leverage in planning and decision making. It provides a platform for you as a leader and planner in short-term change. As you change your organization structure and resources, the plan provides continuity and history in terms of current state IT architecture. The plan will allow you to coordinate IT changes with business initiative changes in a prioritized manner. If you envision business initiatives on the horizon, it will enable you to determine what kinds of changes need to occur within your infrastructure.

An example worth sharing comes from a client who asked me how it might change its infrastructure to support the addition of two new branches in different jurisdictions. The organization was small and had a core set of applications and file systems on a shared set of servers in the head office. The new branches would be the first step in its distribution of IT services. I explained to the client how it would have to make changes both in expanding its network and infrastructure to support the offices and application changes.

A change in software distribution and change deployment was necessary. Multiple considerations for efficiencies, including a change for support staff wishing to run the application remotely versus locally, were key drivers behind the decisions. Differences existed in system availability, and the schedule changed the manner in which backup and recoveries were to be run. These are just a few of the considerations, but by reviewing and discussing the architecture plan, the methods by which applications were currently structured, and the technology, my client was able to make snap decisions as to the direction he wanted to take to make these changes.

Similarly, you'll want to use your enterprise architecture road map as a means to plan change in business direction and strategies. If the business understands and accepts the enterprise architecture plan, the organization can use it for reference repetitively without spawning new research projects for each proposed change to IT assets. Use a consistent format for the solution space laid out by domain architectures to allow you to maintain the context for business architecture changes and strategies the business wishes to deploy.

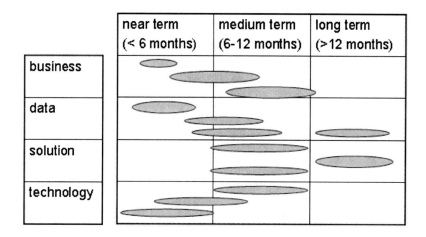

Figure 16 Transition Plan organized by Domain Architecture

The enterprise architecture should provide a migration strategy to steer technology change decisions. It should allow the organization to migrate in a timely fashion away from the older technology and system solutions you no longer wish to support. Change is then planned, articulated, and expected. Your installation path for new solutions allows you to replace the old with the new in a predictable manner. By having a strategy that is renewable and maintainable on an ongoing basis, you get a head start each time in your planning activity. Your enterprise architecture plan provides views in which you may analyze emerging technologies, consistently apply technology change, and manage its life cycle.

Consider the life span of many of the technologies you have used in the past twenty years. Desktops, servers, networks, and software have all undergone changes over the years, and some of the more mature technologies now have a relatively predictable change cycle. Think of these as your first stop when analyzing your portfolio of IT assets. Consider the planned life expectancy for productivity tool suites. Plan their replacement as you introduce any new technology to your road map. Expected change is more readily accepted.

As a change master, one major consideration is the annual requests you get to ensure your systems meet legislative and legal compliance. These are typically not negotiable and must be inserted when the external source dictates. You can, however, control the extent to which you plan for and expect these changes to come and the flexibility you include to complete them quickly. When considering a business decision and the amount of documentation required for purposes of an audit or legal history, it may influence the timeline, especially considering other planned changes. Your enterprise architecture plan will offer you quality and flexibility in your application opportunities. Employ considerations such as SOA and component design, especially when you have a known portion of work that you must complete each year.

Technology will reach a reasonable end of life if you properly mitigate risks to avoid situations that could embarrass IT and highlight poor planning. The enterprise architecture will provide you with a multiyear planning and budget strategy for both projects and infrastructure. Of course, there may be surprises, but if you plan to replace or upgrade your most critical or risky components and plan to undertake all necessary legislative regulatory and maintenance projects, it should allow you to include some capacity to add new capabilities for the business plus the ability to respond to emergencies and last-minute unplanned changes.

The enterprise architecture should also allow IT to limit the resources dedicated to legacy architectures and to schedule a replacement with technology recess. If you see that a legacy application is due to be replaced within a year or two, you can limit the effort you pour into supporting and changing such an application. It gives you a controlled environment from which you may evaluate projects and effect change.

In short, the enterprise architecture plan provides a reliable communication vehicle for change because you have documented target business functionality opportunities. By using established, standard vocabulary around the plan, you are able to demonstrate or show the impacts to business resources when they want to make changes to their business. For example, if you have functionality to technology map a diagram, and a business stakeholder arrives with a proposed solution, you can overlay where that proposed solution would fall on this diagram. This will enable you to demonstrate where the overlaps and gaps exist, then demonstrate how the supporting technologies would either be reused or must be implemented. The plan allows you to manage your services and evaluate change more effectively.

Drive Change Gracefully

If you know what you have, what you need, when you'll need it, and who will implement and manage it, you are able to effect change in a much more controlled, acceptable, and efficient manner. Most people resist change because they are afraid and can't see how it will affect them. If the business can better realize how change through technology will lead to efficiency gains in its business process or reduce complexity in technology, it is easier for you to provide the decision and business rationale behind requests for IT-driven projects. If you must create a business case for your stakeholders, it is important that you have information at hand to show them how you will employ such a request with as little risk as possible. Having an enterprise architecture plan already in place short-circuits the effort at the beginning of the project and allows you to focus on creating any necessary business plan. Standardized vocabulary within the enterprise architecture plan enables your team to communicate more freely with not only business stakeholders, but also all of the domain resources within the IT organization.

When you are the change master, you will meet resistance and you'll have to very vigilantly and strategically pick your battles. If you focus on large enterprise issues as you work with the business and subject matter experts, you can ensure that your enterprise's top three concerns are also those of the enterprise architecture team. If you can keep your eye on the big picture, you can become the enterprise architecture program crusader.

How are you going to drive ongoing change? Best practice would have you achieve this through the portfolio management perspective in concert with the enterprise architecture plan. Optimally, we use the enterprise architecture to drive portfolio management activities. You may embrace the job of identifying and communicating the risks involved along the way. An enterprise architecture plan can highlight business function priority and importance. Focus on areas where the highest value application opportunities exist, as well where components change the most and should be most flexible.

Most often, when projects arise, we have the opportunity to slate them within some type of schedule; sometimes they become emergency projects implemented irrespective of your plans. The enterprise architecture plan should allow you to reduce the number of emergencies by proactively planning upgrades and the evergreen nature of your infrastructure. In harmony with your project portfolio planning exercises, all of this should allow you to adjust the transition plan on an annual basis, yet continue to move it forward.

Zoom In—Action Steps You Need to Succeed

Try to architect out barriers to change when given a choice. Consider these samples:

- ☐ Solutions based on proprietary software
- ☐ Solutions based on beta versions or partial solutions based on purchases of partial code sets, accompanied by long, loosely defined consulting engagements
- ☐ Large numbers of permutations associated with disparate technologies

- [ ] Configurations that inhibit change
- [ ] Solutions requiring massive customization vs. configuration
- [ ] Solutions that swim upstream from business process
- [ ] Very large solutions (the "big bang" approach) that rock many interlocking business processes across the company and have multiyear horizons to realization of value
- [ ] Solutions known to include large upgrade cycles and lead to being "out of version"
- [ ] Services based on emerging concepts, markets, or partners
- [ ] Solutions based on vendors who are insolvent or financially unstable
- [ ] Solutions based on legislation
- [ ] Tier or pillar solutions
- [ ] Solutions that are intolerant of unanticipated change (long change cycles are standard)
- [ ] Solutions with few or complex integration points
- [ ] Solutions based on only the opinions or input of only a few people
- [ ] Custom solutions that replicate industry standard functions (such as finance, accounting, banking, asset management, human resources, etc.)

Zoom Out—Big-Picture Concepts

Change will be your daily staple. Consider these success ingredients for change:

- [ ] Ensure business perspectives surpass IT perspectives.
- [ ] Observe the styles, agendas, focus, and priorities of:
  - o Stakeholders
  - o Customers
  - o Innovators
  - o Creator of the solution you aim to replace
  - o Peers
  - o Operational managers
  - o CIO

      o   Staff management.

☐ Ensure the change provides the absolute best value for the corporation.

Pick Your Battles

☐ Focus on large enterprise issues as you work with the business resources.

☐ Ensure the enterprise's top concerns align with those of the enterprise architecture team.

☐ Keep your eye on the big picture.

☐ Zoom in and out frequently to assess different perspectives.

Demonstrate Desired Behaviors

☐ Identify, analyze, and understand key business processes.

☐ Use a repeatable process to analyze business needs and repercussions on the enterprise architecture plan, models, and artifacts.

☐ Prioritization of the goals, features, and functions of the solution by all interested parties.

☐ Be prepared to retrofit the existing plan and processes with change.

☐ Prepare and use consistent decision-making and governance processes.

☐ Know how you will include change using review and compliance processes.

☐ Promote the practice of reuse.

☐ Create transition plans and road maps that are flexible and reviewed consistently.

☐ Support stakeholder IT teams and projects on the road to implementation.

☐ Include others beyond the enterprise architecture team in the enterprise architecture process.

CHAPTER 21:
GAINING ALTITUDE

A passion for excellence means thinking big and starting small:
excellence happens when high purpose and intense pragmatism meet.
—Tom Peters, A Passion for Excellence

Your Career-Building System

When I started researching this book, I found no career guides for
EAs. I set out to change that and provide what I couldn't find when I
needed it. The system assembled in the preceding chapters should
incite you to set your sights upon becoming a successful EA. You
now have the steps and the information you need to gain enterprise
architecture altitude. I wrote this book based on three premises:

1. Most EAs who excel in their work have the common skills,
   traits, and abilities as outlined in the chapters of this book.
2. The skills, processes, and abilities these chapters describe can
   be learned.
3. The fastest path to excellence is to gain these skills first and
   avoid getting caught in many of the time traps such as learning and choosing a framework, becoming an infrastructure
   guru, and being the multiple methodology mastermind.

So why do so few architects make it neither their goal nor their
priority to be excellent at their job? The answer is sadly that most are
drowning from the day they took on the role. Many can't even
remember their first six months as an EA. They quickly become
confused and frustrated and then fear that they will lose the very role
that they coveted. They should all take some relief in knowing that
finding success can be a process they enjoy and that comes quickly.

Your career is in your hands. Architect it. This book relies on this
conclusion: the clearest path to a goal is a straight line, knowing the

price points on which the line is plotted. Recall that my resting point after research was that excellent EAs possessed twenty common skills and attributes. Compare this to the flow of the chapters in this book, and you'll see that an excellent EA system emerged. All excellent EAs rely on plans for their enterprise and for their careers.

If you are building a team, be sure to follow the steps in Chapter 17. Don't make your team a collection of *yous*. You need those architects who will complement your strengths that you reviewed throughout this book.

The earliest chapters qualified you as an architect. After you decided to pursue enterprise architecture, you should have confidence that you are indeed qualified to be an EA. The second part described a baseline and critical skills for an architect, ramping up to EA skills toward the end of the step. Those were the key skills required to focus on the solutions, systems, and services your company needs. The third part focused on soft skills that should be seeded and grown in all architects but are mandatory for the solution, system, and enterprise levels. If you interact with the business or propose solutions to them, this step is a must.

The fourth part centered on perspectives and abstract thinking and looked at how an architect evolves to taking various lines of sight. They flourish and move away from physical perspectives and acquire the skills to look at things from the big picture and conceptually. Finally, we delved into the last part on strategy required for anyone who leads an enterprise architecture group, acts as a chief architect, or resides in an EA leadership role.

Another point worth mentioning is that this book was written in the second-person narrative ("you do this, you do that") directed toward you, the EA. If you don't currently do these things or possess these skills, you can if you apply some tenacity. Many of my coaching clients used the same three words to describe themselves when they first contacted me: confused, afraid, and overwhelmed. It's no wonder: they felt they would be expected to be the technical guru with all of the answers about all of the methodologies and frameworks.

Consider how an organization that doesn't understand the EA role treats new EAs. They are pulled into every meeting that needs a technical decision and become entrenched in many projects. No wonder they are overwhelmed. Worse than all of this, they might be ignored or shut out due to those who fear they will lose their lot in the organization. This is often a big change for EAs. There is no surprise that they become afraid. Where do they go if this doesn't work out?

As a coach, I've heard many of these stories. What do EAs need in all of these situations? They need a plan to focus their thinking and a strategy to prioritize the goals of their enterprise architecture. How can you plan to do this better? By equipping yourself with skills in process, human factors, perspective, and strategy. You can learn these skills. Remember that excellence isn't a quality you came in with: it's one you will build. Looking back at the flow of these chapters, you should see how an excellent EA emerges. An excellent EA relies on an excellent plan.

Master Your Enterprise Architecture Plan

You will need to have a complete plan for your enterprise architecture transformation, and your passion surrounding it will allow it to become reality. Earlier chapters made numerous references to the enterprise architecture plan. The first step in creating an excellent enterprise architecture plan and program should be with your strategy for the plan itself. Set goals and objectives for the program if this is also your responsibility. Is the goal to replace chaos with sensibility? Is it to bring in a new wave of technology to your corporation? Is it to add quality and improve service to the business users? You need an overarching goal before even adding the business objectives. This is your personal mantra:

1. Keep the goal line in sight. What are you striving for? The enterprise architecture plan must have a goal—it can't be everything—yet.

2. Know what enterprise maturity level you are striving for. Describe the attributes of the level of mature enterprise architecture program you are striving for with your vision and acknowledge as your starting point. You'll choose some CMM to start with, and you'll assess your current position and describe your target destinations in writing to your team and to your stakeholders.

3. Measure your progress and communicate it often. How will you share your status, your point of reference, and proof of progress? What tools will you use to measure and display progress? To whom will you communicate your victories? How will you do it and what is the expected frequency? It is critical to choose a medium that will enable you to show the progress that you are making in your program. Refer to Chapter 19 and the topic of metrics if you need methods to establish your efforts and accomplishments.

4. Get your transition plan into the hands of the Portfolio and Project Managers. As described in Chapter 9, the road maps you create should provide much of this information. Make one last check to ensure your road map, stakeholder value, the IT strategy plan, and corporate objectives align. Is your vision realistic? Achievable? Your enterprise architecture plan and transition strategy must be linked to all that you set out to do. Success depends on the marriage between your project management office (PMO), EPfM, and stakeholder support of your architecture vision.

5. Define, know, and review often what success means. If you can provide more agility to your organization and drive up the value of the information your department provides, you will be on your way. If the organization reaps the benefit of reduced cost and risk, your success will become well known. If it becomes simpler to make changes to systems and add business functionality to your solutions, your plans will be marked genius.

Enterprise architecture plans are lengthy, and the transition plans they contain are mapped over several years. Some EAs do not have the luxury of creating a large-scale plan but must focus on a few key future objectives. Your transition plan, which will include a series of road maps and blueprints, is essential. The details in Chapter 9 will augment your work in understanding and using these plans. The timing and placement of the pieces is only critical in the near term, and what becomes most important is your continuous review to ensure that you are making the best use of resources in the ordering that you choose. Your agility as an architect will be tested as you adjust according to innovation, business change, and resource availability. Without your plan, no transformation can occur, and recognizing that your plan will change along the way is essential.

Your Career Road Map

In the book *Good to Great*, Jim Collins said, "It is no harder to build something great than to build something good." Heed his advice for your career. If you choose to build the right skills on a schedule planned in a straight line, you will get there faster. Set high expectations and develop a plan for achieving a thriving career. Build a can-do attitude. This is very important as you bring your enterprise architecture plan or road map to fruition. As a leader, you must appear confident because followers smell fear.

Your final challenge is planning both an enterprise architecture program and your career. What if you already knew what the end goal looked like? What if you knew what investing in your career was worth to your financial bottom line? What if you could take each step only once, but twenty percent faster? Look at the Zoom Lists in each chapter again. These lists are the result of my trials and tribulations.

You don't have to acquire these skills in order. What is important is that you realize they are the most important and that acquiring them first allows you to accelerate your progress and develop excellence more quickly. An excellent architect gets better assignments and jobs. Better jobs mean better money. After your honest assessment, note the areas in which you need work. See the Zoom

Lists at the end of the chapter for specific details and an action plan. Self-development of the enterprise and excellent architect is paramount to the development of an organization's enterprise architecture program.

Your corporation depends on your desire to build a strong profession. Your financial happiness depends on building a strong career. The effectiveness of your work in both the enterprise architecture program and in developing your career will bring you the most happiness and money. The biggest shift comes at the point when you achieve excellence with improved soft skills in your journey. The cohesion and strength of your team depends on your ability to lead, communicate, and handle the political arena.

To be considered for the EA position, you have demonstrated incredible dedication and professionalism. Only enterprise architecture excellence can enable your IT organization and company to move forward in leaps and bounds. Excellence must be your end goal. You will achieve excellence through focus, experience, and continuous upgrade of your knowledge.

People who have dialed into the Zoom Factor in their careers can auto-focus their career advancement with relative ease. Take the necessary time after you acquire each new skill to review the big picture. As an abstract thinker, this should seem natural. Where are you in completing the framework of your life's work? You become the expert when you are seen as the expert. You can do this when you release your vision to your team and subsequently the masses. You also shore up your expertise when you voluntarily give "lunch and learns" or speak at town hall meetings to help those who are willing to learn more about enterprise architecture.

Center Your Career Plan on Action

Much of the information presented thus far should properly augment your experience as a new or veteran EA with the plan you need to build an exciting career. Be sure that you are ensuring quality and the ability to adapt to change. How are you going to be the best? You will know who you are and what it is you want. You will know where you want to go and how you going to prove it as an EA.

You will need ways to check on your progress. I suggest you use the steps at the end of this chapter at least monthly through the first year of your journey. You will also find a collection of resources at the back of this book to rely upon. These are some of the best tools I have found through my journey.

In addition, you will need a mentor. Where in your organization will you find one? This person may not necessarily be an architect but somebody who has gone through the trials of reaching the pinnacle in his or her career. There are many coaching programs that you may try. References to the architect coaching, training, and career assessment programs that I offer are at the end of this book. You'll find increasingly more architecture training classes are available. I would suggest that you survey to find what is accessible and what fits your needs. Be sure to ask many questions about not just the syllabus but also about the instructor. Finally, you will need some self-assessment. If you haven't already done this self-assessment mentioned in earlier chapters, it is listed again in the resource section.

Your call to action is to plot your plan for both your career and your enterprise architecture. Visit the links included in this book and you will find some great information. Further study areas are also included in the resource section. To this, you will add the specifics of your industry vertical so that you are aware of the latest happenings.

Build on Your Success

One of my biggest concerns when writing *Zoom Factor* was that the suggestion of trying to master each skill would be overwhelming. This is why I have added the Zoom Factor checklists at the end of each chapter. I know it's impossible to tackle all of it at the same time. It took me well over twenty years to develop my abilities in all of these areas. Today, I'm still learning and augmenting my skills. You will orchestrate change masterfully and can plot a road map transition that will win your organization's heart. You'll see it through: by studying the business strategy in detail, you'll gain confidence that you're going to find the best points that will allow you to develop high-quality architecture. You will instill a built-to-last mentality, and take comfort that you won't recommend anything you know to have weaknesses that aren't assessed.

Above all, to succeed, you have to be humble and self-actualized. The reason you are doing all of this is for the greater good, whether for the good of your company or for the good of your career (or both). You've just seen a system for training excellent architects. You can be proactive in changing your own career and are in charge.

The system has been laid out with the intent to be the most effective path to becoming an excellent architect. As mentioned earlier, the skills are listed in a specific order for a reason. I believe you will gain altitude fastest if you follow them in this order.

Many practices exposed to us so far for gaining skills have been backward. With this book, you can now begin with the end in mind. How much time would you spend knowing the physical intricacies of your servers if you knew in the end you wanted to be a chief technology officer? Your strategy would be your killer strategic arsenal, not your knowledge of the bits and bytes of your hardware. Your goal should be to learn the most important skills to make you effective as a high-level strategic technology planner—someone whose primary goal is to bring value to your business.

With the end in mind, you will have taken time to know and trust your personal central values. What will your strategic agenda be? Know the values you want to instill, the processes you want to build, the challenges you face, and your vision for success. At all costs, remember that you were a technical expert: everyone in your organization who knows that will try to consume your time to help them with their personal agendas. Remember why you wanted to be an EA to begin with. It's a win-win for your organization if you become excellent.

See www.zoomfactorbook.com/book-resources to download career plans for the system or solution architect, data architect, service-oriented architect, technical architect, and, of course, the EA.

This should be your overall high-level career plan. If your intention is to become an EA, you may wish to follow this plan.

After reading this book, you may have decided that a career in enterprise architecture isn't for you. Or if you still aren't sure which architecture path you should be following, consider an alternate path.

Do you prefer a technical architecture role above dealing with the business or conceptual design? If designing services that put the pieces together is what floats your boat, then perhaps a solution oriented architect position is better suited for you. You will enjoy the technical, integration of parts and enjoy a very senior application architect's role. You'll need business experience, but you prefer philosophical conversations with developers to discussions of business strategy with the executives.

Do you see solutions from an enterprise perspective? Then perhaps a solution architect role is for you. The solution architect can be considered an EA with a little *e*. Think of your role as a horizontal slice of the enterprise for one comprehensive solution. You include the perspective in each domain of business data and include the application and technology in your studies, plans, and documentation sets. Your design broaches each domain and includes considerations for each. You are less interested in the overarching business strategy and more excited by seeing a solution from vision to fruition.

Take Time to Zoom

You've reached the end of the journey in *Zoom Factor for the Enterprise Architect*. I hope that your big-picture thinking will include the Zoom Lists to make yourself more efficient and build a more satisfying and prosperous career. Take time to focus on the details of your architecture plans, but also be sure to widen your perspectives from time to time to be sure that you haven't missed the crucial points for best business value. You'll see two last Zoom Lists with my hope that you take off to new altitudes in your career.

Zoom In—Action Steps You Need to Succeed

Get a calendar and at the top of each month, write the name of a chapter or topic from the list below that matches one of your target focus areas. If you can, print off a blank calendar for an entire year, one month per page. If you want to chunk it down further, list one topic per week. Take that month (or week), create an action plan, and master the topic. Topics with sample months:

- ☐ Problem definition
- ☐ Architecture analysis
- ☐ Architecture process (January)
- ☐ Modeling
- ☐ Abstract and conceptual thinking (February)
- ☐ Pattern thinking (March)
- ☐ Framework basics (April)
- ☐ Blueprint and road map design (May)
- ☐ Leadership
- ☐ Vision
- ☐ Elevator speech of your program
- ☐ Negotiation
- ☐ Political tactics (June)
- ☐ Relationship management
- ☐ Consulting
- ☐ Communication
- ☐ Writing
- ☐ Presentation (July)
- ☐ Speaking (get yearlong Toastmaster's membership)
- ☐ Document and artifact creation
- ☐ Decision making (August)
- ☐ Risk management
- ☐ Viewing from various perspectives
- ☐ Big-picture thinking
- ☐ Right-sizing architecture/value and alignment
- ☐ Self-awareness (August)
- ☐ Team skills

- ☐ Mentoring
- ☐ Strategic planning (September)
- ☐ Metrics
- ☐ Portfolio management
- ☐ Governance (November)
- ☐ Change management
- ☐ Enterprise architecture planning (October)
- ☐ Career planning/review (December)

Research, learn, and enlist the help of a coach or mentor. Take a class and/or read a book. Practice the ideas. Talk to your mentor about how you can practice the techniques in real time.

Zoom Out—Big-Picture Concepts

Here are my suggestions on how to tackle your career plan and instill these skills within yourself:

1. Rate yourself. See the assessment tool at www.zoomfactorbook.com/selfassessment if you didn't do this previously. Know your strengths, weaknesses, likes, and dislikes.
2. Verify your self-evaluation. Get a colleague and mentor or friend to review it and grill you.
3. Pick two strengths that you have and find the chapter that most aligns with those strengths. Review the chapter and see whether any suggestions would make you even stronger in these areas.
4. Pick one weakness and then do the same as you did in number three. Find the chapter and plan to work in this area.
5. After sixty days, reevaluate your progress in the areas you picked in #3 and #4 that you wish to improve.
6. Repeat the above until you become excellent.

This sounds like a crazy cookbook, but please consider it carefully. You were an excellent technician before you were ever considering becoming an architect. As you reflect on what you've learned so far in your career, be confident in your ability to learn and grow.

RESOURCES

For more information about Zoom Factor Architect Coaching for individuals or teams, see www.architectcoach.com

For more information about Personal Development Assessment for yourself, or team, see www.architectcoach.com/PDP

Book Site Links – Extras, and book Updates:

- www.zoomfactorbook.com/book-resources
- www.zoomfactorbook.com/selfassessment
- www.zoomfactorbook.com/links
- www.zoomfactorbook.com/bookshelf
- www.zoomfactorbook.com/education
- www.zoomfactorbook.com/order

REFERENCES & BIBLIOGRAPHY

Boar, Bernard. *Constructing Blueprints for IT Enterprise Architectures.* New York: John Wiley & Sons, 1999.

Benson, Robert J. "The Critical Role of EA in the Financial Management of IT" (presented at the Shared Insights Enterprise Architecture Conference, San Diego, California, October 24-26, 2006).

Branson, Bill; "Giving Good Whiteboard: The Art of Effective Diagramming"; (presented at the IIR Enterprise Architecture Conference, New Orleans, Louisiana, March 27-29, 2007).

Bernard, Scott A. "Building a Winning Enterprise Architecture Team" (presented at the Shared Insights Enterprise Architecture Conference, San Diego, California, October 24-26, 2006).

Collins, Jim. *Good to Great: Why Some Companies Make the Leap…and Others Don't.* New York: Harper Collins Publishers, 2001.

Cullen, Alex. "Comparing EA Frameworks" (presented at the DCI Shared Insights Enterprise Architecture Conference, Las Vegas, Nevada, Oct 25-27, 2005).

DeBoever, Larry R. "Mis-Match.com: The Truth About Finding Good Architects" (presented at the IIR Enterprise Architecture Conference, New Orleans, Louisiana, March 27-29, 2007).

DeBoever, Larry R. "The iPod As An EA Metaphor: 2005-2010" (presented at the DCI Shared Insights Enterprise Architecture Conference, Las Vegas, Nevada, Oct 25-27, 2005).

Evans, Sharon C. "Enterprise Architecture Framework Overview," *Architect Boot Camp*, www.architectbootcamp.com, March 31, 2003, Firefli Consulting Inc.

Evans, Sharon C. "Project Portfolio Prioritization: Optimizing the Project Portfolio," (presented at the Manitoba PMI Conference, Winnipeg, Manitoba, April 25, 2006).

Evans, Sharon C. "Good to Great: Paving the Road to Excellence for the Enterprise Architect" (presented at the IIR Enterprise Architecture Conference, Las Vegas, Nevada, October 23-25, 2007).

Evans, Sharon C. "Analysis at Internet Speed," *The Architect Abstract*, vol. 2, no. 25, July 2004, pp. 2-3.

Evans, Sharon C. "Mining for Architecture Skills" (presented at the IIR Enterprise Architecture Conference April 7-10, Orlando 2007).

Evans, Sharon C. "Soft Skills for the Enterprise Architect: Tips and Techniques for Architecture Excellence!" (seminar presented at the IIR Enterprise Architecture Conference April 7-10, Orlando 2007).

Frankel, David et al; "The Zachman Framework and the OMG's Model Driven Architecture", Business Process Trends, August 2003.

Goetsch, David L. *Building a winning career in a technical profession: 20 strategies for success after college.* 1st ed. Pearson Prentice Hall. 2007.

Malan, Ruth and Bredemeyer, Dana; "Leadership Architect Competency" www.bredemeyer.com ,2002, Bredemeyer Consulting.

Martens, China. "Enterprise Architect", CIO Magazine, www.ciomagazine.com , August 2007.

Michaelson, Brenda. "IT Linchpin 2006: The (Business-Driven) Enterprise Architect" www.elementallinks.com/

Orr, Ken; "Aiming for the Big Picture: EA Goes Beyond 3D", Cutter Consortium, www.cutter.com, May 2009.

Paras, George. "The Past, Present and Future of Enterprise Architecture" (presented at the Shared Insights Enterprise Architecture Conference, San Diego, California, October 24-26, 2006).

Porter, Michael E. *Competitive Strategy*. New York: The Free Press, 1980.

Rimnac, George. "From Architect to Innovator: Do Something Innovative" (presented at the IIR Enterprise Architecture Conference, Las Vegas, Nevada, October 23-25, 2007).

Robert L. Nord, et al. "Integrating the Architecture Tradeoff Analysis Method (ATAM) with the Cost Benefit Analysis Method (CBAM)". Pittsburgh: Software Engineering Institute, Carnegie Mellon University, December 2003

Roam, Dan; "Back of the Napkin Workshop" (presented at the IIR Enterprise Architecture Conference April 7-10, Orlando 2007).

Ross, Jeannie et al. *Enterprise Architecture as a Strategy: Creating a Foundation for Business Execution. Boston: Harvard Business School Publishing, 2006.*

Schekkerman, Jaap. "The Entended Enterprise Architecture MaturityModel", Institute for Enterprise Architecture Developments, www.enterprise-architecture.info ,July 2003, IFEAD

Scott, Jeff; "The 7 Habits of Highly Effective Architects" (presented at the IIR Enterprise Architecture Conference, New Orleans, Louisiana, March 27-29, 2007).

Scott, Jeff; "Re-Architecting EA". (presented at the Shared Insights Enterprise Architecture Conference, San Diego, California, October 24-26, 2006).

Scott, Jeff. "Innovate Now" (presented at the IIR Enterprise Architecture Conference April 7-10, Orlando 2007).

Scott, Jeff. "The Enterprise Architecture Strategist" (presented at the IIR Enterprise Architecture Conference, Las Vegas, Nevada, October 23-25, 2007).

Setter, Jannine. "Enterprise Architecture: Shelf-ware or Analysis Tool for Strategic Planning" (presented at the IIR Enterprise Architecture Conference, Las Vegas, Nevada, October 23-25, 2007).

Sessions, Roger. "Exclusive Interview with John Zachman, President of Zachman International, CEO of Zachman Framework Associates" (presented at Perspectives of the International Association of Software Architects, April 2007)

Spewak, Steven H. *Enterprise Architecture Planning.* New York: John Wiley & Sons. 1992;

Steward, Bruce A. "Getting the Business Deeply into IT"; (presented at the IIR Enterprise Architecture Conference, Las Vegas, Nevada, October 23-25, 2007)

The Open Group; TOGAF, Version 9.0. www.opengroup.org

Vaidyanathan, Sundararajan. "Enterprise Architecture in the Context of Organizational Strategy" BPTrends, November 2005

Weiler, John, and Schemel, Bob; "ICH Value Chain Method: Actionable Architectures forValue Chains and Value Coalitions®: Taxonomies for Efficient Information Flow, Effective Decision Making and Performance Management"; www.ichnet.org, 2003

Zachman, J.A. and J.F. Sowa. "1992: Extending and Formalizing the Framework for Information Systems Architecture", *IBM Systems Journal.* (31) 3: 590-616 (1992).

Zachman, J. A. "The Zachman Institute for Framework Advancements", www.zachmaninternational.us/index.php/

Zachman, J. A. "Enterprise Architecture: Managing Complexity and Change" (presented at the Shared Insights Enterprise Architecture Conference, San Diego, California, October 24-26, 2006).

Zachman, J. A. "Zachman Framework 2™ ENTERPRISE Engineering and Manufacturing" (presented at the IIR Enterprise Architecture Conference, Las Vegas, Nevada, October 23-25, 2007)

INDEX

ABOUT THE AUTHOR

 Sharon C. Evans is the Principal and Founder of Firefli Consulting Inc., where she provides coaching and mentoring to enterprise architects and focuses on ensuring excellence and success in their professional development. Her consulting and advisory work centers on improving strategic impact, creating value, and obtaining fast results by using architecture in enterprises. Her mission is to see that architects do not spend too much time in the mire and circumstance of IT departments, remain focused on the big picture, and maintain their "Zoom Factor".

Her career experience spans more than twenty-three years in information technology as an architect coach, mentor, chief architect, analyst, strategist, and consultant. She has worked with more than one hundred companies in various industries and the public sector. In 2003, Ms. Evans created a system known as the Architect Boot Camp, and she has delivered her simplified methods through this architecture- and methodology-related training to architects on six continents.

Ms. Evans has been a sought-out expert advisor on various online architecture forums, and she has several electronic newsletters and membership portals through which she shares architecture knowledge with her readers. An accomplished speaker, Ms. Evans is a frequent presenter and educator at various industry events, forums, conferences, and executive education and university programs.

Ms. Evans was born in Winnipeg, Manitoba, Canada and has degrees in economics, computer science, and management from the University of Manitoba. She resides in Winnipeg with her husband and child. For more information about Ms. Evans, visit www.zoomfactorbook.com

Firefli Media

Focus and Accelerate Your Career

QUICK ORDER FORM

Fax orders: 204-489-1964. Send this form.

Telephone orders: Call 204-488-2819. Toll-free 1-800-983-5308

Email orders: orders@zoomfactorbook.com

Postal Orders: Firefli Media, 210-1600 Kenaston Blvd Suite 305, Winnipeg, MB Canada R3P0Y4.

Please send the following books or media. I understand that I may return any of them for a full refund – for any reason, no questions asked.

_____

_____

_____

Please send more FREE information on:

☐ Coaching   ☐ Speaking/Seminars

☐ Other books   ☐ Newsletter

Name: _____

Address: _____

City: _____Prov/State _____ Zip: _____

Telephone: _____

Email address: _____

Sales tax:
Please add 5% GST for products shipped to Canadian addresses.

Shipping by air:
North America: $8 for first book or disk and $2 for each additional product.

International:
$10 for first book or disk; $5 for each additional product (estimate).

9 780981 260907